THE COMPLETE
RV HANDBOOK

A Guide to Getting the Most out of Life on the Road

Jayne Freeman

Ragged Mountain Press / McGraw-Hill

Camden, Maine ▪ New York ▪ Chicago ▪ San Francisco
Lisbon ▪ London ▪ Madrid ▪ Mexico City ▪ Milan
New Delhi ▪ San Juan ▪ Seoul ▪ Singapore ▪ Sydney ▪ Toronto

The McGraw·Hill Companies

1 2 3 4 5 6 7 8 9 10 DOC DOC 9 8 7 6 5

Library of Congress Cataloging-in-Publication Data
Freeman, Jayne.
  The complete RV handbook : a guide to getting the most out of life on the road / Jayne Freeman.
      p.   cm.
  Includes bibliographical references and index.
  ISBN 0-07-144339-8 (alk. paper)
  1. Recreational vehicle living. I. Title.
  TX1110.F74 2005
  796.7′9—dc22   2004027385

Questions regarding the content of this book should be addressed to
Ragged Mountain Press
P.O. Box 220
Camden, ME 04843
www.raggedmountainpress.com

Questions regarding the ordering of this book should be addressed to
The McGraw-Hill Companies
Customer Service Department
P.O. Box 547
Blacklick, OH 43004
Retail customers: 1-800-262-4729
Bookstores: 1-800-722-4726

Photographs by the author unless otherwise noted. Photos on pages i, 3, 65, and 161 courtesy RVIA.
Illustrations by Jim Sollers unless otherwise noted.

CONTENTS

Introduction 1

Part One: Getting Started

Chapter 1. Why RV? 4
   Convenience 4
   Affordability 6
   A Wider Range of Choices 8
   The Chance to Travel with Family 9
   Flexibility 10

Chapter 2. Choosing an RV 11
   Truck Campers 13
   Motor Homes 15
   Towables 30

Chapter 3. Choosing the Features and Options You Want 39
   The RV Kitchen 39
   Bathroom 43
   Washer/Dryers 44
   Bedrooms 46
   Electrical Features 48
   Awnings 50
   Slideouts 51
   Storage Space 52
   Diesel vs. Gasoline Engines 53

Chapter 4. Buying a New (or Used) RV 54
   How Much Is It Worth? 55
   Financing 58
   Making the Best Deal 58
   Taxes, Registration, and Insurance 60
   The Walk-Through 62

Part Two: Using Your RV

Chapter 5. Driving Basics 66
Driving Forward 66
Turning 69
Highway Driving: Entering, Exiting, and Passing Safely 71
Driving Safely 72
Parking, Backing, and Leveling Your RV 75

Chapter 6. Towing and Hitching 83
Towing a Car 83
Hitching and Unhitching a Trailer or Fifth Wheel 88

**Chapter 7. Understanding and Caring for Your RV,
  Its Systems, and Its Features** 92
The RV Toilet 92
Gray- and Black-Water Drainage 95
Freshwater Supply 99
Stove 103
Refrigerator 104
Washer/Dryer 107
Heating and Cooling 108
Power Supply/Electrical Systems 111
Awnings 120
Roof 122
Floors 123

**Chapter 8. Engine, Tires, Suspension, Brakes,
  and Transmission** 124
Light Maintenance and Tune Ups 124
Tires 131
Suspension 134
Brakes 134
Transmission 137

Chapter 9. Finding Places to Stay 138
County, State, and National Parks 140
Membership Campgrounds 142
Dry Camping 145

Chapter 10. Preventing and Responding to Disasters 148
Dealing with Roadside Mishaps 148
Personal Safety 151
Fire Safety 152
Propane Safety 154
Preparing for Medical Emergencies 155

Chapter 11. Leaving Your RV 158
  Choosing the Right Storage Location 158
  Preparing Your RV for Storage 159

Part Three: The Joys of the Open Road

Chapter 12. Loading the RV and Preparing to Leave 162
  Getting It All In 162
  Departure Checklist 165

Chapter 13. Arranging to Be Gone 168
  Mail Services 168
  Getting Cash 169
  Internet Banking 171
  Cellular Phone Service 171
  Medical Care 173

Chapter 14. Traveling with Kids and Pets 178
  On the Road with Pets 178
  RVing with Kids 180

Chapter 15. Taking Long Trips 182
  The Advantages of a Long Stay 182
  Becoming a Snowbird 183

**Chapter 16. Crossing Borders: Taking Your RV to
        Canada or Mexico** 185
  Visiting Canada 186
  Adventuring in Mexico 188

Chapter 17. Technology for the Traveler 193
  Television 193
  Audio Entertainment 197
  Internet Access 198
  Digital Cameras 206
  Using GPS: Never Get Lost Again 207

Chapter 18. Going Full-Time 209
  Getting Started at Full-Timing 211
  The Frugal Full-Timer 215
  The Full-Timer's Social Life 220
  Citizens of Everywhere: Selecting a Domicile 221
  Start Your Engines 225

Appendix: Resources for the RVer 226

Index 231

"Go confidently in the direction of your dreams! Live the life you've imagined. As you simplify your life, the laws of the universe will be simpler."
—*Henry David Thoreau*

Introduction

I envy your lifestyle, but I could never sell my house." I've heard that from hundreds of people over the past decade as I've traveled the country in my motor home. I truly understand how they feel. Before my husband, Dan, and I became full-timers, I was sure I could never part with our home of twenty years.

It was true that our house was too large for a retired couple, but the property was filled with memories. We'd raised our children there. I'd planted trees in the backyard in memory of my parents, and those trees stood large and sturdy now. Could I ever leave them and the memories that were such a part of this house?

All our married life, as we worked and struggled to raise our seven children, Dan and I had talked about things we would do "someday." Well, the kids were grown, we were retired, and "someday" was now. Throughout the years, our dreams had centered around travel. Our retirement income, however, while not marginal, isn't lavish—and travel can be expensive.

The logical solution for us was to sell the house and buy a motor home. We placed our home on the market, and it sold in a month.

Eight years into the full-timing lifestyle, do I regret burning my bridges? The answer is an emphatic no. It was what we had to do at the time to break from the conventional lifestyle that kept us from our travel dreams.

But over these past eight years, I've learned there is more than one way to reach cherished travel goals. I know people who rent out their homes, planning to return to them when they've finished traveling. In fact, Dan and I have bought a second home and we've done exactly that. I've met other travelers who adopt the "snowbird" lifestyle—people who live in their homes for six months and spend the rest of the year in their RVs. Of course, there are also RVers who take to the road just a few months or even a few weeks a year.

But for us, selling the house when we did bought us the freedom we enjoy now. Over these years, snug in my 38-foot motor home, I've been to wonderful places and seen wonderful things. I've lain in bed at midnight with the blinds up while lightning turned the sky a brilliant white and thunder rocked my bed. I've visited with hummingbirds, pelicans, squirrels, deer, ducks, and even alligators. I've been to the Alamo to see a reenactment of that historic battle, to Cape Canaveral to see the space-shuttle launch sites, to the French Quarter of New Orleans, to a half-dozen historic forts that dot the Gulf of Mexico, and to Washington, D.C. I've gambled in Biloxi and gamboled in Florida. I've lived the champagne life on a beer budget.

In a journal entry from our first week on the road, I wrote, "I have always believed, that one should not allow the material things of this world to have possession of one's soul. That the lighter we can travel through life, the better. I'm traveling light, and I'm going to travel far."

And so we have.

But selling the home and setting yourself free is not without obstacles. Before all this became a reality for us, Dan and I had to find creative solutions to problems that never confronted us as homeowners. We discovered that there are dependable ways to get mail while never being in one place for more than a week or two, and similarly simple ways to handle the monthly bills. Keeping in touch with children, grandchildren, and friends is easier than you might imagine. You have a variety of options for getting online as you travel, and those options are getting better every day. If you intend to travel a long distance or be gone for a long time, you may have to wrestle with the problem of finding a medical plan that will provide coverage to fit your itinerary, but it can be done.

RVers can now have television and Internet access, and nationwide cellular service. To receive each of these services—taken for granted by people who live in a fixed location—you may need to bend some rules and regulations of the providers, some of whom are not interested in serving RVers.

If you want to know how to accomplish all these things, read on!

PART ONE

Getting Started

1

Why RV?

There are as many reasons to RV as there are RVers. Whether you're looking for a home away from home, to live more simply, or if you want a convenient way to take your little ones on the road with you, RVing has something to offer. Lets examine some of some of the main reasons to consider RVing.

Convenience

There is something to be said for gazing at the beauty of the Grand Canyon from your dining room table; or for pulling over to the side of the road, starting the generator, and setting up the satellite dish to watch crucial late-breaking news just as it happens; or for standing in awe at the scarlet glory of a desert sunset. There's even more to be said for being warm and cozy inside your rig while the sky turns blue-white with lightning and rain pounds against the roof.

Kids travel more happily and with less quarreling when they have space of their own—a table to hold their coloring books and crayons, snacks to grab from the refrigerator, a bathroom to visit as needed—and when they don't have to miss their favorite TV shows at night. Many parents today are coming to appreciate these facts. The number of young families buying and using RVs is growing all the time.

RV travel can bring you to many if not all the beautiful wilderness places in the United States and Canada. You can tailor your camping experiences to fit your needs and desires of the moment, instead of having to plan your trip far in advance.

A desert sunset can be just a part of your journey, or it can be the destination.

If all your vacations to date have involved planes, hotels, rental cars, and restaurants, consider this: On those vacations, don't you usually lug suitcases crammed with everything you think you might need? You're never sure exactly which clothes you'll need while you're traveling or what the weather will be like, so you probably bring along way too much stuff: shorts in case it's warm, sweats in case it's cool, jackets, sweaters, rain gear, sunscreen, beach chairs, hiking boots . . . the list seems endless. Foreseeing the future is difficult, so you pack everything you can think of, more junk than you want to carry into a hotel or bring into Aunt Maude's house for your annual visit.

What if all your things—swim fins and snowshoes, parkas and Hawaiian shirts—were within arm's reach? Or, what if you never again had to stop at an interstate exit, starving, and eat greasy hamburgers at the only available restaurant? Instead, think about dining in style on what's in your own fridge, maybe barbecuing a steak under shady trees, or munching your lunch beside a babbling

MAKING A HOME ON WHEELS FOR YOURSELF AND YOUR BROOD

In an article in the October 31, 2002, travel section of the *Washington Post* called "RV? Me?" Steve Hendrix related his reluctant conversion to RV travel. An avid backpacker, Hendrix and his wife continued to backpack even after their first child arrived. His wife carried the baby on her back and Steve carried everything else. But with the arrival of his second child, "we ran out of backs," he reports, and Steve believed for a while that his outdoor experiences were over.

Then his sister-in-law persuaded him to try an RV. He was pleasantly surprised to discover that RVing didn't have to involve parking on concrete pads too close to your neighbors as he'd feared. He discovered he could enjoy the beauties of the wilderness while camped in an RV. He could even pull over to the side of the road, gaze at nature's beauty, and enjoy an ice-cream cone from the RV's freezer with his children.

In a few years, Hendrix and his wife will probably be backpacking again with their somewhat older children. But in the meantime, they and many other families with young children explore and enjoy a variety of nature's magical wonderlands in a 25- or 30-foot "home on wheels."

brook. What if you could sleep in your own comfy bed every night while you travel? That's the way it is when you travel in your RV.

Affordability

As well as being convenient, RV travel is also very affordable. A tourism research firm, PKF Consulting, compared nine different ways of taking a vacation to popular destinations such as the Grand Canyon and Disney World. PKF compared travel in three different types of RVs to travel by car, bus, train, airline, and cruise ship.

RV travel was by far the least expensive. Travel with a folding, popup trailer was 50 to 70 percent less expensive than the non-RV modes of transit. Travel with a conventional trailer was 24 to 57 percent less expensive, and travel in a Type C motor home (an RV body built on a cab-and-chassis pickup truck) was 9 to 49 percent less expensive. The study factored in the cost of buying an RV, as well as the actual travel expenses on the road. The table opposite shows the results of that study.

The costs of a typical RV vacation break down differently from the costs of vacationing in a hotel or on a cruise ship. Traveling in your RV, your expenses consist of fuel, insurance, food, RV campsites, and the cost of the RV itself, rented or purchased. Your expenses will vary from trip to trip, based on the distance you travel and the current cost of fuel, but the costs are definitely less than plane fare to your destination, renting a car after you get there, staying in a hotel, and eating in restaurants. For example, if you travel 500 miles in a motor home that averages 10 miles to the gallon, you'll use about 50 gallons of gas at approximately $2.30 per gallon, for a total of $115 in fuel costs. A 500-mile plane ticket often costs twice as much—more if several people are flying—and then there's the rental car to factor in after you arrive at your destination.

Campground fees are a lot less than hotel fees, too, averaging about $25 per night compared to at least twice that for even a low-budget motel. Food you prepare in your RV costs far less than the food you eat in a restaurant—and the bonus here is that you can fix exactly the meal you like to eat and not have to compromise by eating whatever you can find or afford.

If you're buying your RV, you'll have certain expenses including monthly payments and insurance. The cost of buying an RV ranges from around $5,000 for a small, very old RV to $350,000 for a new, luxury-model, 45-foot motor home. Most RV purchases fall somewhere in between these extremes. If you buy an older RV, remember to factor in costs of unanticipated repairs into your travel budget, just as you would with an older car.

The typical rental cost of an RV depends on the size and type you rent. A small RV (Class C, cab-over, 22 to 25 feet long) rented for two weeks in the fall of 2004

AVERAGE TRAVEL COSTS BY TRANSPORTATION TYPE

Vacation Type	Trip Duration		
Type of Travel	2 Nights	7 Nights	21 Nights
Car/folding trailer	$149	$483	$1,413
Light-duty truck/truck camper	$152	$492	$1,441
Van conversion	$155	$501	$1,464
Light-duty truck/travel trailer	$158	$504	$1,461
Motor home	$188	$590	$1,704
Car/motels or hotels	$339	$1,169	$3,544
Intercity bus/motels or hotels	$484	$1,589	$4,534
Train/motels or hotels	$538	$1,588	$4,591
Airline/motels or hotels	$1,338	$2,918	$5,835
Cruise-ship vacation	N/A	$3,310	$5,951
All-inclusive package vacation	N/A	$4,317	N/A

This chart is taken from one published in *Western RV News*, August 2003.

cost about $1,000, insurance included. This breaks down to $72 per day. An intermediate RV (26 to 27 feet long) cost about $1,100 for two weeks. A large RV (28 to 30 feet long) ran around $1,260. Many RV rental companies also charge for mileage. An estimated 1,400 miles for these rentals would cost about $400, making for totals of $1,400, $1,500, and $1,600, respectively, or daily costs of $100, $108, or $115, respectively. If you don't use all the miles you pay for in advance, the difference can be refunded. Compare these costs to a typical round-trip plane ticket, plus hotel rates, plus meals in restaurants, and you can quickly see that you save a lot of money traveling by RV.

You also pay more to rent an RV than you do to buy one, but that doesn't mean you should rush right out to your nearest RV dealer and buy. If you aren't sure whether you're going to like the lifestyle, you need to try it out first. Renting (or borrowing) an RV is the best way to do that. Even if you're totally sold on RVing, renting may still be more cost-effective if you plan to be on the road only a few weeks per year.

The length of each trip you take relates directly to the costs of RV travel. Maybe you're dreaming of going full-time—selling or renting your home and traveling permanently in your RV. Saving money is not a compelling reason for adopting the appealing vagabond lifestyle of a full-timer, but it can prove to be a bonus, depending on several factors. Living and traveling in your RV can eliminate the expenses you have in your home—mortgage, utilities, insurance, property taxes—but on the other hand, you'll have some other expenses as a full-timer, such as satellite-TV service, mail-forwarding service, nationwide cellular-phone service, and a different kind of health insurance. You'll also have expenses on the road like fuel and campground fees.

A Wider Range of Choices

Now that you know how affordable RV travel can be, give some thought to destinations. You can go places in your RV that aren't accessible otherwise, places with no hotels or restaurants. Each state maintains a series of state parks—often, little-known scenic treasures where you can camp among the trees, beside streams, or in the shadow of mountain peaks, and experience the beauties of a wilderness while enjoying all the comforts of home. The U.S. National Parks dot the country like a string of priceless jewels, each with a unique appeal, and each with one or more campgrounds.

In your RV, you can take a trip that combines the best of vacation worlds. If you visit Orlando, for example, you can camp at one of many RV parks there and take the kids to Disney World, and then head south along Florida's fabulous coast to experience a scenic world complete with a sandy, sea-splashed coastline, great blue herons, turtles, alligators, superb fishing, unbelievable sunsets, and the Everglades.

Instead of planning for that highly organized vacation of a week or two, you can simply take off spontaneously in your RV for months at a time, if you can get the time off. When you travel by plane, your itinerary and hotel reservations need to be tightly scheduled, so you can be sure to get to your destination and have a place to stay after you arrive. Traveling by RV, you can head out in the morning and, when you get tired, simply pull into a nearby RV park and find that they probably have space for you. (Don't try this in Yuma, Arizona, in January, however.) And if the park you choose is full? You still have options. Wal-Mart, Camping World, and some shopping malls often permit RVers to stay overnight in their parking lots. You're free to go as far in a day as seems comfortable, and you can stop when the spirit moves you.

In your RV, you can visit destinations that fit your particular interests and spend as much time as you want at each place. Whatever excites you, from history to geology to small-town museums, you can explore it from coast to coast in a leisurely fashion.

The Chance to Travel with Family

"What?" you say. "Travel for months at a time? I couldn't leave my grandchildren that long."

It's true that relating to grandkids is one of the real joys of a grandparent's life. But so is travel. You can reconcile these two apparently conflicting personal goals in a couple of ways. The most fun one is to take the grandkids along. The old saw about quality of time spent with children being more important than quantity really applies when traveling in an RV.

You'd be surprised at how cheerfully parents will let you borrow their kids for a week or more. As for special occasions, you can be there instantly for school plays, high school graduations, weddings, and the births of babies. A couple of guys called the Wright brothers took care of that a hundred years ago.

And if your kids are still at home—whether they're babies or toddlers, children or teens—RVs can make for a great way to hit the road as a family. Your kids will have so much room, and they'll be able to see such interesting views out the windows, that they'll never ask, "Are we there yet?"

Flexibility

There are many patterns to RV travel. Many people rent or borrow or buy a used RV so they can travel during their two or three weeks of annual vacation. Some people, usually retired, are dubbed "snowbirds" for their practice of traveling to warm climates in their RVs every winter. In the summer, snowbirds return to live in their homes. Over time, many snowbirds forget about the returning-home part, and become full-timers. The amount of time you spend in your RV is entirely flexible and up to you.

Starting small with RVing, with weekend and summer vacation trips, is a good idea. Get used to the lifestyle. Be sure everyone likes it. Then extend your dreams to encompass bigger chunks of time.

So why RV? In a nutshell, because it's affordable, it's comfortable, it's flexible, and it's just plain fun.

2

Choosing an RV

Vs are generally divided into categories as a way to understand their similarities and differences. Self-propelled RVs include truck campers and motor homes. Motor homes are subdivided into Class A, Class B, and Class C. This alphabetical classification system is not organized by size or desirability; it's simply a grouping together of similar types of motor homes. The final category of RVs, towables, includes popup (soft-sided) trailers, conventional trailers, and fifth-wheel trailers (which hook into a pickup truck bed while being towed).

The type of RV you select depends on several factors, including your budget, family size, and the type and amount of travel you plan to do. RV lengths range from something as small as a truck camper or van conversion (typically about 18 feet long) to giant motor homes and fifth wheels longer than 40 feet. Prices for used or new RVs vary from a few thousand dollars to half a million. In fact, there's an amphibious motor home that sells for more than a million, if you're interested in both driving and floating.

Small RVs, those smaller than about 25 feet in length, have benches, couches, or dinettes that convert into a bed at night. One classy model, the Safari Trek, has a bed stowed overhead that you lower electrically when needed and simply raise again in the morning. Many newer RVs have rooms that slide out to create more room. These slideouts add considerably to the interior living space. RVs are becoming more than just shelter for a short vacation; they're becoming homes on wheels.

Before choosing an RV, analyze carefully what you plan to do with it. In van conversions, truck campers, small trailers, and Class C mini motor homes like the Minnie Winnie made by Winnebago, space is at a premium. They're good for small families or couples taking short trips. If you have more than three people in your group, or if you're going to travel for more than a month, you might not have much fun if you're traveling in one of these mini RVs. On the upside, pop-ups, minis, and other small RVs are very affordable. A new popup costs from $6,000 to $11,000. You can save even more money by buying a used RV. Look at the accompanying table to get an idea of typical new and used RV prices. One RV in each category was selected as an example and priced both used and new. New prices are those listed by the manufacturer or found on dealers' websites and represent what is called the MSRP (manufacturer's suggested retail price). Used prices were obtained from the website of the National Automobile Dealers Association (NADA). Actual prices of used RVs vary widely, depending on many factors such as condition and mileage, but these figures will give you a ballpark idea of what you might spend.

The RVs discussed here are just a few examples out of hundreds of new models of RVs available. Study their appearance and ponder their floor plans to get an idea of the latest RV features, but remember there is no substitute for visiting RV shows and sales lots to view the real thing. I'm not advocating any of the RVs listed here or discussed in the following pages. All RVs have features to make them worthy of recommendation, but choosing an RV has to be your own personal decision.

TYPICAL PRICES OF RVs BY CLASS

Type of RV	Length and Brand	Used: 10 years	Used: 5 years	New (MSRP)
Truck camper	Bigfoot, 2500-series 15+-ft models	$5,740	$9,080	$25,000*
Class B van conversion motor home	Roadtrek 21-foot	$16,900	$40,000	$67,000
Class C motor home	Jayco 28-foot	$16,190	$28,760	$61,650
Class A motor home	Winnebago Adventurer 35-foot	$26,020	$52,520	$144,000
Popup trailer	Coleman/Fleetwood Bayside 22-foot	$3,200*	$6,500*	$11,000*
Conventional trailer	Bigfoot 25-foot trailer	$6,490*	$9,520*	$19,650*
Fifth wheel	Nu-Wa HitchHiker 32-foot	$18,160*	$26,680*	$44,000*

* Note that towables also need a vehicle to tow them, a truck that is large enough and strong enough for the job. Truck campers likewise need a truck on which to place the camper top. You must add the cost of the truck to the cost of the RV.

Truck Campers

Truck campers are among the most affordable of RVs, at least if you already have a pickup truck. Truck campers are living and sleeping quarters loaded onto the bed of a pickup. The entry door is usually at the rear of the unit, and you sleep in the area over the truck's cab. This cab-over bed has traditionally been small and cramped, but recently manufacturers have addressed that problem and improved the space.

One advantage of a truck camper is that, when you get to your destination or return home from a trip, you can remove the camper from the truck bed and set it up on its own jacks. You can then use the truck as you do normally, to go to town or run errands. A truck camper is a good entry-level vehicle for beginning RVers, especially if you own a pickup truck to put it on.

Small, older truck campers have just the basics in their shell: a dinette, small stove and sink, and a bed over the cab. They don't have holding tanks for sewage and sink water, and they don't have bathrooms. However, new truck campers offer these amenities as standard features; the Bigfoot 2500 series among them. Priced in the

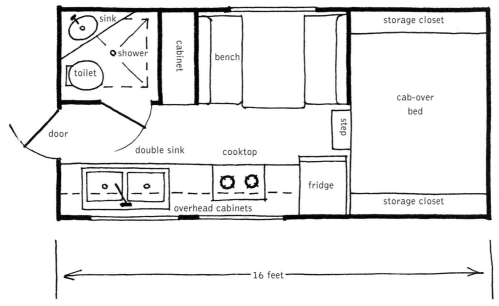

Typical floor plan for a truck camper. Note that there isn't a "living room" in this compact layout. You have space for eating, sleeping, cooking, and bathing—and that's all.

The camper shell can be removed and set on its own jacks.

The Bigfoot 2500's kitchen has a three-burner stove, microwave, plus storage cupboards and drawers.

midrange of the new Bigfoot truck campers, the 2500 series features a nicely organized space in a compact interior. Storage cupboards and closet space line the walls beside the cab-over bed, and more overhead storage is located on the walls over the dinette.

Bigfoot campers in the 2500 series have a 60-by-74-inch bed in the cab-over space. One advantage of a truck camper is that it has a bed that is always made up. In a van conversion and some popup trailers and very small motor homes, you must convert other space such as the dinette into a bed each night.

Bigfoot campers are made of molded fiberglass with a gelcoat finish. The top and bottom sections of the campers fit together like the hull and deck section of a boat. They have 1½ inches of polystyrene insulation to keep the interior warm in winter and cool in summer.

The 2500 series are "basement models," which means that the camper has storage space under the living area as well as freshwater and waste-water holding tanks. The camper shells range in length from 15 feet 11 inches for the smallest model, the 25C8.11, to 17 feet 11 inches for the largest, the 25C10.6. Interior headroom is 6 feet 4 inches. Even Abraham Lincoln would have had no trouble standing upright here.

The specifications for the Bigfoot 2500 series show that the 25C8.11B Shortbox holds 47 gallons in the freshwater tank; 24 gallons in the gray-water (shower/sink waste water); and 14 gallons in the black-water (sewer water) tank. Other models have even larger capacities. With careful use, you can go several days without needing to drain these tanks. The 20-gallon propane tank is standard for small RVs.

Motor Homes

Motor homes are just what you'd expect. Unlike campers and towables, these RVs are quite literally homes with motors in them. There are many different types of motor homes, all of which I cover in the following sections.

Class B Motor Homes

The smallest motor homes are the Class Bs, which are also known as "van conversions." Basically, a van conversion is a standard van with the interior redesigned to allow cooking and sleeping inside. Sometimes the roof is raised by the manufacturer to make standing in the van easier. Van conversions are very compact—good for two people taking the occasional vacation. The smallest Roadtrek van conversion is 18 feet 6 inches in length, and this is probably a typical size. The largest Roadtrek is almost 22 feet long.

Van conversions' main advantages are affordability and maneuverability. You can maneuver with confidence down those narrow, winding country roads in a

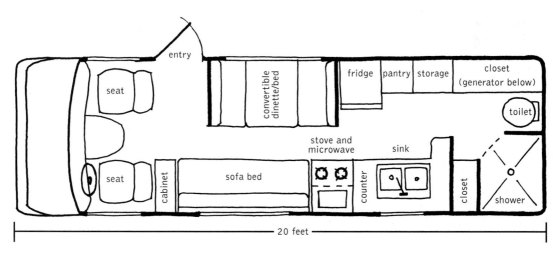

Typical floor plan for a Class B van conversion. Note that both the sofa and dinette convert to beds, allowing enough sleeping space for a family.

Class B and not have to worry about whether you can turn around if you're lost—not the case in a 40-foot motor home or fifth wheel.

Because of their limited size, Class B van conversions have been cleverly designed to pack a lot of features into a small space and to sleep up to four people. However, calling a van conversion a motor *home* might be a bit of a stretch. I don't know anyone who actually lives in a van conversion.

ROADTREK: A TYPICAL, POPULAR CLASS B The Roadtrek Class B, which claims to be the best-selling Class B in the industry for the past fifteen years, costs around $60,000 new. Something to note here is that the Roadtrek is based on a Chevrolet chassis. In general, smaller RVs are based on chassis from the major automobile manufacturers. Even in large Class A motor homes, mechanical components are often from major engine and transmission manufacturers. A number of manufacturers, including Spartan and Workhorse, make chassis especially for Class A motorhomes. Also, some companies like Monaco manufacture their own chassis in order to get a larger size and a particular design.

Roadtrek touts the fuel efficiency and easy handling achieved from the lightweight, aerodynamic design of its vans (gross vehicle weight of 8,600 to 9,600 pounds, depending on the model). Class Bs are a good choice if you're a little uncomfortable with the idea of driving the big RVs, because they aren't much different from driving your family car.

Note that the manufacturer has raised the roof, a common feature in Class B vans, which makes it possible for even a 6-foot-tall person to stand up inside. The interior height of the Roadtrek is 6 feet 1 inch.

Other features of the Roadtrek are a roomy interior with forward-facing seating for up to six, private sleeping sections, easy access to the bathroom, and aisles between the beds after they're set up. You can set up the rear bed and leave it that way because it isn't part of another section like the dinette—a feature you'll really appreciate if you travel for extended periods. Older van conversions typically trade off the bed and dinette, but some of the newer ones have this feature.

Speaking of dining, the driver's and passengers' seats in this van can be swiveled to face a small collapsible table.

The Roadtrek 210 Popular.

Interior of the Roadtrek 190, a moderately sized and priced Class B van conversion, showing four seats and table at the front of the van.

The rear dining arrangement and galley of the Roadtrek 190.

The Roadtrek 210 Popular is 21 feet 11 inches long, compared to the 20 feet 5 inches of the Roadtrek 190. The 210 has a relatively large refrigerator (4 cubic feet compared to 3 cubic feet in the 190) and even a 1-cubic-foot microwave, compared to 0.7 cubic feet in the 190.

Refrigerator sizes are especially important to consider when purchasing a van conversion, or any RV for that matter. The smaller the fridge, the more trips to the grocery store you'll have to make. Out in the wilderness, this can be a problem. Of course,

The Roadtrek 210 Popular, showing kitchen and dinette. Note the amount of space that's devoted to storage cupboards or shelves.

in a van conversion, you won't find household-size refrigerators, but there is a significant difference between 3 and 4 cubic feet.

CLASS B WITH A SLIDEOUT: THE CLASSIC SUPREME Another Class B van conversion, the Classic Supreme, is offered by Great West Vans in Canada for about the same price as the Roadtrek. A unique feature of the Classic Supreme is the optional slideout in the sleeping/dining area, giving some important added living space to this compact unit. A slideout is a portion of the side wall of an RV that remains closed while you're on the road. But after you park the vehicle, you extend the slide. The wall typically moves out from 1½ to 2 feet and allows for a much roomier feeling inside. Older RVs generally do not have this feature, but for the past eight or nine years, newer models of all kinds of RVs have increasingly offered slideouts. Like the Roadtrek, the Classic Supreme has a raised roof to allow for additional headroom.

The dinette area in the Classic Supreme also converts to a bedroom. This feature is not as convenient as a bed you can leave made up, but the additional space gained from the slideout is worth considering. You can also select an option for the two-person bunk bed instead of cab-over storage.

Van conversions do not have the same bathroom facilities as larger RVs, but both the Roadtrek and Classic Supreme have a shower as well as a toilet.

One advantage of the van-conversion type of RV is that the van can be your

only car. During the week, you can take it to work and take your kids to school and to their soccer games, and on weekends or vacations the same vehicle becomes your camper. It's definitely a dollar stretcher, but I don't advise trying to live in one year-round. Everything in a van conversion must, by necessity, be compact, from the refrigerator to the pantry to the closet space.

The Classic Supreme 2004 model.

Before.

After. (The folded-down table is stored below the mattress.)

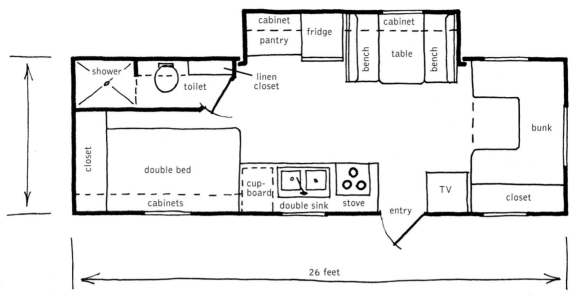

Typical floorplan for a midsize Class C motor home.

Class C Motor Homes

Class C motor homes are built on a truck chassis. They usually have a bed over the cab of the truck. Class Cs used to be small, around 20 to 25 feet in length, but recently they've grown to lengths of 35 feet. Many people feel that Class Cs are more maneuverable than Class As, because they handle like a pickup truck. Bigger Class A motor homes can feel like you're driving a city bus. Class Cs used to be less expensive than Class As, but the price of the new, larger Class Cs, such as the 35-foot Endura made by Gulf Stream, is edging close to the price of Class As.

SMALL BUT ELEGANT: COACH HOUSE CLASS C One small but very elegant Class C is made by Coach House. The Platinum 232XL has a patented one-piece fiberglass body that comes in two lengths, 23-foot and 27-foot, and both are available with a bedroom/living room slideout. The 23-foot model is built on a wheelbase of 158 inches; the 27-foot model on a wheelbase of 170 inches.

Wheelbase length determines the turning radius of a vehicle. A shorter wheelbase is more maneuverable than a long one, while a longer wheelbase provides a smoother ride, and is more stable at high speeds. Of course, you can also fit a bigger coach onto a longer chassis.

The one-piece fiberglass body has become a selling point for this Class C: it is

Coach House Platinum 232XL. The slideout increases the living space dramatically.

The bathroom in this popular Class C includes a large, enclosed shower. In most van conversions the interior of the bathroom itself becomes the shower stall.

lightweight, it minimizes the possibility of leaks (because fewer parts are welded together), and it shuts out a great deal of road noise. The base suggested retail price for the 23-foot model is $108,540, making it the high end of small Class C motor homes in terms of price.

If you're interested in buying a Platinum Supreme, your first decision is to choose between the 23-foot and the 27-foot model. Leaving out the fact that the 27-foot model costs more, deciding on the right size RV is a complex matter, involving comparisons of living space, maneuverability, and parking options. Large motor homes of course have more room inside, but one tradeoff for interior comfort is the need for a larger parking space. This can be a problem on a visit to a mall or supermarket.

If you buy the Platinum 232XL, you may want to consider the optional 6.0-liter diesel engine. The Ford 450, standard on this RV, is a gasoline engine. Gas engines work fine but don't have quite the power or mileage of a diesel. Also, in most parts of the country, diesel fuel costs less than unleaded gas. The nasty little secret no RV salesperson will voluntarily tell you is that all RVs get terrible

Before.

After. The couch easily converts to a bed with the push of a button.

mileage. Gas models probably average between 6 and 7 miles per gallon (mpg). Diesel does a little better at 8 to 10 mpg.

You may have been surprised to see that this small Class C motor home is priced at over $100,000. Don't worry—you don't have to spend that much to buy an RV. To begin with, you don't have to buy it new. Study the chart on page 12 to get an idea of how affordable an older RV can be. Even a new one may cost less than you expect. Chapter 4 explains in more detail pricing an RV and discovering its actual value. You shouldn't have to pay the manufacturer's suggested retail price (MSRP) for a new RV.

The kitchen with a microwave/convection oven, three-burner stove, double sink, refrigerator/freezer, drop-leaf countertop, and slideout pantry.

MODERATE SIZE, MODERATE PRICE: JAYCO ESCAPADE The Jayco Escapade is a larger Class C than the 23-foot Platinum, and it's priced more affordably because it isn't as elegant and doesn't have all the features of the Platinum (for example, the Escapade doesn't have a slideout). The manufacturer's suggested base price on the 2005 Jayco Escapade is in the $60,000 range—the midrange for Class C sizes at 28 feet in length.

The Jayco Class C Escapade.

The Escapade's compact but cozy bedroom.

The interior of the Escapade. The kitchen includes a stove, microwave, large refrigerator/freezer, and lots of storage space overhead.

The bathroom of the Escapade.

The lengths of Class Cs are limited by the size of the chassis on which they are built. Some Gulf Stream RVs and some Jayco RVs are built on the 2-ton Chevy Kodiak chassis which allows these Class C motor homes to stretch to 35 feet.

Inside and outside, the Escapade is well organized for living and for storage. With a longer RV like this, you get larger holding tanks as well as larger propane and gas tanks. The Escapade has 35-gallon gray-water, 37-gallon black-water, and 39-gallon freshwater tanks. Compare these to the 23-foot Platinum, where gray-, black-, and freshwater tanks are 30, 25, and 25 gallons, respectively. The larger tanks mean you can go more days without needing to drain (or fill) the tanks, an important feature if you're dry-camping (camping without hookups).

Jayco owners I've talked to are enthusiastic about their RVs. They mention in particular the excellent service they've received, not only from the dealer where they purchased their Jayco RV, but from dealers across the country as they traveled. Jayco advertises itself as "family owned, family focused" and it certainly seems to be trying to live up to this slogan.

LARGER CLASS C WITH A SLIDEOUT: COACHMEN FREELANDER Not many Class Cs have slideouts, a feature you'll really admire when you see it, but newer Class Cs are beginning to offer this option. One large Class C with a slideout room is the Coachmen Freelander. The base retail price for the Freelander 2490SO is about $63,000.

This model has generous sizes for the gas tank (55 gallons) and fresh- and gray-water tanks (50 and 35 gallons, respectively). Generally, as I mentioned earlier, the rule is the bigger the better for these features.

The Coachmen Freelander Class Cs range in length from 25 to 31 feet.

The Freelander's dinette area. These dinette benches come with seat belts, a great feature if you're traveling with kids.

Freelander's interior.

WINNEBAGO'S POPULAR MIDSIZE CLASS C: THE MINNIE WINNIE Another Class C is Winnebago's beloved Minnie Winnie. The 2005 31-foot model 31C of the Minnie Winnie is priced at about $78,000.

Some models of the Minnie Winnie come with two slideouts, one in the bedroom and one in the living room. Another option is the large, four-door refrigerator.

There is not a lot of propane capacity in these models: just 18 gallons. Since

The 29-foot model Minnie Winnie.

The entertainment center.

The Minnie Winnie's interior. Note the expansive living area, aided by the slideout.

A cab-over bed. Sleeping in one of these requires a little agility to climb in, but once you're there, it's cozy. Kids love it.

propane tanks can only be filled to 80 percent of their capacity, this leaves an actual capacity of 14.4 gallons of propane. On the other hand, the 55-gallon fuel tank will lessen the number of fuel stops.

Class A Motor Homes

Class As are usually larger and more powerful than Class Bs or Cs. Instead of being built on a truck chassis like Class Cs, Class A motor homes are built on a large chassis designed for motor-home use.

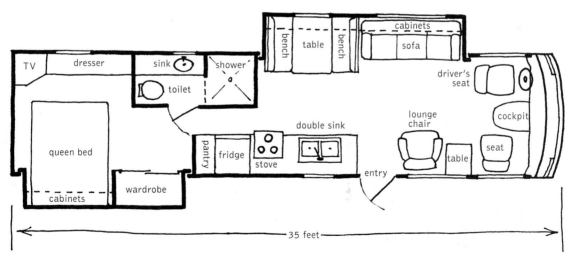

The floorplan for a typical Class A motor home with two slideouts.

Class A motor homes can be powered by either gasoline or diesel engines. Diesel models generally have better performance due to higher torque, but they're also more expensive. Most newer Class As have slideout rooms that increase the living space when the vehicle is parked.

A SMALL CLASS A THAT SEEMS SPACIOUS: THE SAFARI TREK Among the small Class A motor homes, I'm partial to the Safari Trek because of one important feature: the bed is suspended completely out of the way in the ceiling, leaving a nice-sized living space remarkable in such a small motor home. The 26-foot Trek I toured had many of the same features and a feeling of nearly the same space as my 38-foot Monaco Diplomat. The manufacturer's recommended starting price for the 2004 Trek is $111,000.

The Workhorse chassis available on this coach is a new design, specifically manufactured for motor-home use. It replaces the traditional Chevrolet P-30 chassis previously in wide use in the industry. For such a small RV, the Trek has generous 40-gallon water and waste tanks. In 2004, the fuel-tank capacities for different models of the Trek were between 60 and 75 gallons, capacities that would take you a long way between fuel stops.

If you're thinking of living in your motor home full time, you'll want to consider something larger than 24 or 26 feet. The typical full-timer lives and travels in an RV around 35 feet long, and 45-foot motor homes are becoming more and more common.

Treks come in 26- to 31-foot lengths. The Trek does not have a slideout.

Before. (Look carefully and you'll see the bed suspended crossways in the ceiling.)

After. (Here's the same room with the bed lowered.)

A compact kitchen with a lot of work space and a fold-out counter addition.

A LARGER CLASS A: THE MIDPRICED WINNEBAGO ADVENTURER The Winnebago Adventurer is a midpriced, Class A, gas-model motor home. Priced at $144,000, the 2005 35-foot model 35U has two slideouts: one on the driver's side in the living room area and the other on the passenger's side in the bedroom at the back. If you think a slideout is a luxury you can do without, I suggest you visit a sales lot and tour motor homes with and without slides—you'll soon see what I mean.

Is Bigger Better?

Although motor homes come as large as 45 feet in length, there are some drawbacks to this large size. Before you rush out and buy a 45-foot motor home, you need to know that if you hope to visit British Columbia, the maximum allowable combined length for an RV and trailer (meaning motor home plus a tow car) is 20 meters (65.6 feet).

Another real problem with a 45-footer is finding a space in an RV park. Older parks may not be able to accommodate a rig that big, unless the parks have been

The Winnebago Adventurer.

You can easily see how spacious the slideout makes the interior.

Note the large shower, on the right.

The free-standing dinette allows for flexibility. We prefer this design because we can move the chairs for entertaining.

This kitchen offers a lot of counter space.

remodeled. You'll need to check carefully before choosing a place to stop. One RV park where we stayed recently had a few "premium sites," which cost more but were very large. If you have a large rig, you might want to purchase a book called *The Big Rig Best Bets Campground Directory*, available online for $16.96 (www. newrver.com/bigrigbook).

Towables

Unlike towable RVs, motor homes have the advantage of being completely self-contained during travel. There is no barrier between the area where the driver sits and the rest of the motor home. While you're tooling down the road in a motor home, a passenger can go to the fridge and get a cold drink, use the facilities, or even in some cases watch TV. However, towables do have some advantages over motor homes.

Towable RVs are either trailers or fifth wheels. Trailers come in sizes from very small to very large. Towing a small trailer or popup is an inexpensive way to test out the RV lifestyle, especially if you already have a pickup, SUV, or van to tow it with. Some trailers are designed to be ultralight and can be towed by regular cars or SUVs. The smaller trailers and popups have convertible beds: before you go to sleep at night, you have to change the dinette or the couch into a bed and then put that sleeping platform away the following morning, similar to what you have to do in a van conversion. One solution to that dilemma is to cook and eat outside. Some people set up an outside kitchen and dining area wherever they camp, using the interior of their small RV strictly for sleeping.

Popup Trailers

Popups are easy to tow with an ordinary (large) vehicle, easy to manage on the highway, and especially easy to back into a space. All this is because the living space is compressed in size for towing, and height is compressed to around 4 feet.

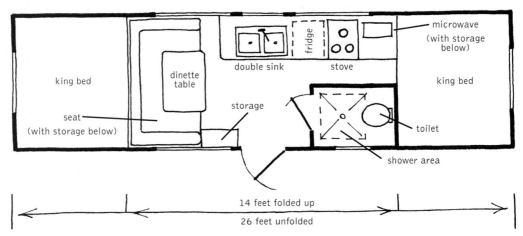

The floorplan for a typical pop-up trailer.

A popup trailer on the move. Note the short bed and low profile.

When you reach your destination, you unfold your trailer out and up, to make a relatively large living space. When expanded, a popup is more like a tent than a solid-side motor home, but within its limitations it's cleverly designed.

Most popups have what is called a "cassette toilet," which must be dumped when full. In a popup, the shower most likely consists of pulling a curtain around the whole bathroom area, which has a drain in the floor. To get a full-size shower, a more convenient way to dump waste, and a larger water tank, you need to move up to a conventional trailer. A popup offers a lot for what it is, but naturally, it can't provide all the conveniences that a larger, fixed-side trailer can offer. That said, popups are relatively inexpensive—only about $11,000 new—so they're

Set up and ready for camp.

The Fleetwood Destiny's interior.

less expensive than many fixed-side trailers.

Let's examine a typical pop-up. The Fleetwood Destiny, shown in the accompanying photos, has a stated sleeping capacity of eight, but I think eight people would have to be very good friends to crowd into a trailer this size at night. Nevertheless, it is relatively roomy for a small RV. The Des-

The Highlander galley.

tiny Bayside has a galley, refrigerator, and Porta Potti, with storage and options for an outside grill. The closed length of this popup is just 19 feet, and the expanded length is 24 feet. Likewise, the height grows from 4 feet closed to 8 feet open.

The Highlander Sequoia is a slightly larger popup made by Fleetwood. Priced

The interior of the Highlander Sequoia.

at around $12,800, the Highlander Sequoia features (among other things) a 16,000 BTU furnace, a three-burner stove and oven (compared to 2 burners and *no* oven in the Destiny), a 3-cubic foot gas/electric refrigerator, built-in 20-gallon water storage tank, and a double sink for easy cleanups.

Travel Trailers

A travel trailer is the first step up from a popup trailer and has the advantage of rigid sides. When you arrive at your destination, your home on wheels is ready to inhabit. You don't have to pop up the trailer. This is also true of fifth wheels, of course, but a travel trailer is somewhat less expensive than a fifth wheel. For many people, the travel trailer is the first step into the world of "real" RVs.

However, traditional travel trailers are falling out of favor with some RVers because they are less stable under tow than fifth-wheel trailers. A fifth-wheel provides more stability due to an extension that locks into the bed of the truck pulling the trailer, directly over the axle. A travel trailer uses a conventional towing connection, which makes it tend to "wag the dog" when you least expect it—something you have to keep in mind when towing. It's very important when towing a travel trailer that its load is balanced and that you drive defensively, because your tow may become unstable under certain conditions. Do not accelerate rapidly to pass someone on the highway or make sudden movements while towing a travel trailer. Also, be careful when a large truck is passing you because his "bow wave" can jostle your trailer and cause it to sway.

Trailers tend to have a low center of gravity relative to the towing vehicle, which creates the potential for "wagging of the dog." This problem can be alleviated by using a stabilizing hitch. PullRite is just one company that manufactures a specially designed hitch to control sway. The PullRite changes the pivot point of the towing apparatus, relocating it to a point immediately behind the rear-axle housing, making the trailer less subject to seesawing motion. If you buy a travel trailer, think about getting a hitch like this. The Standard PullRite has a manufacturer's suggested price of $2,245.

Despite towing problems, there are still a lot of traditional travel trailers on the road—as well as numerous happy customers purchasing and enjoying them. The one I'm most nostalgic about is the classic Airstream, which has been around longer than I have. Yes, you can still get an Airstream trailer in their distinctive aluminum aerodynamic design that has been the company hallmark since 1931.

The Bigfoot 21-foot trailer.

If you're thinking trailer, give Airstream a look. Its trailers are well engineered and carefully designed.

Fleetwood also makes a line of well-designed, popular travel trailers. The Fleetwood Pioneer, for example, comes in lengths of 17 through 30 feet, and its interior reveals a compact but efficient design.

Travel trailers come in all sizes and prices, from as small as 12 feet to as large as 35 feet. Prices range from $8,000 to $80,000, with the average price around $16,000. Remember, though, that you have to have something to tow your trailer. Adding a midsize diesel truck, or something else large enough for the job, will more than double your investment.

The travel-trailer industry has become aware of this dilemma, and some companies are manufacturing compact, aerodynamic trailers that can be pulled by the family SUV—something you could never do with a fifth wheel because fifth wheels are designed to hitch into a pickup-truck bed. Bigfoot is one of the popular models of compact trailers that can be towed by SUVs and some minivans. The Bigfoot is a comfortable home on wheels, well-designed for inside storage with a lot of cupboard space. Some Bigfoot trailers also have a pull-out pantry for extra storage. Bigfoots range in length from 21 to 25 feet.

The bedroom and galley of the Bigfoot.

The dinette area.

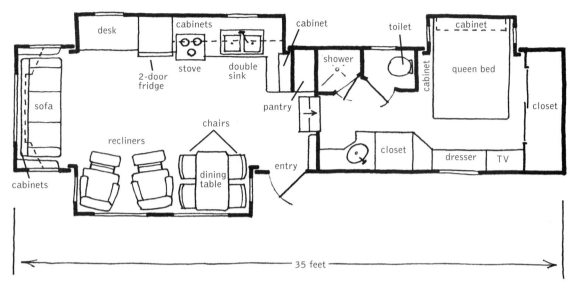

Floorplan of typical fifth wheel with three slideouts. Because the driving space is located else-where, the interior of a fifth wheel is roomy.

Fifth Wheels

Most full-timers I know live and travel in either a fifth wheel or a motor home. Each of these has advantages and drawbacks, and the choice actually comes down to personal preference.

A fifth wheel is a kind of large trailer with a forward section that rests in the bed of the pickup truck that pulls it. Large fifth wheels require large trucks to pull them, making the price of a fifth-wheel/truck combination equivalent to the price of a Class A motor home of about the same length. Most fifth wheels have a bedroom in the part of the trailer that extends over the truck bed.

A LIGHTWEIGHT MIDSIZE FIFTH WHEEL: THE HOLIDAY RAMBLER SAVOY

In 2004, Holiday Rambler started making a lightweight fifth wheel called the Savoy, which can be towed by a standard half-ton truck instead of a commercial-weight vehicle. The Savoy comes in 27- through 30-foot lengths.

Like most fifth wheels, the Savoy's cab-over bedroom space above the hitch is accessible via a short flight of stairs. The Savoy comes with an attractive living space, complete with slideout. Most models of this RV have only one slide, but the 27-foot 27RKD has two slides on opposite sides of the living area.

The Holiday Rambler Savoy lightweight fifth wheel.

THE NUWA HITCHHIKER: A LARGE TRIPLE-SLIDE FIFTH WHEEL The HitchHiker by NuWa is another popular fifth wheel with a number of attractive features, the most appealing of which to me are the triple slideouts, two in the living room and one in the bedroom. The 2005 33-foot LK TG model of the HitchHiker Premier has an MSRP of $62,500. The 35-foot model is priced at $64,400.

To pull a large fifth wheel like the HitchHiker requires a very large truck. You can easily be persuaded that a less expensive, smaller truck will do the job, but if your tow vehicle is underpowered, you risk burning out the transmission. Consider a midsize diesel truck to pull a large fifth wheel.

The exterior of the HitchHiker Premier.

The HitchHiker Premier's interior.

The HitchHiker Premier's kitchen.

The HitchHiker Premier's bedroom.

THE GREAT DEBATE: CLASS A MOTOR HOME OR FIFTH WHEEL?

Price doesn't seem to be a factor in choosing between fifth wheels and motor homes. Initially, you pay about the same, although you can change the dwelling part of your rig a lot less expensively when you have a truck and a fifth wheel. You keep the truck and buy a newer, larger, or better-designed house on wheels. Also, you may pay more insurance if you have a motor home and a tow car. You're insuring two vehicles with engines that way.

Motor homes have the advantage of being self-contained on the road. You can leave your seat and get a drink or use the restroom while your partner guides the motor home down the highway. A motor home can hold three children belted safely on the couch, with their books and games spread out beside them. You can't do any of that in a fifth wheel, because you're more or less captive in the truck while your house follows behind. You can't get at the house until you arrive at your destination.

In choosing a fifth wheel, you have to be sure you have a truck with enough horsepower, whereas with a motor home the manufacturer has made that decision for you. Any motor home will have enough power to get itself and a reasonably sized tow car down the road and up the hills, although a diesel-powered motor home will do this better than a gas-powered one.

Some fifth wheel owners like the appearance of their interiors better than the "living rooms" of a motor home. In a gas-powered motor home, even if you turn the driver and passenger chairs around to face the room, you still have a "doghouse" above the engine. Diesel-powered motor homes have the engine in the rear, eliminating the "doghouse," but in any model of motor home you have a cockpit up front with steering wheel, gear shift, and instruments—not quite as elegant.

Ultimately, choosing one rig over the other comes down to which one you feel drawn to. If you're trying to make this decision, there is no substitute for cruising the RV lots or going to RV shows. Walk in and out of a lot of rigs and get a feeling for what they're like and which one you'll be happiest in.

3

Choosing the Features and Options You Want

When you're choosing an RV, you need to consider exactly what features you want. Think about mechanical options like the engine type (diesel or gas), the engine size of your motor home or tow vehicle, the size and type of the RV, the storage capacity of the rig, sleeping arrangements, cooking and refrigeration, and heating and cooling. All of these features will loom large in your life as you travel, so make sure you look at enough RVs to make a considered decision. The RV you ultimately choose may not have all the features you want, but in that case you'll at least knowingly accept its limitations as a trade-off for something else, like price.

The RV Kitchen

Realtors will tell you that the kitchen of a house can make or break a sale, especially for the person in the family who does most of the cooking. Many RVers tell me that the kitchen design was an important factor in their choice of RV.

Some people do the majority of their RV cooking outside. They have hot plates and barbecue grills, and enjoy cooking and eating outdoors most of the time. If you prefer eating outdoors, your kitchen might not be as important to you. That said, even if you plan to do your cooking outdoors, you'll undoubtedly get pinned inside by rainstorms or (heaven forbid) snowstorms once in a while. On those occasions, you'll want and need a kitchen that works, as well as a pleasant dining area inside your rig.

Stove and Oven

The stove is the most important item in most kitchens. The cooktop on your RV stove will probably have three or four burners. Something to check is how those burners ignite. Newer models generally have an igniter on the stove next to the burner controls, but in older or smaller stoves you may need your own—a hand-held igniter or a match. The built-in igniter is a nice feature and saves having to find, buy, dig out and use something else.

Another consideration is the oven. The conventional propane oven that comes in many RVs, located below the cooktop, has one advantage, and that is its large size. You can roast a turkey or bake a large pizza.

A drawback of the full-size oven is that it uses a lot of propane, which you also need for your furnace, hot water, and on-the-road refrigeration. In addition, propane ovens heat up the RV while you're baking.

Instead of a full-size oven, your RV kitchen may have a convection oven/microwave combination, usually mounted on the wall above the cooktop. Con-

Most RV cooktops have a folding cover, adding to counter space for meal preparation, and three or four burners.

The galley of the Prowler Regal fifth wheel.

vection ovens are the size of their microwave partners, which isn't very big. If you have a convection oven, you may have to shop for small baking dishes—such as 12-inch pizza pans and 6-cup muffin tins—to fit it. With a propane oven, you can probably use the baking pans you already have.

Because of their smaller size, convection ovens have one advantage: they're terrific space savers. With the oven mounted above the cooktop, the entire space below is free for storage.

If your RV has a convection oven, you need to make some adjustments when using it. Convection ovens work a little differently from conventional ovens. They cook a little faster, so you may want to set the baking temperature a little lower or check for doneness sooner than you would when baking in a regular oven. Some convection ovens radiate the heat down from the oven top. In this case, you'll need to cover cake pans when baking so that a skin doesn't form over the batter before it has time to rise. These adjustments aren't hard to make, and convection ovens can generally produce the same quality product as the larger conventional oven.

Don't ignore the microwave when it comes to cooking, either. It's not just for heating leftovers. You may be surprised at the variety of foods you can cook in your microwave—everything from scrambled eggs to fresh vegetables.

Sink

Be sure to weigh sink options in the rig you're considering. A porcelain sink is attractive in appearance but subject to chipping. A fact of RV life is that things tend to fall out of the cupboards the first time you open them after you've been traveling, and a cup or bowl can easily make an ugly chip in your porcelain sink. A stainless steel sink is impervious to whatever may fall on it.

The other consideration about sinks is size. The smaller your rig, the smaller your sink will probably be. Consider whether your dishes and pots will be a match for your sink. If you like to make soup or cook corn on the cob in a large pot, your pot may not fit into a tiny sink when the time comes to wash it.

A double sink this large makes washing up a snap.

Dinette

All RVs have some kind of dinette. The major differences are usually the size of the table and the seating arrangements. Some tables are extendable, pulling out to increase the size from a table for two to a table for four or even five. Bench dinettes, fixed benches on either side of a built-in table, are the most common seats, but the freestanding dinette, with two or four chairs instead of a bench, has more flexibility. You can use the chairs as extra seats if you have a lot of visitors, or stand on one to reach something in an upper cupboard. When traveling, the chairs ride comfortably beside the table. On the other hand, bench dinettes often have extra storage under the bench seat. In a small RV, that extra storage can be important.

If you aren't really into cooking, and you plan to have a lot of outdoor barbecues, some of the kitchen and dinette features may not be important to you. Make your own list of priorities, and keep them in mind when you look for your RV.

Refrigerator

Any rig you buy will have a refrigerator already installed. The refrigerator may be something barely large enough to keep your beer and sodas cool to something almost as large as your fridge at home. As you're looking at RVs, keep in mind what size refrigerator you want, or decide what size you can live with.

RV refrigerators are very specialized. They have to operate under conditions that don't occur in a stationary location like a house. For example, they have to work while bouncing down the road and while going through external temperatures that might differ 50 degrees during the course of a single travel day.

A household refrigerator works only on 120-volt AC, but an RV refrigerator must be able to keep things cold when the rig is not plugged in to electricity. "Two-way" RV refrigerators are powered by 120-volt AC while the rig is hooked up to power, and by propane gas while dry camping. They will also run on propane while you are traveling down the highway (see discussion in Chapter 10). Three-way models also work on 12-volt DC (battery) power. The way RV and house-

Two companies, Dometic and Norcold, manufacture most RV refrigerators.

hold refrigerators cool things also differs. The RV system uses an evaporator to cool, while the home refrigerator uses a compressor.

One final note about RV refrigerators: if you can, try to get one with an icemaker. If you've never lived with an icemaker, you'll quickly find how addictive they are. The RV lifestyle goes hand in hand with tall cool drinks (lemonade, ice tea, etc.) outside on patios under the shade of awnings. You'll wonder how you ever lived without an icemaker.

Bathroom

RV bathrooms come in many different sizes and arrangements; as you can guess, they're larger and more comfortable in the more expensive models. When you inspect the bathroom in an RV you're thinking of buying, keep in mind a few important features, including privacy. Do you care if your bathroom has a door? Surprisingly, not all RV bathrooms have this feature.

Also, check the bathroom for storage. Is there a medicine chest with enough room for your medicines and cosmetics? Remember that having toiletries standing on your sink countertops isn't practical in an RV, because you have to put them away every time you move. Is the area under the sink roomy enough for storing soap, shampoo bottles, and other large items? Where are you going to keep clean towels and washcloths?

Look at the shower itself. Is it big enough to suit you? Showers are small in less expensive rigs.

Along with small-size showers go small hot-water tanks. A 6-gallon hot-water tank makes for a very short shower. If that's how much hot water you can expect, you have two choices. The first is to learn how to take a quick shower (turn on the water to get wet; turn it off while you soap up; turn it on

The shower in this popup trailer occupies the entire bathroom space. Note the drain in the bathroom floor.

again for a quick rinse, and follow the same pattern for washing your hair). The second option with a short supply of hot water is to use campground showers. Many folks like to do that—you'll see them traipsing across campgrounds, often in bathrobes, with their towels over their shoulders, carrying tote bags full of soap and shampoo. Others dislike the bother of gathering up soap, shampoo, and towels and leaving the comforts of "home" to shower.

How you feel about showering in your rig will help determine your choice of bathroom. It's something worth considering, because it'll be part of your daily life as long as you're traveling in the rig you choose.

Washer/Dryers

If you have a washer/dryer in your RV, you're giving up some storage space. You need to ask yourself if you can spare that space. If you can, there are still some special considerations associated with RV washers and dryers.

Two kinds of washer/dryers are used in RVs. The front-loading combination washer/dryers are the most common in RVs, and they come in two types: vented and unvented. A vented machine requires cutting a hole in the RV wall so the hot air and moisture from the drying process can be vented outside. Non-vented machines don't require a hole in the wall; moisture extracted from the clothes becomes steam, which is then condensed into water and drained into the gray-water tank. The non-vented machines have a bad reputation due to leaking and flooding, and I don't recommend them. Go ahead and cut that hole. You'll be happier—I guarantee it.

The main drawback of the combination machines is that they're small. They can wash and dry a load no bigger than the clothes two people wear in one day, so to keep up you need to use them almost daily. Many people don't wash their sheets in the RV machines; instead, they use Laundromats to do these larger loads or loads that dry slowly like jeans and towels. Those who do wash sheets in their RVs run a separate cycle for each sheet. The drying process in a combination machine is much slower than that of the dryers in a house or Laundromat, because home machines use 220-volt power, while the RV models use only 115 volts. Drying a load can take from an hour to an hour and a half. As for towels? They take even longer. But, on the other hand, you don't have to sit around and watch them dry as you do in a Laundromat.

Some people wash and dry their clothes while they're traveling down the road, running their generator as they go to accomplish this time-saving feat. Others put the clothes in the washer and then go to town, or go for a walk and swim, and when they return the load is done, clean and dry. Still others run the wash at night while they sleep.

If you're staying where 30-amp power is all you can get, you have to be careful when you use the washer/dryer, because it draws a lot of current (about 15 amps by itself, which can be a lot because most rigs also have hidden loads like the house battery charger, electric hot-water heater, instant-on television, etc.). People who have washer/dryers in their rigs often choose to run their machines at night, when the machines aren't competing for power with the microwave, heater, air conditioner, and other appliances. There is nothing more annoying than tripping a breaker in the middle of whatever you're doing. Sometimes it's only a circuit breaker inside the coach, but sometimes it's more complicated than that—a problem best avoided if possible.

The most common RV washer/dryer combo is made by Splendide. Users of newer Splendides are generally satisfied with their machines. If you have an older model, a few problems may arise, such as difficulty removing parts to replace them, or leaking when you remove the lint filter to clean it. The older Splendide models have lint filters that must be cleaned regularly, but the new models have a recirculating pump design, which allows lint to pass through the pump and out the drain. Splendide claims that this feature completely eliminates the need for a filter. However, these new machines do have a strainer to catch coins and larger items. As for problems removing parts, Splendide has eliminated many mechanical parts in its newer models by making them electronic and adding built-in self diagnostics.

A large motor home or fifth wheel can accommodate a stacked individual washer and dryer, with the dryer on top of the washer, as you find in some apartments. The stacked units are larger than the combination single washer/dryer unit that most RVs have. That means they can do more wash per load, but it also means they use more space, more

The Splendide washer/dryer combination.

Kenmore's stackable washer and dryer will handle a lot more laundry than a combination unit.

water, and more electric power as well. An advantage of the stacked units is the fact that you can wash one load while another is drying, if you're plugged in to enough electric power to handle the draw.

Kenmore makes a pair of stacked units that many RVers use and almost universally praise. These machines are designed to run on 120 volts. The height of a stackable combination is a factor, however. The height of the Kenmore combination is 71½ inches. That's pretty tall for an RV but not impossible to consider. The capacity of the washer, 1.5 cubic feet, is about the same as the Splendide, but the dryer is twice that size at 3.4 cubic feet.

This is the only "laundry center" Kenmore makes that runs on 120 volts. Kenmore also sells individual units that can be stacked, but this model, the 88732, is the most popular with RVers. To stack these units, you must buy a stacking rack, or you can install them side by side or in two different locations if you have the room.

Having your own washer/dryer is convenient, but with the combination unit, the loads are small and the water and power usage is high. In order to have the stackable washer and dryer, you need a large rig plus the capability to plug into 50 amps of power, although my friends with stackables have managed to use them with 30 amps by making sure everything else is turned off. You have to decide for yourself how much you want the convenience, and which kind of machine you can handle in your rig.

Bedrooms

The majority of RVs of any size, even some truck campers and popup trailers, come with a queen-size bed. "Island queens" are bed arrangements that provide ample space to walk around them—a highly desirable feature when it comes to making up the bed in the morning. Otherwise, in a bedroom where the bed reaches from wall to wall, you have to be something of a contortionist and crawl across the bed to perform this daily chore.

Another factor to notice in the bedroom is the amount of closet space. Many RVs have only a half-size closet, on the theory that you're going to be wearing mainly shorts and shirts as you travel and won't need to hang up long articles of clothing. However, that isn't always so. If you're going to bring long pants, long skirts, and dresses, check whether there is a closet to accommodate them.

This tight-fitting popup trailer bed doesn't provide enough space to walk around it while making it.

The closets on either side of the bed in the picture below are small and narrow, but they are not the only closets in that bedroom. A wardrobe runs the entire length of the wall to the right, and a dresser is opposite the foot of the bed. This bedroom, which slides out, also has space for a washer/dryer combination.

Smaller RVs have a variety of space-saving sleeping arrangements. Truck campers have a bed in the area over the cab. The space can be claustrophobic, but newer truck campers are tall enough to allow a little more headroom up there. Kids love these beds, while adults tolerate them if the price of the rig is within their budget.

Most RVs, even popup trailers, have some space that can be converted into an extra bed (by adding a mattress to a dining table, for example). Think about how these will work for you in actual practice. Making your dinette into a bed is fine for the occasional overnight visitor, but it can get old fast if you have to do it every night during longer stays. You may want to dig into your pocket for enough money to buy a rig with a couch or spare bed you can leave set up all the time while traveling with a guest.

If your rig has a couch in the living area, the couch probably converts into a bed. However, some couches are short, and the bed they convert to may be long enough only for a child. An adult might have to sleep

The Prowler Regal's "island bed" has walking space on both sides.

at an angle in order to stretch out. Whether an extra bed, and its size, are important to you depends mainly on how many guests you intend to have overnight in your RV, as well as their ages and sizes.

Electrical Features

Depending on the size, newness, and type of your RV, you may have a generator and an inverter. These are very useful features if you plan to dry-camp in some beautiful wilderness areas without electricity. Generators and inverters provide electrical power when you can't get it any other way. They're also useful in case the power goes out at the campground where you're staying. That happens more often than you might expect.

You'll also want to check whether the RV you're interested in is wired for 30-amp or 50-amp service. Larger, newer RVs often have 50-amp wiring. With 50 amps, you can run almost all the electrical equipment in your RV simultaneously. You can have both air conditioners on at the same time, a factor that's probably only important if you go to visit someone in Phoenix in August. Many camp-

A 30-amp plug, like the one shown here, will have two prongs plus a ground plug; a 50-amp plug has three prongs and a ground plug.

50 amp outlet

30 amp outlet

You can tell whether the electricity is 30- or 50-amp by a quick inspection of the receptacle.

grounds are only set up with 30-amp service, so you need to purchase an adapter for your 50-amp RV so it can plug into 30 amps.

Generators

A generator uses gas, diesel, or propane to create electrical power. A generator's power is measured in watts; to figure out how many electrical items it will power, you can add up their individual watts.

If you buy a motor home, it will most likely come with a generator. The generator in a motor home usually runs on the main fuel source—gas or diesel—and will be located near the fuel tank from which it draws. For example, in a gas-powered motor home with the engine in the front and gas tanks in the rear, the generator will be in the rear. In a diesel pusher, which has gas tanks near the front and the engine in the rear, the generator will be located near the front. Trailers and fifth wheels don't usually have generators as standard equipment, partly because they don't have a ready fuel source. The generators in these RVs are usually optional items, and they must be powered by the same propane tanks that provide heat and cooking fuel for the RV.

Some generators are hardwired to your RV's electrical system and can be started from within your RV's interior. Other generators feed electricity into the same external power cord that you use at campsite hookups. This means that during a power outage you'd have to go outside, remove the plug from the hookup, and plug it into the generator. Because power outages are more likely to occur during high winds and heavy rains, this is precisely the time when you'd least want to be outside fussing with the power cord. I recommend you opt for a hardwired generator.

A large enough generator can provide as much power as you'd get from a 50-amp power source. That is, it can power your microwave, small appliances, and two air conditioners simultaneously. If your RV does not come with a generator, you might consider having one installed. Most RV stores can supply and install them. Onan, Honda, and Kohler all make lightweight RV-style gen-sets. They're the ones supplied in most units today. However, aftermarket models

A typical generator.

A typical inverter.

are not always lightweight. Quite the opposite. Before running out to buy one, consider where you'll fit it and how much weight it will add to your total load.

Generators are noisy. Your neighbors—and most likely everyone else—will hate the noise. Be sure to run your generator only during the day and only if you have to.

Inverters

Inverters change DC power to AC power. That is, they draw power from your house batteries and change it to electrical power to run your appliances such as microwave, TV, and VCR. Most inverters don't supply enough power to run an air conditioner, but if the people around you would be bothered by your generator noise, and you want your morning cup of coffee and/or morning TV show, they're a godsend. However, since the inverter draws its power from your house batteries, it can draw them down if you run it for a long time, so inverters remain a short-term power solution. Inverters are more often found in motor homes than in towables.

Awnings

Most fifth wheels and motor homes come with an awning, a feature you'll appreciate on hot sunny days. An awning provides shade and defines your outside living space beside your motor home, trailer, or fifth wheel. The shade provided by an awning can also help keep your interior cool. Some rigs have small awnings over most of the windows as well as a large patio awning.

The newest innovation in awnings is the power awning. After you've set up a conventional awning a few times—it works best if two people can perform this task—you'll appreciate the idea of just pushing a button to extend your awning.

A power awning can be opened with the simple push of a button.

Some awnings, including the Weather Pro (opposite page), are so automatic that they sense wind and/or rain and roll themselves up, but I've heard they have a propensity to roll up when you aren't expecting them to. When the wind and/or rain are not that bad and you want to enjoy the shelter and shade of your awning, suddenly—whoosh—away it goes, leaving you exposed to the elements.

Awnings can be persnickety. They have a lot of little parts that can fail and leave you with the awning permanently extended, unable to roll up, or, if rolled up, unable to come down. But when they work right, they're must-haves.

Slideouts

Slideouts are a popular feature in newer RVs, and are now offered in every kind of RV, including truck campers, van conversions, motor homes, trailers, fifth wheels, and even popup campers. The slideout is a room that, as the name implies, slides out after you're at a site and leveled, to make your living area larger than the conventional width of an RV, which is generally no wider than 102 inches.

A slideout adds from 18 to 32 inches to that width, but you can't measure what it does for your psyche. In a few seconds, by pressing and holding a button, you go from cramped to spacious. The room slides out slowly to its full extension. When you're ready to leave, move anything from the floor or elsewhere, especially cupboard doors or the driver's seat, that would prevent the slideout from coming all the way in, and hold down the button until the slide is all the way in. It's that simple. Slideouts have rubber seals that prevent moisture, dust, or anything from the outside getting into your RV.

Some newer RVs have three and even four slideouts. In most cases, the third slide is a second feature in the living room: both sides of the room slide out. The fourth slide is an additional spacemaker for the bedroom area.

A slideout is a feature you need to look for when buying your RV. Although it is possible to add them on to an older coach as aftermarket items, as in bus conversions, it's an expensive process, costing from $40,000 to $50,000.

Slideouts create a few problems when you're selecting, pulling into, or backing out of a site. In addition to aligning your rig with the electric, sewer, and water connections,

Two slideouts add a lot of interior living space.

you'll need to make sure there are no obstructions such as trees, rocks, pipes, or low walls that will prevent you from extending the slideout.

Slideouts extend from about $1\frac{1}{2}$ feet to $2\frac{1}{2}$ feet. In RVs with three slides, the third slide in the living room on the passenger's side of the coach is usually 18 inches deep, while the one on the other side is about 2 feet deep or deeper. Some very upscale models of RVs have small slideouts. The rationale is that smaller slides are more stable and have fewer problems.

If you want to get an early start each day, or if you are staying overnight in a commercial parking lot like a Wal-Mart, you will probably not want to extend your slideout when parked. In most cases, everything in your RV—your appliances, etc.—will still work. The RV will be just as functional, especially if you'd planned ahead and removed needed items from cupboards that are not accessible when the slideout is in.

Storage Space

A creative RVer made this outdoor entertainment center in a storage locker.

The amount of storage that you have in your RV will depend in part on its size, but design is also a factor. When you go out to look at any RV, go through each area inside and ask yourself what you want to bring along and use there, whether kitchen, bedroom, bath, or living area. Look at the cupboards and the closets. Are there enough? Many RVs have clever storage areas under dinette benches or under beds. Check these out to see how much room they actually have. Look at the closet or closets. Do you need a full-length section for dresses or long skirts, or can you make do with a shorter closet?

Outside, examine the lockers. Some of them will be taken up with batteries and/or propane tanks. Look at the empty ones for ease of access and size. A pull-out tray in a storage locker can be a big plus, making for easy access. Some RVs have an "entertainment center" in an exterior bay, so that you can watch TV or listen to music in your patio.

Diesel vs. Gasoline Engines

When you're buying an RV, the type of engine is an important consideration. The size and type of engine greatly affect the price. The amount of power the engine provides impacts the ease and comfort of your travel.

Classes A and C motor homes come in two basic types: gas-powered and diesel. Trucks that tow trailers and fifth wheels are also available with both types of engines. As mentioned earlier, diesel engines have a lot to recommend them, including mileage, power, and durability. However, diesel-powered coaches cost considerably more than gasoline-powered coaches. The increased power makes a difference when you go up a mountainous road, but it's a difference you pay for. Don't forget, though, that the diesel engine is substantially more durable than the gas engine, because it doesn't work as hard, seldom exceeding 1800 rpm.

An RV with a diesel engine will cost more, so the first question you need to ask is whether you're willing to pay more to get it. You may be willing if you're buying a large RV, in the 34-foot or larger range, especially if you enjoy traveling in the mountains or are planning long trips where the terrain is uncertain and may be steep. In addition, diesel fuel is cheaper in most states and most diesel engines get slightly better mileage than gas models, but note that I said "slightly." In a diesel, you may get 8 miles to the gallon compared to 5 or 6 in a gas-driven RV. If this comes as a huge surprise compared to your car or SUV, consider the fuel cost factor when you're considering how large an RV you want to buy.

An interesting fact about diesels is that, when evaluating a used diesel motor home, you don't even consider whatever mileage it has accumulated. Diesel engines are designed to be so rugged that you can drive them hundreds of thousands of miles with no major problems. Conversely, a high-mileage gasoline-powered motor home will definitely be priced lower than a low-mileage one. The 70,000 miles we had accumulated on our gas-powered Dolphin when it was six years old counted very much against its trade-in value.

When your list of "must-haves" and "nice-to-haves" in your dream RV is completed, it's time to look at your budget and decide what you can afford to spend on your new RV and what your options are for trade-ins and/or financing. The next chapter helps with that.

4

Buying a New (or Used) RV

Before you begin to look for an RV, make a list. What do you absolutely have to have in your home on wheels? What would you really like to have but would give up for the right deal? If you and your spouse or partner are making this purchase together, be sure you both have input into this wish list.

Rank the features you want as "must-have" and "nice to have." "Must-haves" are deal breakers, and "nice-to-haves" are things you really want but may not find in an RV within your budget or things you won't cry over if you don't get.

Then go look at a wide variety of RVs, and see how manufacturers organize them. Think about floor plans. Think about the size of the shower. Does one of you need or want a lot of bathing space or can you settle for using campground showers? Think about the refrigerator. How big a fridge do you need? How long will you be traveling and how many grocery shopping trips are you willing to make? Think about an ice-maker, a feature I recommend in Chapter 3. Do you want a washer and dryer in your rig? Where? In the bedroom? In the hall?

Another question to resolve in the course of looking at a variety of RVs is whether you want to buy new or used. There are arguments to support either idea. A new RV will cost more, but because it's new, you won't initially have many problems. Things can go wrong with even a new RV, but the warranty ensures that at least you don't have to pay for any repairs. Your budget can then consist of only the RV payment plus insurance and registration costs, without the need to factor in repairs. Another bonus of buying new is that you'll get the latest features, like slideouts, that older models may not have. Here's where having made a list of what you want comes into play. If you want, for example, a flat-screen TV, you won't find it in an older model. However, some features, like newer TVs and washer/dryers, can be added on to older rigs. Here you can do a balancing act between the costs of add-ons compared to the cost of newer models that already have those features.

How Much Is It Worth?

You've made your list and decided on the type of RV that is right for your style of travel. You've selected among a variety of makes and models, and you have a list of features that are important to you. Most important, you've gone in and out of a lot of RVs to be sure of what you want, and what you don't want. In short, you're ready to buy.

The next step is finding out the value of the RV you want to buy, and the value of your trade-in if you have one. There are several ways to accomplish this, and I suggest you try all of them. You're going to be spending a lot of money here, and you don't want to part with any more than you have to.

Maybe you've been to a dealership just to look, and a clever salesperson has roped you into considering a deal. Before you place your trust in a salesperson, you need to do your homework and find out the numbers for yourself. Then you'll be so happy when you find a dealer whose price agrees with what you already know.

There are a number of ways to evaluate an RV. Sometimes it's easier if the RV you're interested in is used. In that case, you can go to the NADA website (www.nada.com), click the recreational vehicle tab, and fill out their form with info about your prospective purchase. They'll give you, for free, a high-retail and low-retail appraisal of the RV. This is a good first step. However, the figures you get this way are just approximations. A lot of variables enter into the actual price or value of any RV.

The NADA data assumes that you're looking for the value of an RV you want to purchase and not for the value of a trade-in. Be careful when filling out the NADA form online. It's best to ignore the "optional features" section. Checking the items in that section will unrealistically inflate the value of the RV, because most of the optional items on the list—like air-conditioning and microwave ovens—are standard on most RVs. You'll probably get a more realistic figure if you don't try to list add-ons when filling out NADA's form.

RVs-R-Us (described below), whose evaluation of my trade-in's value I used when purchasing our 2003 Monaco, cautions that people using the NADA website need to be aware that NADA is a dealer's association and the numbers they provide a consumer may favor the dealer. RVs-R-Us also points out that NADA puts out a separate wholesale guide for dealers, which includes "suggested list prices" that are not mentioned in their information for consumers.

NADA figures will give you a place to start when evaluating an RV you're interested in: consider those figures as one piece of the picture but by no means all of it. You may also want to get the Kelley Blue Book appraisal. Kelley and NADA do not absolutely agree; NADA is usually higher.

Kelley Blue Book appraisals are not available on their website (www.kbb.com). Instead, Kelley offers its motor-home guide, which is updated three times a year, and its trailer guide, which is updated twice a year. Each of these guides costs $50. If you want information on just one RV, Kelley will send you a certified copy of that one page from its book for $25.

There is another, more affordable way to get both NADA and Kelley evaluations for less than $50. RVs-R-Us (www.rvs-r-us.com) charges $14.95 for an e-mail appraisal of a used RV, using both the Kelley and NADA values. They'll send you the results via email in 24 hours or less, so if you have a deal pending you can find out quickly if the price is right. As well as evaluating a particular RV by e-mail on the next business day, RVs-R-Us will give you an instant quote over the phone or by fax, within an hour of your telephoned request, for $18.95. For the same price, they'll send by "snail mail" a written response to your written request.

Recently, RVs-R-Us has added a new feature to the services they offer: they'll evaluate a new rig for $24.95. (Both Kelley and NADA give information only about used RVs.) Using the information Dave provides, you can find out how much money a dealer has in any given rig, and then calculate a reasonable profit (or what you're willing to pay to give the dealer a reasonable profit).

What a dealer has paid for a new RV is a closely guarded secret, and some RV dealers try to take advantage of a prospective buyer's ignorance about this information when they mark up their RVs. When people say an RV has depreciated a great deal in the first year, it's a sure sign they paid too much for it.

Dealer costs, taxes, and the value of a trade-in are all fixed. The only option for a dealer to play with is the price. On the other hand, RV dealers need to make a higher profit per item than car dealers do, because RV sales are not as high in volume as car sales are. Many RV dealers sell in a year what a car dealer sells in a month. As a buyer, you have to walk a tightrope between paying too much and giving the dealer a reasonable profit. The best way to succeed at this high-wire act is to have as much information as you can about the rig you want to buy.

Whatever you do to find out the value, it's crucial to enter the negotiations for an RV just as you would when buying a new or used car. Learn as much as you possibly can about the RV you want to buy, especially what it's worth. That way, you know when to walk away and when to jump at the deal.

Optional equipment in the RV is listed on the sticker as an increase in price, but most if not all of those options should actually be included in the price you pay. RV manufacturers include in each production run of a certain model items like a four-door refrigerator, power seats, two air conditioners, and so on. These items are actually standard because all models of that year contain that equipment. This is not to say that you can't get optional equipment added to your RV, but make sure when you're buying one that you don't pay extra for anything that every model will have.

When you've obtained a possible value for the RV you're interested in, through NADA, Kelley, or RV Dave, be sure that you price the RV you want with as many dealers as you can possibly visit. See if their asking prices are anywhere near the numbers you've obtained. The Internet is one way to do this, and visiting RV dealerships is another. Do both of these if you can.

Don't be ashamed to haggle. Offer a much, much lower figure than the sticker price and see what happens. Try offering two-thirds of the sticker price. After all, you have nothing to lose by starting low. Walking away sometimes works well, too. Now is the time to let your head rule your heart.

One final piece of advice. Don't let the salesperson suck you into considering monthly payments. This is a very common ploy. The salesman, instead of talking price, will ask you how much you can afford to pay each month. If you name a figure, he'll probably try to persuade you that you can actually afford a little more. "Just the cost of a few meals out or a movie or two," he may say. Don't fall into the trap. Don't ever tell the salesperson how much you want to spend per month. What you want to have clearly in mind is the full price of the RV you're buying. How much is it going to cost? This is exactly what an unscrupulous salesperson will try to steer you away from. A full price of $100,000 is much scarier than $900 per month.

Financing

You may want to set up your financing before you even look at an RV. Be wary of the dealer's financing, even if it's one of those special low-interest deals that are advertised to get you on the lot. Many deals like that are only for "top credit-rating customers" and even if you have flawless credit, that interest rate may simply "not be available anymore." Or, if you're approved for the low-interest financing deal, the price of the RV may be higher, or the amount offered for a trade-in may be less, to compensate. Don't talk to a dealer about financing until after you have your deal locked in.

If you do business regularly with a bank or credit union where you're known as a customer, it pays to ask them about their rates. Find out how much they'll lend you on a specific year and model of RV, and get pre-approved for a loan that fits your budget. That way you know exactly how much you can spend, and you can stand firm when the salesperson tries to move you up a few thousand dollars to a better or newer model, or one with more features, or with credit terms more favorable to the dealership.

Making the Best Deal

So now that you know what you want to buy and you know what you want to pay, or what is a reasonable price range, where do you go to get the best deal? RV prices vary with the season and the seller, so you'll want to do a lot of hunting before deciding where and when to buy. Many different dealers may offer the same coach under very different terms.

An RV show can be a good place to buy a new RV, especially at the end of the show when dealers must either sell or transport the vehicles back home. You may get a very good price here, but be sure you have all the information discussed in the preceding section before you buy.

The end of the RVing season can also be a good time to buy. Dealers don't want to have their lots full of RVs during the cold winter months, and they may price them favorably just to get rid of them. Dealers have to make interest payments on all the RVs on their lots, and that can add up during the slow season, so you may find a highly motivated dealer. If you're buying a new rig, the manufacturers themselves may be offering price incentives. The end of the winter season, before the spring travel time begins, is still a good time to buy.

BUYER BEWARE

We once went to an RV dealership just to look, and an unscrupulous salesperson took advantage of our complete ignorance. We hadn't planned to buy, and so we hadn't done any homework. We actually wound up with a good quality, 35-foot, three-year-old motor home, but we paid way too much for it. We got caught up in buyer's fever, falling in love with the coach, hypnotized by the fact that it had a slideout and that the interior was attractive and had everything on my list (yes, I had a list—although it was entirely in my head), and the fact that it was eleven years newer than the motor home we were driving at the time.

We didn't know the value of the coach we were buying, and we trusted the salesperson to be fair with us. However, every time I asked to see the blue-book value for the coach we were buying, he changed the subject. I remember expressing surprise at the price, which he quoted at $89,500 and said, "Oh, don't worry. We'll give you a lot of money for your trade-in." Well, he didn't give us enough. We eventually discovered that this three-year-old RV had sold new for $92,000, and when we came to trade it in three years later we discovered that we owed $23,000 more than the coach was worth.

The moral of our story is that before you place that kind of faith in a salesperson, you need to find out on your own the value of the RV you're interested in and the value of one you're trading in. Don't depend on anyone's sales staff to give you this information.

What about buying from a private party? There are two sides to this possibility. One is that you can often get a very good price on a used RV from a private party. People buy an RV and then find they don't use it often enough to make it worth keeping. Or someone dies and the surviving spouse has no interest in traveling alone and just wants to get rid of the thing, sometimes at a real bargain.

On the downside, a private party won't give you the kind of guarantee that a dealer will. If something fails on your used RV two weeks after you bought it, you're out in the cold if you bought from a private party. If you bought from a dealer, you may have some recourse, depending on the sales contract.

One good way to find an RV offered by a private party is to look in the RVing magazines such as *Family Motor Coaching* and *Highways*. In the back sections of these magazines, people advertise their rigs for sale, often at bargain prices. Of course, you can also look on the Internet, where you'll find many dealerships and consignment websites. RVs are also listed for sale at eBay Motors, but I don't advocate bidding on and buying an RV sight unseen.

The advantage to looking on the Internet for the RV you want is that, in a very short time, you can get a good idea of what prices some people and some dealers are asking for them. This doesn't tell you what price the seller is actually getting, but it's one more piece of the puzzle. The more you know, the better deal you'll be able to make.

Before you make a final decision, check out RVs in person. This is the only way you'll know what features you really don't like, such as TVs down low where the driver's chair blocks your viewing, the designs of some bathrooms and some kitchens, and some hideous upholstery patterns and colors. This final visit will firm up in your mind the features you're sure you want. You may find some new features you didn't know about, such as automatic awnings or four-door refrigerators with ice in the door, or plasma TV screens that fold down. Check them out, then check them out again.

After you've decided on just one RV, be sure that you examine it carefully before you buy, especially if it's used. Take it for a thoughtful test drive. How does it feel? How does it maneuver? How does it stop? Look at the tires for tread. Read the dates on the tires to see how old they are; an RV's tires should be replaced every seven years, even if they've just sat in storage all that time, and even if good tread remains. Replacing RV tires is costly.

Inside the RV, examine everything: the fridge, the storage areas, the toilet and bathroom. Examine the ceiling for water stains, a sure sign that the rig has a leak. Turn on the TV, run the microwave, flush the toilet. If possible, bring along someone with some experience in your type of RV who can help you evaluate it. Unless you have complete faith in your own savvy about engines, brakes, and transmissions, have these features checked by a mechanic you trust.

Taxes, Registration, and Insurance

After you purchase your new RV, you'll have to register it in some state. In Chapter 18, I talk about how full-timers can select their domicile state based on their own personal criteria. Among these criteria are sales tax and registration fees.

The states that don't have sales tax are Alaska, Delaware, Montana, New Hampshire, and Oregon. You may want to purchase your RV in one of those states, but after you do so, you still must register your RV in the state where you live and that licenses your vehicles. If you're not in a tax-free state, you may be charged a fee equivalent to your state's sales tax when you register your RV.

A completely legal option is to form a Montana nonresident corporation and register the vehicle in Montana to the corporation. Montana has no sales tax and its licensing fees are reasonable. We have Montana plates on our Monaco motor home, although we're registered voters in Texas, which also issued our driver's licenses.

To form a Montana corporation, you need the help of a Montana-based attorney. The classified pages of several RV magazines, in particular *Escapees*, carry ads that will put you in contact with a Montana lawyer who will manage your corporation (for a fee) and handle the annual re-licensing of the RV. A word of caution: check with your bank or the finance company that will handle your loan to make sure they don't have a problem lending to a Montana corporation. If you're getting your loan through a bank that knows you well, they should trust you. A Montana attorney can refer you to local Montana finance companies, if desired.

Before you drive your new RV anywhere, you'll need to insure it. Just like shopping for the best price, be sure you shop around for the best insurance. And remember that the best RV insurance is not necessarily the cheapest. RVs are not the same as cars; a number of companies specialize in insuring them. That said, don't overlook the company that insures your car. Find out how an insurance company classifies an RV and whether they penalize you for full-timing (if you plan to). Don't be persuaded by a company that professes to provide RV-specific insurance but actually provides coverage that is normally part of a homeowner's or renter's policy and actually costs more than each of these policies obtained separately.

You can find a number of RV insurance companies in magazines like *Family Motor Coaching*, *Trailer Life*, *Escapees*, and *Highways*. Camping World RV stores also sell RV insurance. Be sure to survey many companies, and also ask your RVing friends which insurance company they use and why.

To sum up, follow these steps for a satisfactory RV purchase at the best price:

1. Know what you want.
2. Know the value of what you want.
3. Price it at a variety of different places.
4. Arrange financing ahead of time.
5. Consider options for insurance, sales tax, and registration fees.

The Walk-Through

When you're actually taking possession of your new RV, a dealer will give you a walk-through. If you're buying from a private party, ask the owner to take you through the RV.

A walk-through can be a fairly detailed procedure lasting more than an hour, or it can be cursory. Try to get the detailed one. This is the dealer's or owner's opportunity to show you what you need to know to operate the RV, and also to demonstrate to you that everything is in good working order.

Take notes, take pictures, or even make a video, to solidify in your mind exactly what you're learning about this particular rig. Otherwise, you'll find yourself on the first night asking, "Now where is the sewer hose and how do I hook it up?" (You'll be given an owner's manual, but don't rely on that to tell you everything you need to know.) During the walk-through you can ask any questions that come to mind, and find out where the controls for everything are located. One friend of ours who didn't attend to that during the walk-through regretted his inattentiveness on his very first RV trip. He pushed the button that turns off all power and then wondered why he couldn't start the RV.

If this is your first-ever RV, there are some things you definitely want to learn (for example, which features of the RV are battery-controlled and which can only be used if you're plugged in to electricity). We have friends who borrowed a fifth wheel and the first time they used it, at a campground without hookups, were totally mystified by the fact that the lights worked, the radio played music, and water flowed from the faucet but they couldn't use their electrical appliances (toaster, coffeemaker), which required AC power.

You need to be shown how to run the generator, if your RV has one. Some generators require that you be unplugged from shore power and plugged into the generator before it runs. See where the controls are, inside and outside, and locate the circuit breaker for the generator. Find out the same information for the generator controls that are located in the interior of the coach. (More information about RV electrical systems can be found in Chapter 7.)

Outside, find out what's in the lockers, where the propane tank is located, where the electric cord, hose connection, and sewer connections are, and how you connect each of these to hookups. Find out where the fuel goes in—you'll need to know this before you pull your big rig into a gas station for the first time. On our coach, we can fuel from both sides, which is really advantageous.

Inside, be sure you know where the water tank is located, as well as the thermostat that controls heat, air, and fan. Find out how the microwave works—they're all a little different. Are there any quirks to the TV or sound system, if you have one? How does the couch convert into a bed? There are several variations of toilets in RVs. Make sure you know how to flush your particular toilet. If you have an inverter, how do you turn it on? What does it take to light the stove burners—are they automatically sparked or do you need something to ignite them?

Taking your RV on its first journey will be much more fun if you've figured out all these things ahead of time. And who better to show you how it works than the salesperson or the previous owner?

PART TWO

Using Your RV

5

Driving Basics

Even strong men and women, experienced drivers all, feel intimidated the first time they find themselves driving a 40-foot motor home. It's just not the same feeling you get behind the wheel of the family sedan.

Many people (myself included) have chosen to attend an RV driving school. For around $300 an experienced instructor will give you eight hours of instruction in your own rig, beginning in a parking lot and including freeway driving, backing, and parking. Taking such instruction is a real confidence booster. Contact information for one of the most well-known driving schools is given in the Appendix.

However, with a little practice, you can teach yourself to drive a big rig. After all, your RV isn't all that different from a car, it's just bigger and needs more time and more room when turning or stopping. A little time behind the wheel will make you comfortable with your vehicle's size and performance.

Driving Forward

Many people like to get started driving their new RV in a large empty parking lot. A church parking lot in midweek or a school parking lot during the weekend both provide a perfect opportunity for practice. (And room for error!)

Once you've found the lot, the next step is to get your seat adjusted so the pedals and steering wheel are at a comfortable distance for you. Many trucks and motor homes have adjustable steering wheels and powered driver's seats to facilitate this task.

not safely stop short of the intersection. When you pass that spot, you're committed to going through.

Highway Driving: Entering, Exiting, and Passing Safely

After you're comfortable on city streets, take a deep breath and try a freeway. If possible, get on a freeway that you're familiar with so you'll have a sense of traffic flow and where the exits are. You may find that freeway driving is easier than street driving, because the road is wider, there are no traffic signals, and there are no cross streets to worry about. The trickiest part of driving on the freeway will be *entering* the freeway. As you approach the freeway on the ramp, use your left mirror to see the traffic that you'll soon merge with, then time your entry such that you do most of your accelerating while you're still on the ramp. The goal is to be close to highway speed when you merge with the freeway traffic. This doesn't mean that you have to drive down the on-ramp at 65 miles per hour, but if you're only going 30 mph, you may become a road hazard for other drivers.

Never think that you have to go as fast as the posted speed limit or other drivers unless you're comfortable doing so. Remember that it takes much more time to slow or stop a large vehicle—and the faster you're going, the longer it takes to stop. At speeds below 40 miles per hour, leave a 4-second time gap between your RV and the vehicle in front of you. Here's how to measure the gap: pick a mile marker, highway sign, or any other fixed object on the side of the road and begin counting when the car in front of you passes it. If you can count to four before you pass the same object, you should have ample stopping distance. If you're driving faster than 40 mph, leave a 5-second gap.

If you collect a train of vehicles behind you in a situation where they cannot safely pass you, ignore them and drive at your comfortable speed until you come to a place where you can safely pull over and let them by.

If you decide to pass another vehicle, try to do it on level ground where you can accelerate easily. Remember that a large motor home or truck is slow to accelerate, especially if it's towing something, so you'll need a lot of room and a lot of time for passing. If you're towing a trailer, remember that sudden moves may make it unstable. When passing another vehicle, wait until you have a full image of that vehicle in the right-hand mirror before pulling in front of it; this will make sure you're safely past it. If you change your mind about passing after you've pulled out, be aware you need to make that decision quickly to give yourself enough time and room to safely pull back into your space.

When you're ready to exit the freeway, keep your speed up as much as practical until you're close to the ramp. Remember to signal your intention, and be sure to slow down to the suggested speed for the exit ramp. If the ramp is extremely curved, be extra cautious. Keep your eye open for truck tipping warning signs. You may have ignored these signs for most of your life, but now they apply to *you*.

Driving Safely

Driving an RV—as you've probably figured out—is different from driving a car. You'll need to pay particular attention to weather, terrain, and overhead structures such as bridges.

Wind

Some highway conditions are downright dangerous for an RV. One of these is wind. An ordinary car is not bothered by wind as much as a vehicle with a high, broad profile like a motor home, or a trailer being towed (which can pivot dangerously on its tow-bar like a tail wagging a dog).

A tragic accident occurred in Utah in December 2003 when a motor home went off the highway on a curving road in high wind. The driver, his wife, and five of the seven children in the motor home were killed. The road was icy, curving, and, worst of all, lashed by strong winds. No one knows the details of exactly what caused this crash, but the inexperienced RVer's main mistake was simply being out there in such conditions. Sometimes it's just better to stay off the highway and wait for better weather.

Motor homes are top-heavy and tend to sway. Wind exacerbates this condition. Therefore, when you're driving in wind, slow down and steer carefully. Note highway warnings about windy sections of the road or anticipated gusts. Some particularly notorious locations are marked by wind socks. When you see any of these markers, pay close attention and drive defensively—keep your speed down and maintain a good distance between yourself and other vehicles.

Wind also can cause problems for trailers. Trailer yaw can occur unexpectedly when a gust of wind hits the trailer sideways. When a large truck passes a trailer, it pushes a column of air ahead of it that can also cause the trailer to yaw suddenly. If you see in your mirror that a truck is approaching, be sure you have both hands on the wheel to keep control. If your trailer or tow car starts to yaw, don't panic and don't try to correct the yaw. Steer straight ahead to regain control. If possible, don't use the tow vehicle's brakes. However, the braking systems on some trailers allow you to actuate just the trailer's brakes from the tow vehicle. If you have this option, applying the trailer's brakes alone can be an effective method to correct the yaw.

Rain, Sleet, and Snow

Quickly stopping a motor home or fifth wheel under optimum conditions can be difficult; in wet weather, it can be a nightmare. Here's where an auxiliary braking system for a motor home's tow-car, or electric brakes on a trailer, can literally be a lifesaver.

Even if you have these safety devices, stopping on ice is difficult. Your best bet? Don't go out on ice in the first place. There are situations that call for scrapping the plans, changing the reservations, and waiting until the weather improves. Being an RVer provides its own flexibility. What's the rush? You're already home. Take advantage of it. Modify your plans if you experience inclement weather. It's not worth risking precious lives.

Steep Hills

A roadmap will show you where the highways and streets are located, but the average roadmap doesn't indicate the locations of steep grades. A book called *Mountain Directory*, on the other hand, does. It's actually intended for truckers, but we've found these books a great help in planning our routes. When we know where the steep grades are, we can make a choice to take a different route or plan for extended driving time across the mountain. East Coast and West

Grade signs let you know what to expect from upcoming hills.

Coast versions of the book are available. More information about these books can be found in the Appendix.

The higher the percentage of grade, the steeper the hill. Depending on your engine size and the weight of your rig, you might slow to a crawl when climbing a hill. Be prepared. If you see a steep hill looming ahead, speed up and take it at a run. Hopefully, you won't slow down quite as much. If you do, you don't have many options. Just relax, take it easy, and fantasize about having an engine with more power.

Driving down a steep grade can be as intimidating as going up. It's a good idea to enter a steep slope at a moderate speed so you're sure to maintain control. If you're driving a gasoline engine, downshifting is a good idea in this situation. In lower gears, the engine's compression helps slow you down so you don't have to ride the brakes.

If you're driving a diesel, use the "Jake brake" according to manufacturer's instructions, but watch the tachometer. The Jake brake will slow you down, but the transmission will automatically select a lower gear at the lower speed. This will cause the engine to turn at higher rpms than it should. Accelerating slightly will cause the transmission to shift into a higher gear. This will allow you to maintain a lower rpm. The Jake brake will still retard your speed, although you may have to go down the hill a bit faster than you want in order to keep the engine within the desired rpm range.

A rule of thumb is that the less you use your brakes, the longer they'll last, not only when going downhill but over their entire lifetime. If you apply the brakes constantly while going downhill, you run the risk that they'll overheat and fade or stop working entirely. Continuous light braking is preferred to pulse braking. If you're towing a trailer, you can use the trailer brakes to slow your descent, but put them on only briefly each time. If you're driving a motor home and towing a car, this is one situation in which you'll be grateful if you have an auxiliary braking system on the car. The main consideration in downhill driving is to take it slow and easy.

Bridge Clearances

Be sure you know the height of the highest part of your rig. Almost all bridges or underpasses on freeways will have their height marked, and we have never encountered a bridge clearance too low for our motor home on a freeway. Driving in the country is a different matter. Those colorful, old covered bridges were designed with a horse and buggy in mind. Often, they may have no posted maximum height. If you aren't sure whether your RV can clear a bridge (or anything else for that matter), don't attempt to drive under it. Taking a different route to avoid becoming stuck or ripping the air conditioner off the top of your rig is definitely worth the trouble.

Parking, Backing, and Leveling Your RV

After you drive your rig safely to its destination, the next step is parking. With an RV, parking is not just a matter of pulling into a campsite and turning off the engine. The hookups in nearly all campgrounds are on the same side which means that unless you are lucky enough to have a pull-through site, you will need to back your motor home, fifth wheel, or trailer into the site to connect the RV's utility panel on the driver's side. Then, after you back in, you'll have to level and stabilize your RV.

Backing

Backing can be an intimidating maneuver. It can be even more intimidating if you're towing a trailer or fifth wheel. I recommend you get lots of practice in an empty parking lot.

BACKING A MOTORHOME Backing a motor home isn't any more difficult than backing a car. The main concern when backing a motor home is being able to see any obstacles behind you. Low-down obstacles may not show up in your mirrors, so the best way to back into a campground site is to have someone stand outside your RV and guide you in with hand signals or a handheld radio. If you're the person doing the guiding, use some basic arm motions to indicate forward, right, left, or stop. Be sure to stand where the driver can see you, usually in line with the driver's-side mirror.

   If you don't have a partner to help you back up, back just a little, get out, inspect where you are, get back in, and move a little more; repeat this procedure until you're safely where you want to be. If you keep the motor home parallel to a curb or line on the ground, you'll stay straight. If you're using a mirror while backing, remember that images are reversed. If you have a split-view mirror,

Both hands held apart tells the driver to come straight back. Sometimes the thumbs are used instead of fingers.

Note that one hand is encouraging the driver to keep moving and the other indicates the direction of that move.

change the setting so you can use the upper, undistorted flat section of the mirror and have a clear view of the ground.

If you're towing a car, things get significantly trickier. The general rule for this situation is: Don't back up with the car attached. You need to stop, detach and move the car, and then back up. For this reason, you'll have to be careful not to get in a situation where you have to back up (until you get to a campground). But, from time to time it does happen. For example, you may have taken a wrong turn down a narrow dead-end road. Just relax, stop, get out and detach your tow car so you can back out.

BACKING A TRAILER OR FIFTH WHEEL "Pushing a rope" is an expression that may come to mind the first time you try backing a trailer or fifth wheel into a campsite. Towables have a tendency to "jackknife" when backing, so you'll definitely want to practice this maneuver in an empty parking lot. Otherwise, you may become the evening's entertainment as everyone in the campground gathers to watch you fumble around.

When backing a trailer, start by grasping the steering wheel with one hand at the bottom. As you turn your hand to the right, the trailer will go right, and if you turn your hand to the left, the trailer will go left. Put your other hand on the top of the wheel, so you have complete control, and back very slowly with your eyes on the mirrors. If the trailer moves in the wrong direction, don't panic—just

This fifth-wheel trailer is backing straight into the parking slot while the tow truck is cocked at an angle.

turn the wheel the other way. Again, having a partner to guide you with hand signals is a good idea. You'll probably have to pull forward and change directions a few times, then back up some more, before you've correctly placed the trailer where you want it to go.

Consider the pivot points of both the tow vehicle and the trailer. For the tow vehicle, the pivot point is the rear axle; for the trailer, it's the hitch. Don't be embarrassed to pull out and start over, several times if necessary. Backing a fifth wheel is a little easier than backing a trailer because the pivot point of a fifth wheel is in the truck bed directly over the axle, where it is more easily controlled.

Leveling

If you don't have jacks or levelers, and you do nothing to level and stabilize your RV when you park it, you may find yourself in the predicament faced a few years ago by a couple I'll call Roger and Joan. Roger and Joan had parked their motor home at a terraced site in an RV park. They didn't have jacks or levelers, and they somehow forgot to set the parking brake. They checked everything else and went to bed. During the night, the couple's playful little dogs chased each other inside the RV and one of them knocked the gearshift lever into neutral.

Roger and Joan had a rude awakening as their motor home gently but inexorably slid down a hill to the terrace below. Fortunately, they missed the big tree stump that was almost in their path. Unfortunately, they had to call for a huge tow truck to pull them back up to their site the next morning. Meanwhile, the campsite personnel found them a place to sleep in a rental cabin for the night. Roger banged his knee and had a few cuts and bruises, but he was otherwise unhurt. The dogs were just fine!

Roger and Joan actually made two mistakes here. They didn't level or stabilize the coach and chock its wheels, and they didn't set the emergency brake after putting the gearshift in Park. You don't have to spend a lot of money on stabilizers or levelers—in a pinch, a few sturdy, 24-inch-long 2×8 or 2×10 boards under each tire will do. Lay the board on the ground and drive over it. To make this task easier, you can cut a 30- to 45-degree bevel at each end of the board. Make sure that you have some method of keeping your coach where you want it, and keeping it level.

WHY LEVELERS? Every time you park at a camping spot, you'll need to think about leveling your rig. Being level can very important to the health of your RV's refrigeration system. And even if you don't have a refrigerator to worry about, walking around the inside of an RV that isn't level is like being on a carnival ride or a fun house with a moving floor. Bottom line: You'll need some system of levelers.

TYPES OF LEVELERS Larger, newer motor homes come with leveling jacks that can be lowered from inside the coach. Some will even test themselves every so often to make sure you're still level and straighten themselves automatically if you aren't. The hydraulic leveling system made by RVA in our 2003 Monaco is typical. The three jacks—one in the front and two in the rear—are controlled from within the coach by three controls, one for each jack. A light indicates when the jack is deployed, and another light shows when the coach is level. You can also use a large bubble level placed on the floor or a kitchen countertop. If adjustments are needed, each jack can be raised or lowered from the driver's seat. The controls will also warn you via a loud horn and flashing red light if you attempt to drive off without raising the jacks. Leveling and stabilizing the motor home is a process we can accomplish in minutes.

The situation is different if you have a trailer or fifth wheel, where getting level and getting stable are two different things requiring two separate systems.

First, while the trailer or fifth wheel is still attached to the tow vehicle, check to see which side is low. Then level the trailer left and right by backing the trailer's wheels over the necessary number of 2×10 boards or plastic leveling blocks. You will need one board or leveling block for each wheel on the low side, or a single board long enough to go under all the wheels on that side. The good news is that you only have to place a board under the low side of the RV. If the campsite is completely level, you don't need a board at all.

After leveling left and right with a board, detach the tow vehicle from the trailer or fifth wheel. Next, extend the two front jacks, either manually or with a motor. Motorized front jacks may have a single switch that runs both at the same time, or two switches that permit one jack to be raised independently from the other. The jacks have holes at 1-inch intervals through which a locking pin can be inserted when they're in the correct position. You can use the front jacks to fine-tune the left-to-right leveling, but they're mainly designed to make the trailer level front to back.

The third step involves putting down stabilizing jacks at the rear of the trailer. These are usually lowered with a hand crank, although some new, larger models have a

Boards can provide makeshift footpads for jacks that come without. The board provides additional stability. If the front jacks needed to be at different heights, a second board could be placed under the lower one.

These rear stabilizers are motorized—an uncommon but desirable feature.

Stay well to the side of an RV when sliding a board under the jack.

motor to accomplish this. Lower the jacks just enough to stabilize the vehicle. Stabilizing jacks in the rear of a trailer or fifth wheel are not designed to lift any substantial amount of weight.

The larger and heavier your rig, the larger and more sturdy your jacks must be to support it. At the end of our jacks is a plate called a footpad, which prevents the jacks from sinking into the ground; however, if you're camped on damp, muddy ground, you may sink anyway. On hot, sunny days, it's possible to sink into asphalt. In those cases, retract the jack and place a board under each footpad to increase its surface area.

You can also buy polymer plates that will do the same for you. Level-Eze is one good brand. The advantage of the plates is that they come with a rope to pull them in place and remove them, so you don't have to risk life and limb crawling under your coach and shoving in a board. Also, the plates are rated for 40,000 pounds while a 2-inch board is probably not.

If your motor home doesn't have levelers, you'll have to improvise in some fashion—you can't always camp at a perfectly level site. The most basic way, as described earlier for trailers and fifth wheels, is to have a set of boards or blocks to drive onto. Sometimes you're too high in the front, and sometimes you're too high in the back. After you've leveled your rig on the boards, set the parking brake and chock the wheels to make sure the RV won't slide off the boards and to keep the rig stable.

Many people use plastic blocks like those made by Camco or Tri-Lynx. Camco makes a wedge-shaped leveler that allows you to raise the RV $1\frac{1}{2}$, $2\frac{3}{4}$, or $3\frac{7}{8}$ inches. The advantage of the wedge shape is that it's easy to drive on. Tri-Lynx makes stackable, interlocking blocks that look a little like LEGOs. You pile them up to the desired height, and drive or back onto them. Tri-Lynx levelers are roughly $40 for a set of ten. You can get them on the Internet and at most RV stores.

Tri-Lynx leveling blocks.

You can also add aftermarket jacks to your RV. Jacks come in three basic configurations: straight jacks; kick-down jacks that are hinged so they fold up when not in use; and scissor-type jacks that move apart or together around a fixed center. Scissor jacks are usually used for stabilizing a trailer or fifth wheel.

U.S. Catalytic Corporation and BAL RV Products Group offer aftermarket jacks that come in a variety of sizes to fit different rigs. BAL's QTG levelers cost around $270 for the front and $350 for the rear (according to the latest catalog from Camping World). To use them, remove the travel pins so the jack drops to the ground and then lift the RV to the desired height with a hand crank.

HWH is a major manufacturer of rugged, dependable leveling systems for Type A, Type B, and Type C motor homes. In HWH systems, a panel installed adjacent to the driver's seat indicates which parts of the coach need to be raised to make it level. You can raise and lower each foot independently. HWH also makes a computerized system that does the whole process automatically and checks itself to make sure you remain level. Quadra, another major jack manufacturer, makes a four-jack leveling system called Big Foot for types A and C motor homes.

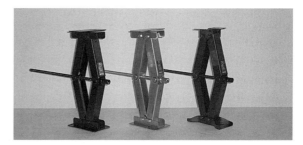

Scissor jacks are used to stabilize trailers.

Professional installation is necessary for

all these systems. You can buy them at such places as Camping World, but if you do, you need to have Camping World's mechanics perform the installation.

A word of warning: Use your levelers only as they're intended. Do not use them to jack up your RV in order to change a tire or work on the brakes. They aren't intended to lift the entire weight of your RV, and they might fail while you're underneath it. Don't risk it!

Also, when leveling a motor home do not accidentally lift the tires of your RV off the pavement. Doing so can stress the frame of your coach and may twist the chassis. The windshield may even pop out of some units. If you find one wheel in the air, redo your leveling procedure to correct this situation.

POSSIBLE PROBLEMS AND HOW TO SOLVE THEM Designs have been improved over the years, and jacks in newer RVs will probably last for years. But if you're starting out in an older rig, you may have some problems with its levelers. There are two basic problems you can have with jacks. Either they won't come down when you want them to, or they come down when you don't want them to. If your jacks fail to lower properly, check the level of hydraulic fluid before you conclude that professional intervention is needed. Low fluid can cause them to malfunction. Refer to your RV owner's manual for how to locate the reservoir, check the level, and add fluid.

If your jacks lower unexpectedly while you're traveling, one of the bolts that holds the jack in place may be missing or stripped. You can temporarily remove the jack until you reach your destination, and then replace the bolt. If the problem recurs, contact the manufacturer.

Whatever type of leveling system you have or select, leveling the rig is a procedure you'll learn to perform almost automatically each time you pull into a site. Your refrigerator will thank you, and you'll be much more comfortable.

6

Towing and Hitching

Towing a Car

If your RV is a motor home and it is fairly large, say 30 feet or longer, you may want to tow a car behind it. That way, when you get to your destination, you can unhook your tow vehicle and go shopping or exploring. Parking a 40-foot vehicle at the supermarket is no fun, and it's also a problem to move your RV in and out of a site after you have hooked it up to utilities and leveled it.

Finding Out Whether Your Car Is Towable—and What to Do If It Isn't
Your first consideration needs to be whether your car is towable on four wheels. Some vehicles require that an auxiliary transmission pump be installed to prevent transmission damage during towing. As a general rule, cars with manual transmissions are more apt to be towable than automatics, but some automatics can be towed.

To find out if your car is towable, check with a local dealership (although it has been my experience that dealers don't always know which of their cars are towable and which are not). Some owner's manuals address this issue; others don't. If you're a member of Family Motor Coach Association, go to their website (www.fmca.com), click on Motorhoming Guide, then click on Towing. Under the category of towing, click on Selecting a Towed Vehicle, enter your member number, and you'll find an up-to-date list of towable cars going back about three years. Another comprehensive list—available without any membership requirements—

can be found on *Motorhome Magazine*'s website (www.motorhomemagazine .com). Scroll down on the home page until you find the Dinghy Towing category (towed vehicles are often called *dinghies* or *toads*), and click on the model year you want to check. (Note: This list requires Adobe Acrobat Reader to read. Most computers come with Acrobat Reader already installed, but if you have trouble opening the file, go to www.adobe.com for a free download.)

If your car isn't towable on four wheels, one solution (short of buying a new car) is to get a tow dolly. With a tow dolly, you run the front wheels of your car onto the dolly, fasten it safely, and then tow the dolly and car to your destination. Dollies cost about $1,200. A drawback of this arrangement is that when you're parking your motor home, you also have to park both the dolly and your car. Tow dollies can take up a considerable amount of space in a crowded campground.

Buying a Tow Package

If you have a tow vehicle, you have to get a towbar. Be prepared to spend some money on this—about $1,000. Although that price may seem steep, this is not an item to skimp on. You want to be able to trust your tow bar to do the job and not release your car in the middle of a freeway somewhere.

The two most common brands of tow bars are Blue Ox and Roadmaster. Both of these are easy to hitch and unhitch.

In the case of the Blue Ox, the two bars that hook the car up to the coach are placed in the front of the car where they're inconspicuous. Most of the tow equipment stays on the motor home, folded up neatly in back. Older Roadmaster towbars had the majority of the equipment bolted to the front of the car, making it ugly and awkward-looking to drive around town; newer Roadmaster models stay attached to the motor home in a similar manner to the Blue Ox. Keep in mind that appearance is not why you buy a towbar—the Roadmaster towbar is as rugged and durable as the Blue Ox. Look into both brands and see which works best for you.

A number of federal and state laws regulate the towing of vehicles. You must have a tow bar that is rated for the weight of your vehicle. If you're towing a relatively small, light car like our Hyundai Elantra, which weighs around 3,000 pounds, you can get by with a Class III tow bar, which is rated up to 5,000 pounds. Actually, I wouldn't recommend doing that because if you buy a larger car in the future, say an SUV, you would have to replace your tow bar and that would be

The two tow bars jut out just a little from the front of the car.

expensive. We have a Class IV tow bar, rated for 10,000 pounds. You must also check the weight capacity of the receiver on the back of the coach, the device to which you hook up the tow bar. Ours, like most newer coaches, is rated for 10,000 pounds.

If you plan to tow a larger vehicle, such as an SUV, you should consider that the more weight your motor home tows, the lower its gas mileage. Given that typical motor home mileages are in the 7–8 mpg range, towing a heavy vehicle could get expensive.

The laws in most states require that you have two or more safety cables or chains attached between the motor home and the tow car, crossed underneath the tow bar to prevent it from falling to the ground and lifting the car up in the air in a breakaway situation. Safety cables are rated the same as tow bars:

CLASS WEIGHT LIMITS FOR
SAFETY CABLES AND TOW BARS

Class I	2,000 pounds
Class II	3,500 pounds
Class III	5,000 pounds
Class IV	10,000 pounds
Class V	14,000 pounds

You also need a base plate attached to your tow car—bolted on rather than welded. Finally, you need to have the lights on your car (turn signals, brake lights, etc.) wired so they'll work in sync with the motor home. The RV store where you buy your towing gear will likely have technicians who can install and wire your towing equipment. It's not a do-it-yourself project, in most cases.

Towing Your Car Safely

Every time you start up your coach to go somewhere, as part of your getting-on-the-road checklist, make sure the brake lights, flashers, and turn indicators are working properly. At the same time, make sure the car has been set into neutral gear, with the emergency brake off, and that the ignition key is turned to the "accessory" position so that the wheels are free to turn and the steering wheel is not locked. Newer cars will not show an increase in the mileage on the odometer while they are being towed, but older models might.

Here are the steps for safe towing of a car:

1. Inspect all the parts for loose bolts or excessive wear. Make needed repairs before hooking up. Bolts can be secured with either Loctite or a double nut.
2. Connect motor home and tow car on a level surface. Hooking up on a slope complicates the whole process.
3. Hook up the tow bar to connect the car to the rear of the motor home.

Attaching the tow bar to the motor home.

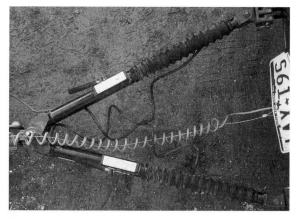

Crossed safety chains.

Hooking up electrical connections.

4. Make sure the car's key is in the ignition and turned to the accessory position

5. Rotate the steering wheel to make sure it moves freely.

6. Make sure the parking brake is released.

7. Cross the safety cables between the motor home and car, attach them, then wrap them around the tow bar legs so they won't drag on the ground.

8. Attach the electrical cable, and make sure the lights work on both the motor home and tow car. Include headlights, turn signals, and brake lights in this review. Note: the car's headlights do not need to be on. If you turn on the motor home's headlights, the car's tail lights will be lit. To make sure that the car's battery does not get drawn down during towing, make sure that the car's radio, air conditioner, and other electrical devices have been turned off.

Driving a Motor Home with a Car in Tow

Driving a motor home with a car in tow is no different than driving the motor home by itself—at least while you're driving straight. The tow car will follow wherever the motor home goes. The only difference is you'll need extra room to complete the turn.

Remember not to back up while your tow car is attached. You may need to detach the car before parking unless you can park by pulling straight ahead into a large space, such as a campground "pull-through" slot.

One more hint: A rear camera with a screen mounted in the motor home is a useful device for monitoring your tow car as you go. With a camera, you can make sure your "toad" is obediently following along on all four wheels.

Supplemental Braking Systems for a Towed Car

Some states require that a towed car have a supplemental braking system, which is a box you put in your tow car and attach to the brake pedal. It either uses a radio signal from your motor home or is wired into the braking system of your motor home. In the photo below, note the rod that protrudes over the brake pedal. Stepping on the brakes in your motor home activates a 12-volt air compressor (powered by a cigarette lighter adapter) on the supplemental braking device and pushes the rod against the brake pedal in your car. This becomes important in any kind of highway emergency where you need to stop your 32,000-pound motor home and your 3,000-pound car as quickly as possible.

Supplemental braking systems are expensive, around $1,000, but if it saves your life even once, you'll know it's a good investment. Even if you're lucky enough to never *need* one, a supplemental braking system is still a good preventive measure. Be sure to choose a model with sophisticated electronics that can sense the amount of braking force you're applying to the RV and automatically apply a similar amount to the car brakes. Not every supplemental braking system has this feature; some apply a constant pressure whenever they sense that the RV brakes have been applied. A light installed in the motor home's cockpit will flash to let you know that your car brakes have been activated. A list of supplemental brakes manufacturers appears in the Appendix.

The Apollo supplemental braking system, hooked up in a tow car.

Hitching and Unhitching a Trailer or Fifth Wheel

If your RV is a trailer or fifth wheel, you'll need to know how to hitch up the RV to the tow vehicle before you can hit the road. Fortunately, RV manufacturers have done their best to make this procedure as simple as possible.

Fifth wheel kingpin.

Notched tail gate.

Hitching and Unhitching a Fifth Wheel
To hitch a fifth wheel follow these steps:

1. First raise or lower the jacks to align the fifth wheel's kingpin (the part of the fifth wheel that slides into the hitch) with the truck's hitch.
2. Open the tailgate on the truck. An alternative is to have a notched tailgate so the kingpin will move over it without the need to open it.
3. Open the locking bar on the hitch.
4. Back the truck under the trailer until the hitch engages the kingpin.
5. Push the locking pin through the hole in the kingpin and fasten it into place.
6. Put the truck in forward gear but do not step on gas pedal. "Bump" the hitch to be sure it's locked.
7. Raise the landing legs.
8. Connect the wiring, safety chains, and breakaway switch cable.
9. Check the trailer lights and brakes.
10. Raise the truck tailgate.
11. Remove the wheel chocks from the trailer wheels.

Attaching the kingpin to the hitch.

Caution: Unplugging the electric cord is the last thing you do inside your fifth wheel, so that you can use the electricity to adjust the height of the kingpin. Otherwise, you're using battery power to raise or lower your fifth wheel to the proper level, and you can run down your coach batteries. Just be sure you don't forget to unplug that cord—some unpleasant things can happen if you drive away still plugged in.

To unhitch a fifth wheel follow these steps:

1. Pull into the site and get your trailer where you want it. Chock the wheels so the trailer won't move.
2. Disconnect the cables and safety chains.
3. Lower the landing legs.
4. Drop the tailgate.
5. Gently put the truck into reverse so the kingpin moves off the locking bar.
6. Disengage the locking bar.
7. Drive away.
8. Raise the truck tailgate.
9. Adjust the fifth wheel height.

Hitching and Unhitching a Trailer

Because stability is an important safety factor when towing a trailer, hitching up a trailer is a bit more complicated than hitching a fifth wheel. In addition to your hitch, you also need load-distributing bars and breakaway cables, which are required by most states. You need to make sure that the load carried by your trailer is distributed as evenly as possible.

When first embarking on the process of connecting your trailer to a tow vehicle, it helps to know the terminology. The tongue of the trailer is the A-shaped part in front. The coupler is the part in the front of the tongue that slides over the receiver on the tow vehicle. Load distributing bars disperse the trailer's weight among the tow vehicle's axles. This improves handling and steering of the trailer. Breakaway cables apply the trailer's brakes if the trailer breaks away or becomes disconnected from the tow vehicle.

1. The first step in hitching a trailer is to align your tow vehicle's hitch to the coupler on the trailer. Raise the tongue, if necessary, and back the truck until both ball hitch and coupler are perfectly aligned, with the tongue slightly higher than the ball.

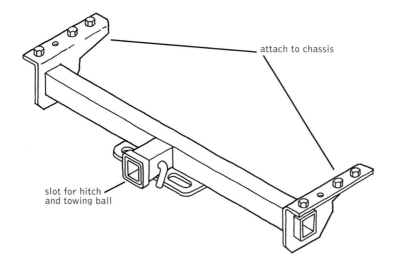

A weight-distributing trailer hitch evens the load between the tow vehicle's axles.

2. Lower the coupler so it fits over the ball.
3. Latch the coupler and raise the leg to a safe height.
4. Install and tighten the spring bars. You're almost but not quite done at this point.
5. You need to connect electrical cables that transmit signals for both the brakes and the brake lights from the truck to the trailer. Check that the plug and receptacle fit together and are in good condition. Wind the wires carefully so they don't snag on anything and so they're long enough that you can turn without disconnecting them.
6. Most states also require you to have a breakaway device to apply the trailer brakes in case the trailer becomes uncoupled from your tow vehicle. Make sure that the cable spanning the breakaway switch on the trailer and the anchor point on the towing vehicle has enough slack that it won't inadvertently apply the trailer brakes as the trailer turns or goes uphill.

When the time comes to disconnect the tow vehicle, make sure you level the trailer from left to right by backing the trailer over a board placed under the wheels on the low side. The rest of the leveling and stabilizing actions are performed after unhitching. This process is described in detail in the section on parking and leveling in Chapter 5.

7

Understanding and Caring for Your RV, Its Systems, and Its Features

Your RV has several systems. These include interior living systems like the toilet and its associated black-water drainage system; the sink/shower/ freshwater system and its associated gray-water drainage systems; the stove, refrigerator, and the washer/dryer if you have one; and heating and cooling systems (furnace and air conditioner). The electrical systems in your RV provide power to your RV either through a power source at a campsite, through house batteries, or by using a generator or inverter. The vehicle mechanical systems, including the engine, transmission, brakes, and tires, will be dealt with in Chapter 8.

The RV Toilet

The RV toilet works a little differently from toilets in houses. In the RV, waste material drains from the toilet into the black-water holding tank, and is later drained from that tank through your sewer hose to an external sewer line. The bowl is filled from either your freshwater holding tank or an exterior water source.

Toilet System Care

Because the toilet drains through a narrow system of hoses, you need to use a special kind of toilet paper, and never put anything other than that into the toilet. If the toilet paper does not dissolve in water, it can form large wads of soggy paper that completely plug up your tank or your drainage hose.

Thetford makes a toilet paper designed for RVs (get it at Camping World or other RV stores). You can also use any single-ply toilet paper that you find in a supermarket if it says "Safe for Septic Systems" on its label. (Scott is the brand we use.) Just to be sure, test a sheet of the toilet paper you plan to use in a glass of water and watch it dissolve. If it won't dissolve readily, don't use it.

Adding chemicals to your toilet will help dissolve solids so that they'll easily flush out when you drain the black-water tank. These chemicals use enzymes or bacteria to break down the wastes. Some brands use formaldehyde, but many campgrounds do not permit formaldehyde to enter their septic systems, and it's not used much anymore. The chief advantage of formaldehyde was that it blocked odors. Enzyme-type products control odors by helping break down the solids in your tank. They also have a useful tank-cleaning and valve-lubricating function. Add these chemicals after each dumping. A variety of chemical products for toilets are carried at most camping stores. We use RVTrine concentrate, an enzyme product manufactured by Valterra, but you'll find many other good choices.

Read the label to determine how many ounces of product you must put in the toilet at each use. Divide that into the price to see how much it will cost for each application, and compare those figures with similar information from other brands. Some brands give fewer doses for a similar price. Ultimately, you'll need to try the chemical and decide if it does the job. If you decide to change chemicals after using a particular kind, it's a good idea to empty and rinse your tanks thoroughly before you switch.

Periodically clean the toilet bowl using a mild bathroom cleaner. Avoid cleaners containing chlorine or caustic chemicals, because they may damage the seals on the toilet as well as interfere with the enzymes you add to break down solids.

Toilet Problems

Occasionally, you may find that the toilet bowl is not holding water. This can cause problems, as the water helps provide a barrier against holding-tank odors,

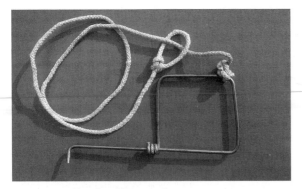

Homemade cleaning tool.

just as the trap on a conventional household toilet holds water to seal out sewer odors. The problem may be due to a leaky bowl seal. One common reason is toilet paper trapped between the flush valve blade and its seal. Thetford offers a tool for under $10 that allows you to clean the groove in the seal on its toilet.

My husband, Dan, being something of a miser, created his own by bending a wire coat hanger. Note the tether line that you attach to your wrist so you won't drop the tool into the tank. (Thetford's tool doesn't come with a tether. Be sure you add one.)

If scraping for paper clogs doesn't solve the problem, you may need to repair or replace the seal, the flushing mechanism, or even the entire toilet. If it gets to that point, you may want to call in an expert.

Another common problem is water constantly running or dripping into the toilet bowl. Normally, water fills the narrow area at the bottom of the bowl to a height of 1 or 2 inches. If the valve fails to shut off, you need to replace it. You can buy a new flush valve at an RV store, or call a repairperson.

Removing your toilet to replace the seal or another part is not as hard as you might think. Here's how to go about it:

1. Be sure the water supply to the toilet is turned off. Check in your RV owner's manual how to do this. If all else fails, disconnect the external water supply and turn off the water pump.
2. The toilet is probably fastened to the floor by bolts. (If it is a Thetford, those bolts are behind the foot pedal and behind the toilet.) First look closely and be sure you have located all these bolts. They may be hiding behind a skirt which must first be removed. Then remove all of them and lift the toilet straight up. If you have an electric model, you may also have to disconnect the toilet from a power source. Consult your manufacturer for details.

Note: Whenever you remove the toilet, replace the wax seal between the toilet and the floor. These seals are not reusable.

Gray- and Black-Water Drainage

The water from your kitchen and bathroom sinks is called *gray water.* The water from the toilet is called *black water.* Gray and black water drain into separate tanks, and when these tanks become full, they must be drained into a sewer. Your sewer connection hose looks like a giant Slinky toy and is usually stored in the compartment of your RV where the drain valves are located. To drain your gray- and black-water tanks, you connect one end of the sewer hose to the exterior of your RV. The other end of the sewer hose goes into the sewer drain.

The completed sewer hose hookup.

Inside the locker where your sewer connection is, you'll find two handles attached to slide valves. Note that these handles are attached to two different sizes of pipe. The larger-diameter pipe is the black water, and the smaller-diameter pipe is the gray water. Pull one handle to drain the gray water and the other to drain the black water. Drain the dirtiest water first, so that the cleaner water that follows will clean out the hose as it flows through. If you want to flush and clean your tanks, fill them with water for three to five minutes (the greater the water pressure, the fewer times you'll need to flush it) or until the tank is about one-quarter to one-third full, and drain again. Until you know your system well, have someone monitor the toilet while you're filling the black-water tank. Never walk away or get distracted while you're filling this tank. You don't want an overflow inside the coach—trust me.

After draining your tanks, be sure to close both valves and replace the cap on the outlet pipe (required by law in some areas).

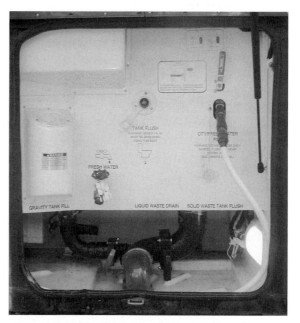

Gray- and black-water drainage handles are just under the labels in the bay: "Liquid Waste Drain" and "Solid Waste Drain." Liquid waste is gray water; solid waste is black water.

Remember to replace the holding tank chemicals in the black-water tank for the next usage cycle.

After connecting your sewer hose and draining your tanks, set the gray-water tank to drain continuously into the drain by leaving the valve open while you're camped, but leave the black-water tank closed until it's almost full. It will drain more efficiently that way. If you leave it open, the liquids will drain out but the solids won't, and you'll have trouble emptying the tank completely. Just don't forget to drain the black water every three or four days.

Sewer hoses come in a variety of lengths, the longest of which is about 20 feet. We have two 12-foot hoses and a collapsible 20-footer. When not in use, the hoses fit into a storage locker under the RV. You may want to purchase a variety of lengths because the distance between your rig and the sewer connection at a campsite can vary widely. Sometimes you may want to face in a different direction than was intended by the people who put in the hookups. To run the hose under your coach and connect on the other side requires a much longer hose. That said, we've never needed more than two 12-foot hoses connected end-to-end.

Unfortunately, there is no standard method for connecting your sewer hose to an external sewer line at a hookup, and you may need to purchase a variety of fittings at an RV store so you have whichever type is required. Some will screw into the hookup and some will just press in, using what is called a doughnut connector or a sewer seal. Some RV parks require the latter type of connector. Obviously, the connector needs to fit tightly so nothing leaks out. We like the red plastic connectors made by E-Z, but there are many others available.

If you find a large rock sitting next to your sewer connection at your campsite, it's not for tossing at wild critters. Set the rock on top of your sewer fitting to make sure it doesn't pop up when the liquids start to flow. Remember that your tank has 35 to 50 gallons of liquid in it, can weigh up to 350 pounds, and can generate considerable force at the discharge end. Open the valve slowly and be sure everything is securely connected and going into the sewer when starting the drainage process.

A sewer hose connector.

A transparent plastic sewer adapter.

To connect the sewer hose to the coach, Dan uses a transparent plastic adapter so that he can see the flow as the gray-water and black-water tanks are draining. This helps determine when the black-water tank is actually clean. You can buy these adapters at most RV stores.

Drainage Problems

Nothing is more disconcerting than to hook up your sewer hose and find it has sprung a leak. You can't always rush out and buy a new one. Pinhole leaks can be temporarily repaired with a couple of wraps of duct tape, but a leaky hose needs to be replaced as soon as possible. This is a situation when spending a little more money on a good-quality sewer hose will pay off over time—you'll find the heavier materials more dependable.

If liquids are draining slowly from your tanks, or seem not to be draining at all, check the angle of your sewer hose. Sewer hoses use gravity to allow the water to flow from your holding tanks to the dump, so it's important that the hose slopes downhill. You can buy or make a hose support to achieve this. Dan made ours out of pieces of 3-inch plastic gutter supported by little blocks of

Dan's homemade sewer hose support.

wood at a total cost of about $4. He can change the pitch of the drain by changing the number of blocks at each end.

If making your own sewer hose support seems like way too much trouble, you can buy one at most RV stores. A company called Slunky makes a popular design that sells for between $20 and $40 depending on length. Another brand, the Sidewinder, costs about the same as the Slunky but has a different design. Its angled shape is flexible enough to curve around obstacles, promoting better drainage, and it collapses for easy storage.

Knowing When to Dump the Tanks

You always need to know how full your tanks are so you know when to dump them. You should have a monitor panel inside your rig that tells how full your gray-water, black-water, and freshwater tanks are.

Unfortunately, the probes and sensors that yield this information are inside the tanks themselves, and they often get clogged with waste materials or corroded, so these readouts are not all that reliable. Immediately after emptying the black water and flushing the tank, you may be surprised to see that the monitor panel reads that the tank is full or partly full. The only monitor you can depend on is the freshwater level.

People have devised various ways of cleaning these probes. Some recommend putting ice cubes down the gray- or black-water tanks and then driving the rig around. The ice cubes will supposedly slosh around, bump into the probes, and knock stuff off of them. Then the ice melts and flows out next time you drain the tank. However, this plan is somewhat risky. The ice cubes in their solid state could do some damage as they roll around inside the tank. Instead, fill the tanks with plain water before you leave on a trip. The water will slosh around and if you're lucky it will clean the probes. You can also buy probe-cleaning chemicals at an RV store.

The best solution to unreliable tank information is to remember to drain the black water every three or four days. You can also view the water level in the tank with a flashlight when the toilet valve is open.

Another hint: while you're traveling, you may want to dump your tanks on the way. Perhaps you left in a hurry with your tank almost full and you know you'll be washing dishes at your lunch stop. Go to www.rvdumps.com. This website gives information on the location of more than 1,200 dump sites. You can find similar information in campground guides published by *Woodall's* and *Trailer Life*, but the advantage of consulting the website is that the information is constantly updated. You can download and print out information for every state in the union, or buy an e-book from the site.

Freshwater Supply

Fresh water flows to your taps in the RV from one of two sources. Either you receive the water directly from a hose connected to an exterior water source at a campground, or you receive it through your RV's freshwater tank using an interior pump.

Maintenance

Keeping your drinking-water supply clean begins outside the RV: attach a clean hose to the drinking-water faucet and use that hose only for that purpose. For obvious reasons, you don't ever want to hook up to your freshwater supply a hose that you've used to clean the black- or gray-water tanks. The easiest way to avoid confusion is to have a different-colored hose for each purpose (for example, white for clean water and green for flushing the tanks).

A water-pressure regulator is an essential device to have attached to your hose. Most RVs are designed to use pressures of around 40 pounds per square inch (psi). If the pressure is higher than that, the regulator will protect your system from burst pipes or hoses.

There are three things to notice about the regulator:

- It's attached to a Y-connector with valves that allow attachment of an extra hose.
- A tether holds the assembly together to diminish the possibility that you'll unscrew the pressure regulator and leave the Y-connector behind.
- The quick-release connection at the bottom facilitates attachment and removal of the coach water hose.

From time to time, you'll need to put water into your RV's freshwater tank so

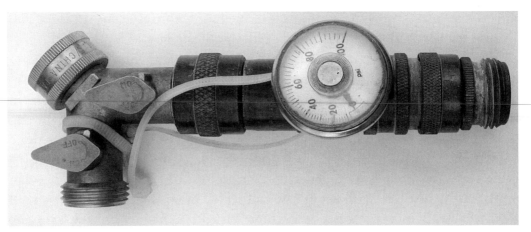

A water-pressure regulator between hose and faucet keeps excessive water pressure from damaging your system.

that you can have a supply of water as you travel. You probably have one of two systems to connect your RV's water tank to a hose. Either you have a separate connection from your hose to your internal tank, or you have a valve that turns one way to provide water directly to the RV's interior plumbing system, and another way to fill your tank. This valve is one of those items to locate before you make your first RV trip. Be sure to monitor the freshwater tank while you're filling it so that it doesn't overflow. Check with the readout inside your RV until the tank has reached the level you want, or visually inspect the tank itself as it fills. In some RVs, the tank is under the bed. If so, you can lift the bed and watch the water level rise through the translucent material of the tank. In other RVs, the tank is not accessible and you must rely on the readout. Fortunately, freshwater readouts are generally dependable. Completely filling your freshwater tank isn't a good idea, unless you're going to be dry camping; water is heavy and will add to the total weight of your RV, negatively affecting your gas mileage.

The electrical switch for the water tank's pump is located at different places in different RVs. Before you take possession of a new RV, ask the dealer to show you where the switch is located so you aren't left searching for it later. Ours is in the bathroom, with a second switch in the external utility bay, but some are part of the electrical panel, which may be in the hall or the bedroom. When this switch is turned on, water flows automatically from your freshwater tank whenever you turn on a faucet in the RV. Don't be worried if you hear a pulsing noise when the pump is running. This is normal. The pump is a battery-powered device.

Freshwater Problems

As with other parts of your RV, you may encounter a problem with your freshwater supply. Here are some of the more common ones.

LOW WATER PRESSURE Your water pressure regulator protects your rig from damage due to too much water pressure, but many campgrounds have the opposite problem, especially if the campground is full and everyone seems to be running water at the same time. You may step into your RV's shower and find a pathetic little dribble coming out of the shower head.

That is the time to switch to your internal water tank. If your water tanks are empty, you can fill them with your hose from the local faucet, (although if pressure is low, this may take a while) and then switch to internal water. Your built-in water pump will provide the good water pressure you want. We spent an entire season using internal water one year in Mexico. The following year, we connected a supplemental water pump in series with the water hose to boost the water pressure delivered to the coach from the external water source.

BAD WATER Before hooking up to a campground's water supply, you may want to run a little water from the faucet to check its color or even to taste it. If it smells or tastes bad, don't hook up. Instead, use water from your freshwater tanks that you'd filled in a more desirable location. If the water is especially good somewhere, drain and replace the supply in your freshwater tank for use at a later location where the supply is not ideal.

Fill your freshwater tank from a reliable source—from home before you set out, for example—and you'll always have a good water source with you. Whether or not you want to completely fill your water tank depends on several factors. The main one is the length of your trip and the quality of water you expect to find along the way and at your destination. Balance this information with the fact that water is heavy and carrying a full tank of water will reduce your fuel efficiency. If you are dry camping, you need to arrive with a full water tank and empty drainage tanks. In other situations, you can opt for one-third tank to get you along the way to your destination.

WATER DRIBBLES FROM THE KITCHEN FAUCET BUT RUNS FREELY EVERYWHERE ELSE If you experience this problem, your internal water filter—the one under your sink—has probably become clogged. It's easy to forget to

CAN THE WATER MAKE YOU SICK?

You want to be sure that the water you use in your RV is as clean as possible. Many RVs come with a water filter under the sink. This is intended to protect your drinking water by filtering out the disease-causing parasites like those that cause amoebic dysentery and other unpleasant illnesses. A good filter will also remove things from the water that affect the taste, but it isn't guaranteed to completely purify your water supply.

A typical pair of water filters. Note the hose connection at each side.

If we're worried about the quality of water where we're camped (anywhere in Mexico, for example), we buy and use bottled water for drinking and cooking, and use our freshwater supply only for bathing and washing dishes. We also disable our icemaker, which draws local water to make the ice cubes. I fill old-fashioned ice trays with bottled water, and complain every time I struggle to empty them, but staying healthy is a priority.

An inside water filter may clog quickly if a water supply contains too much dirt and sediment. For this reason, many RVers elect to filter the water as it comes from an external source. The most common way to do this is to use a pair of filters and place them in the water connection to your rig. The first filter uses a string filter cartridge and the second uses a charcoal cartridge. The string cartridge filters out rust and sediment, and the charcoal filters out bad-tasting chemicals like chlorine and also reduces—but does not totally eliminate—bacteria in the water. You may want to buy your filters from a hardware store like Lowe's or Home Depot rather than an RV supply store; the filters are the same, but the ones at RV supply stores are often a little more expensive.

To store them, you should drain the filters of excess water when you depart the campsite. To do so, disconnect them from the hose, point the inlet end at the ground and press the air bleed valves on the top. They'll drain out the excess water they have collected in about 15 seconds.

change this filter, and when it gets clogged it basically stops working. Replacing this filter every six months is a good rule of thumb, but it may need to be replaced sooner if you've been camped where the water has particulates. Unfortunately, internal water filters are expensive.

HOSE LEAKS OR KINKS Your hose may leak after you've connected it to a campground's faucet. Carry a supply of hose washers in your tool kit so you can replace them easily. If the hose itself has a pinhole, cut it off below the leak and replace it with a hose mender. This strategy will help you out in the short run—for example, if you've pulled into a campground after hardware stores are closed—but you'll need to have a hose clamp handy. The best solution is to replace the hose as soon as you can.

Rather than one long hose, try several shorter ones such as one 8-foot and one 6-foot hose. A long hose tends to kink and form flat spots in its structure that will always collapse no matter what you do to fix it. Multiple shorter hoses may cost more, but they won't kink as readily and they'll last longer. However, just as with sewer hoses, you may find that you need a long run to the water faucet, and carrying a long hose just for emergencies is also a good idea.

PUMP RUNS CONTINUOUSLY As I said earlier, it's normal for the water pump to make a pulsing noise when you're using water from your internal tanks. However, if you shut off the water at the faucet and you continue to hear the pump running, or if it runs when you haven't turned on any water, you have a problem—most likely a leak in the water system or a leak in the pump.

One common cause is a leak in the pump's check valve, which prevents water from back-flowing through the pump into your tank. You may need to replace the water pump in this situation, or at least replace the check valve. Water-pump parts and new water pumps can be found at most RV stores. Seek the advice of the parts people, who generally can point you toward what you need.

Stove

Propane flows to your stove burners from the exterior tank or tanks. To use propane for cooking, you must light the burner flame at your stove. Depending on the age and sophistication of your rig, you may have a built-in igniter for your burners. You turn on the burner, turn the igniter knob (which emits a spark), and your burner is lit. If you don't have a built-in igniter, purchase a handheld one—the kind you use to start a propane barbecue. If you need to light a pilot light for your refrigerator or stove, refer to the directions that came with those appliances, because they vary.

Stove Problems

Here's a list of some of the more common stove problems and tips on how to fix them.

BURNERS DON'T STAY LIT If your burners don't light or don't stay lit, you may have air in your propane tank. Most LPG dealers can purge this for you.

YELLOW FLAME The flame on your burners should be blue with a light blue tip. If the flame is yellow or tipped with yellow, you have an incorrect ratio of fuel to air. The burner will work less efficiently and carbon may build up. You may notice a black residue on the bottom of your pots or pans. To correct this problem, adjust the flow of air by turning the shutter located near the burner, or have a technician make this adjustment. If this doesn't solve the problem, you may have a bad regulator at the propane tank. Have this checked by an expert. If you're at high altitude (5,000 feet or above), the ratio of air to fuel is altered by altitude, and you may have to live with a yellow, wimpy flame.

IGNITER WILL NOT LIGHT BURNER This problem is generally due to the absence of a spark. To check for a spark, first remove the wire between the igniter and the burner, hold the wire near the surface of the burner, and turn on the igniter. If the igniter does not create a spark this way, you may need to replace it. If you do get a spark, your igniter is fine and the problem is in the wire between the igniter and the burner, or in the burner itself. Check to see if the burner is clogged. If you've recently cleaned the burner, for example, little bits of cleaner may have plugged the holes. With a toothpick, probe the holes in the burner near where the igniter sparks to take care of this problem. Try cleaning the surface of the stove where the burner is fastened down to be sure you have a good ground. Also clean the contact at the side of the burner and the one under the burner connected to the wire. Steel wool works well here.

Refrigerator

Your RV refrigerator can run from either of two sources—propane or electricity. If you set it on "automatic," your refrigerator will run on propane when you're unhooked, and automatically switch to electricity when you're hooked up. Some refrigerators use a third method—the RV's house batteries—while traveling, thereby avoiding the hazards of propane use on the road, but be warned that this system can run down your batteries in short order even if the engine is running.

Refrigerator Maintenance

The most important thing you can do to maintain your refrigerator is to always level your RV when it is parked. When the refrigerator is not level, the combined chemicals that cause cooling can separate, crystallize, and block the circulation of the cooling unit. Once this has happened, it is irreversible. To be sure the refrigerator is level, put a bubble level inside the fridge or place one on a flat countertop when you're leveling your rig. Get it as close to level as you can. If you're comfortable walking around your rig, it should be fine. Also note that newer fridges can tolerate being off-level better than old ones, due to some design improvements.

Incidentally, if your fridge is running on propane while you're traveling, be sure to turn off the refrigerator when you pull into a gas station to fuel up. This is just a sensible precaution to make sure the refrigerator flame will not ignite nearby gasoline vapors. Remember to turn the fridge back on after you've pulled away from the station. We seem to forget this a lot, but a fridge will keep itself cold a long time when it's turned off as long as you don't open the door. For this reason, many safety-conscious RVers simply turn their refrigerators off while they're traveling.

To keep your refrigerator running at its happiest, try to always keep it cool. If you come into the RV with a huge load of groceries, it helps if most of the items that need to be refrigerated are already cold. We carry a fold-up cooler in the trunk of our car, and put the cold stuff directly into it at the supermarket. If you fill up your fridge with room-temperature stuff, it may warm up alarmingly. In that case, just leave the door closed for a few hours and check the temperature again later. We have a fast-reading darkroom thermometer for that purpose. It serves double-duty, telling us the temperature inside the coach and inside the fridge, depending on where we place it.

My RV refrigerator gets very unhappy when I open both doors and hunt around inside for something. In fact, after whining at me (beeping), it will even shut itself off if the hunt takes too long. It's a good idea to have in mind exactly what you're going to remove and where those items are located inside the fridge, and then open the door quickly and remove them.

Completely defrost the refrigerator and remove all items from inside if you're going to be storing it without it being plugged in. Wash the interior with a mild detergent. Prop the doors open so air circulates inside the box.

Refrigerator Problems

Here are some of the more common refrigerator problems and how to handle them:

INTERNAL TEMPERATURE NOT COLD ENOUGH If you suspect that your refrigerator is not as cold as it should be, test with a thermometer to verify your concerns. The internal temperature should be around 42 degrees Fahrenheit. If it's significantly warmer than that, you have a problem. If you notice that the cooling problem only arises when the refrigerator is using propane (or while you're dry-camping), the problem may be that the propane flame has gone out. Remove the rear access cover on the outside of the RV. On the lower right, find and remove a cover over the propane burner. Sometimes the burner may become clogged by debris from the chimney. In that case, you can blow out the debris and relight the flame. The flame should burn blue with no yellow tip.

If you have a cooling problem when plugged into shore power, use an ohm meter to check the electric heater element located at the rear of the refrigerator and generally accessed through an outside panel. If there is a reading of either zero or infinity, it is called an "open circuit." That means there is a gap in the heating element and it cannot conduct electricity. In this case, you'll need to replace the electric element. See your owner's manual for the correct reading. Be sure to disconnect the RV's power cord before performing this test.

You can purchase an ohm meter (or a multimeter which measures voltage, current, and resistance) at RadioShack or a hardware store.

AMMONIA SMELL COMING FROM THE REFRIGERATOR If you smell ammonia, you probably have a coolant leak, and the likely outcome is that you'll need a new cooling unit or refrigerator. Upon smelling this distinctive odor, consult a repairperson. Be sure that what you're smelling is ammonia, however. A while ago, when I kept noticing a sulfury rotten-egg smell near the fridge and in the ice cubes, we nearly bought a brand-new replacement. In the end we realized that our under-the-sink water filter was delivering smelly water to the icemaker, a problem not related at all to the refrigerator. The refrigerator was cooling normally, a clue that all was actually well.

ICEMAKER PROBLEMS If your icemaker is not producing much ice, or not working at all, defrosting the freezer may correct this problem. The few times that our icemaker quit making ice have all been due to a buildup of frost that blocked the tube that delivers water for ice production or prevented the system from ejecting ice cubes.

The icemaker works only if the freezer temperature is low enough, so if you've recently placed a large number of items in the freezer so that its temperature has warmed up, that may cause a reduction in ice production. Wait patiently, and your icemaker will deliver.

Make sure your icemaker is receiving a supply of water. You must either be hooked up to shore water, or have the internal pump on to deliver water from your water tank. You must also be on AC power, or turn on your inverter, for your icemaker to work.

Washer/Dryer

If you've opted for an RV that has a washer and dryer, you'll most likely have a combination washer/dryer that runs on 120-volt AC power. This means that, in order to operate it, you must be hooked up to shore power or you must run your generator. You also need a water source. The typical washer/dryer uses about 16 gallons of water per load.

To begin a wash load, sort the laundry, and add the amount of detergent recommended for this particular machine (generally no more than 2 tablespoons). Remember that this machine is probably much smaller than what you're accustomed to in a house; don't overdo the soap. Place the laundry items inside the machine, close the door, set the wash and rinse cycles, and start the machine. It's as easy as that—but remember that each complete wash and dry cycle takes a very long time (as much as two hours), so it's a good idea to do something else for a while before checking on the status of your laundry.

Because RV washer/dryers are rather small, laundry can be a daily chore. To make the job less bothersome, you might set it going just before you take your daily walk. Or, if you like the idea of arriving at your destination with a clean set of clothes for the day, you could arrange to do laundry while traveling down the road. Just be sure to turn on your generator and your water pump, and make sure there is enough water in your tank.

Depending on its age and manufacture, you may need to clean your washer/dryer's drain screen—which protects the pump from lint and foreign matter. When you do, make sure that any water has been emptied from the machine. Even so, some water may dribble out, so place a cloth or shallow dish under the drain-screen housing before you remove the screen. After you clean the screen, replace it carefully and check for leaks before you use the washer again.

Repairs on your washer/dryer are not a do-it-yourself operation. Know when it's time to call an expert. Some repair facilities will send a repairperson to an RV park to work on your washer/dryer right there. Don't try to remove the washer/dryer by yourself if it needs repair: at 185 pounds or more, they're heavier than they look.

Heating and Cooling

From Baja to Bar Harbor, and all points between, you're going to experience extremes in temperature. Nights may be too cool for comfort, and days may be too warm. Your RV's heating and cooling systems are complex, and require some maintenance to keep them in good working order. It's important to know how the heating and cooling systems work, how to maintain them, and what to do if problems arise.

Heating

PROPANE TANKS Most likely your furnace, stove, and on-the-road refrigerator obtain their heat from a propane tank. For safety reasons, the propane tank in an RV is never located inside a locked compartment. In a trailer, two tanks are typically mounted on the tongue. In a fifth wheel or motor home, the propane tank, or tanks, are located inside a vented, unlocked compartment. The flow of propane from your tank is controlled by a regulator, which reduces the high pressure in the tank to the proper pressure for use in appliances.

To use propane for heating or cooking, you must first turn on the flow at the tank outside. As you open this valve, the initial flow may cause the tank to shut down temporarily. To prevent this, open the valve slowly.

PROPANE FURNACE In our motor home, the furnace is operated through the 12-volt DC house batteries. That means we can stay toasty warm while dry camping without external electric power. Be warned, however, that the typical RV furnace uses up a great deal of propane, especially in freezing weather. If you are dry camping, be sure your propane tank or tanks are full before you arrive at your destination.

When you are camped where you have a source of electricity, use a small electric heater as a backup, to conserve propane.

FURNACE PROBLEMS You can troubleshoot a few items on the furnace, but most of the time, be prepared to call for an expert. Here are some problems you *can* fix yourself:

Fan Doesn't Run The problem may be with the anticipator that controls fan operation. Under the thermostat cover, locate the anticipator, a control that slides over a wire. Set the temperature on the thermostat to "high," and move the slider on the anticipator. Listen for the fan to start, remembering there is a time lag between setting the thermostat and the fan starting up. If the fan starts when you move the slider, adjust the slider to a position where it will continue to operate even as the RV warms up. If the fan doesn't start, you may need a new thermostat. You can purchase a new one from an RV store, and install it yourself.

Fan Runs but There's No Heat The furnace will fail to heat if the regulator at the propane tank is bad. Check the color of the flames on your stove. If yellow, the regulator may be bad.

A WORD ABOUT PROPANE TANKS

When your propane tanks need refilling, you must take some precautions. Propane tanks can only be filled to 80 percent of their capacity, so if you have a 40-gallon propane tank, the most you can put in is 32 gallons. Since 1998, all propane tanks must have an overfilling protection device. If your rig, and therefore your tank, was manufactured before 1998, you should replace your propane tank, or install an overfill protection device, because refilling a tank that does not have this device is illegal.

Propane tanks can only be filled by a trained operator. When your tank is being filled, exercise a few safety precautions. Turn off your refrigerator, electrical power, and pilot lights, because these may generate a spark that could cause the propane to explode. Make sure your RV is turned off as well. Most states' regulations—and good common sense—dictate that everyone should be outside the RV at the time the tank is filled.

The furnace will also refuse to heat if the air flow is insufficient. Make sure all the registers are open and not blocked by anything. (Remove that file box you placed on a register!) Finally, check the level of your house batteries. If they aren't producing enough voltage, the fan may run too slowly to adequately circulate the hot air.

Cooling

Air conditioner maintenance is simple. Make sure the vents are clean and free of dust and periodically clean the air filters inside the vents. A dry sponge makes a good tool for wiping dust off the air conditioner vents. To clean the filter, first remove the vent cover and the filter, then wash the filter in warm soapy water. Rinse and let it dry. When dry, replace it inside the vent cover.

AIR CONDITIONER PROBLEMS You may encounter the following problems with your RV air conditioner:

The Air Is Too Cool or Too Warm If you find that your thermostat setting doesn't seem to produce the desired result with the air conditioner, check where the sensing mechanisms are located. In our motor home, they're up front, and if the sun is pouring in, the air conditioner thinks that the whole motor home is too hot and cools down more than we find comfortable. Adjusting the thermostat should take care of this problem.

The Air Conditioner Runs Continuously When Turned On Check the fan setting. If your air conditioner fan has three settings—low, high, and auto—it will probably run continuously if set on low or high. Only on auto will the fan shut off when the air conditioner has cooled the room to the set temperature. If your fan runs continuously when set on auto, you may have a problem with either the thermostat or the fan mechanism. Have an expert check it out to see if you need to replace one or the other.

The Air Conditioner Doesn't Work Because it's a closed system, you really can't repair your air conditioner yourself. If it fails, you'll have to take it somewhere for repair.

However, sometimes an air conditioner can "freeze up." If the air is very humid, the moisture will freeze and ice will collect around the vents. In this case, turn the AC off, allow the ice to thaw, and try turning it on again later. For my air conditioner, the owner's manual recommends setting the blower fan on high in humid conditions. Just be aware that if you do set it on high, it may not turn off at a set temperature.

Power Supply/Electrical Systems

Your RV will have two electrical systems. One runs off the coach batteries (DC), and the other runs off 120-volt AC, which you obtain by plugging into a campground receptacle. AC runs such things as your air conditioner, microwave, appliances, and so on, while DC runs your lights, heater, fans, and water pump.

Most U.S. RV parks offer either 30-amp or 50-amp electrical service. Not all RVs, especially the older ones, are equipped to use 50 amps. If your RV is equipped for 50 amps and you are plugged in to 50-amp service, you're in electrical heaven. You don't have to worry about how much current you are drawing. You can run two air conditioners and a microwave oven simultaneously without worrying about blowing a fuse.

When you're plugged into 30 amps, you must be careful how much power you draw. For example, you can't run an air conditioner and microwave simultaneously.

CROSSED WIRES

We were watching TV in our motor home on a balmy, warm winter evening in Guayabitos, Mexico, when suddenly my husband Dan spotted smoke coming from the compartment that contains our satellite receiver, VCR, video distribution box, and surge protector. He reacted quickly, shutting off the TV and rapidly unplugging everything. The smoking culprit was the surge protector, which was doing what it was supposed to. It burned itself up, preventing the electrical problem from destroying our TV and other valuable equipment.

The problem turned out to be caused by a neighbor in the RV park working on his own electrical system. He had miswired the hot, neutral, and ground pins, and the result was that his ground wire became energized. When his ground wire became energized, so did all the ground wires in the park, causing problems throughout. We were not the only ones to suffer a burned-out surge protector, but fortunately no one suffered greater damage than that. Everyone's TVs and VCRs remained intact.

The contrite amateur electrician insisted on reimbursing us for the cost of our new surge protector, so actually no harm was done, but the event was a kind of wake-up call to me. It's easy to take electricity for granted, expecting a reliable continuous flow, but in an RV that's not always the case. Mistakes can happen, and having a surge protector will add to your peace of mind.

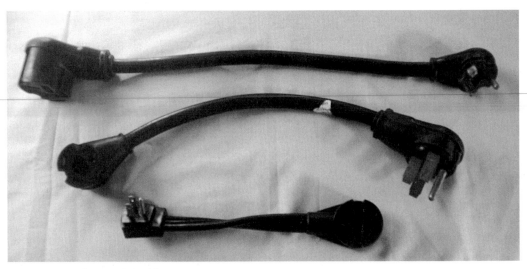

30-amp and 50-amp adapters.

Using the electrical power in your RV when it's plugged into 30 amps, or less, becomes a matter of calculating the available power and also calculating how much of a drain on that power comes from the appliances you're using.

You probably have a thick power cord in the rear of your RV for plugging into a power source at a campground. If the cord terminates in a 50-amp plug, you need to buy an adapter to use at those sites that don't have 50-amp power. Many older RV parks in the United States, and most parks in Mexico, have 20-amp or 30-amp connections. If your RV has only 30-amp service, you'll need an adapter for 50-amp power and an adapter for 20-amp service.

Make sure the power switch is turned off before you plug in.

Using External Power

Before you plug into a campground's power system, examine the connector or plug on your power cord to make sure it's in working condition. Look for melted plastic or corroded terminals. If you see the latter, try to clean off the corrosion, or replace connector as a preventive measure. Replace at the first sign of excessive wear; don't wait until your cord goes into meltdown. Always carry a spare connector just in case.

Most parks in the United States have at least 30-amp circuits, but at some older parks the flow of electricity can be undependable. If the electrical pylon looks battered or rusted, you should check this out before you plug in your RV. We have a circuit/polarity analyzer, a little device that plugs into any outlet. To check the electricity at your site, plug the analyzer into the outlet where you plan to plug your RV. The analyzer has three lights that should light in a specific pattern. Two yellow lights on the left and a red light on the right indicate the correct reading. If the pattern is different, you have a problem such as reversed polarity. Reversed polarity occurs when the outlet is wired incorrectly, and it can damage appliances. If you discover that a site has reverse polarity, move to a different site and notify campground management of the problem. If the readout indicates that the ground wire is energized, do not plug in your rig, or if you are already plugged in, unplug your rig right away. A hot ground wire can cause a fire or severe electrical shock. We keep our analyzer plugged in to one of the outlets in the bathroom, so we'll know if a problem develops.

A circuit checker. The guide on the front shows readouts and how to interpret them. Two yellow lights on the left and one red light on the right is the correct reading.

LOW OR HIGH VOLTAGE Monitoring the flow of electricity with an AC voltmeter is a good idea. The voltage should be 120 volts, but frequently it is not.

If your voltage is markedly low, turn off your computer to avoid damaging it. Complicated electronic devices don't respond well to low voltage. Low voltage occurs if a campground is not properly wired to support the demand. This is particularly true on hot days when everyone's running their air conditioners, or on cold days when everyone's running portable electrical heaters.

Voltage that is too high can also cause problems. Many RV stores sell a device called an *auto transformer* that will take care of voltage variations, but be warned that these transformers are expensive, costing from $350 to $600. Auto transformers have only a limited range and may not be useful enough to justify their high cost. They do not totally correct the problem—they merely minimize it. And they will not increase the number of amps available to you. They can't add power that isn't there to begin with.

UNRELIABLE POWER SOURCE If you don't like the readout on your circuit checker, and either no other sites are available or all the others read the same, just don't plug your RV in. Many if not most RVs are designed to work efficiently without electrical input. We have both a generator and an inverter in ours, and although the generator is noisy, it provides all the electricity we could want as long as there is fuel in the tank to run it.

The inverter, which converts DC power to AC, is good for two or three hours, enough to watch our favorite TV shows at night or make a pot of coffee in the morning. Be aware, though, that the inverter runs off the house batteries and can draw them down. Also, if you have an inverter in your RV, you can power these same devices from a solar panel. (More about that later in this chapter.)

DON'T CHEAT THE (ELECTRICAL) SYSTEM

Some parks have a 20-amp and a 30-amp plug in their power boxes, and you can buy a cheater box that will connect your 50-amp coach into both of these simultaneously. You plug into the box and the box has two cords, which plug into the 20- and the 30-amp receptacles at the same time.

Sounds good, right?

It isn't.

The wiring of an RV has two circuits. The current gets split evenly between these two circuits: 15 amps per circuit on 30-amp service, or 25 amps per circuit on 50-amp service. A cheater box, on the other hand, puts 20 amps on one circuit and 30 amps on the other—a dangerous imbalance.

Fifty-amp power can run all your electrical systems simultaneously—air conditioner, microwave, laundry—without the danger of tripping a breaker or causing other problems, so I understand why people would "cheat" to get it. However, if several rigs are using cheater boxes, they may be drawing more current than the park's system is designed to supply. If they're lucky, a tripped breaker will be the only bad result. More-disastrous results—such as widespread power disruptions throughout the entire campground—are also possible.

At a campground located in a fairly large city in Baja California, RVers are given a note upon check in. The note warns that the electricity for the whole region is unreliable and the use of a microwave or air conditioner could result in a citywide blackout. This is a situation when it's best not to plug in. Either run on your own internal power, or hunt for another campground.

POWER SURGES It's easy to take electricity for granted, expecting a reliable continuous flow, but in an RV, that's not always the case. A neighbor tinkering with electricity may produce a power surge that affects your rig. Inexpensive surge protectors protect only the devices plugged in to them, but new RVs have numerous surge-sensitive microchip-equipped devices in their control circuitry that need protection. The good news is you can get 30- or 50-amp surge protectors that will protect the entire RV. The bad news is they're expensive. You need to weigh the risk against the cost.

Electrical problems don't happen often in RVs, but just in case, Murphy's law being what it is ("If it can happen, it will"), it's a good idea to have a surge protector, circuit polarity analyzer, and voltmeter in your RV bag of tricks.

HOW MUCH IS TOO MUCH? Be aware that unless you have 50-amp power, you'll need to do a kind of triage when using electrical appliances—you'll have to shut one off in order to use the other. Our 2003 motor home has a power-management system that shuts things down in case of an overload, but it always seems to shut

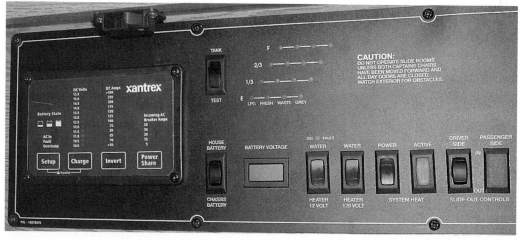

A power-management panel.

down the system that I'm currently using. It's best to plan ahead. I turn off the air conditioner when I need the microwave, and I've checked most of my appliances to find out how much current they draw.

Because the power readout in your RV is in amps, you may need to do a little math to get the numbers for each appliance. The basic equation is:

$$amps = watts \div volts$$

For example, according to its label my toaster uses 120 volts and 850 watts. 850 divided by 120 equals roughly 7 amps. This equation is not precise, because circuit voltage is not always exactly 120 volts—120 volts is actually an average figure. However, to find out what appliances you can safely use while plugged in to 30 amps, this estimation will suffice.

The accompanying table shows the typical power draw in amps of some appliances that you may have aboard your RV. If you're connected to 30 amps, add these up and make sure the total simultaneous usage does not exceed 30, or to be safer, 25, because you probably have a "hidden load" of things like thermostats or a battery charger.

GFI The electrical outlets installed in most RV bathrooms are ground fault interrupter (GFI) outlets. A GFI outlet houses a device that automatically shuts off

POWER CONSUMPTION BY APPLIANCE

Appliance	Current Draw in Amps
Air conditioner	18
Coffeemaker	8.3
Convection oven	12
Electric water heater	up to 12.5
Hair dryer	7.5
Iron	8.5
Microwave oven	10
Mixer	1
Refrigerator	3.5 to 4 (depending on size)
Space heater	8 to 12.5
Toaster	10
TV, 20-inch	1.5
Vacuum	9
Waffle iron	7.5

electric power if an unsafe electrical condition occurs. If the outlet trips, press the reset button (usually red or cream in color) directly on the outlet—flipping breakers in the circuit panel won't restore power to a GFI. GFIs also have a black test button that will simulate a short and disable the circuit. This tells you the GFI is working properly. GFIs are used on outlets near water sources—bathrooms and kitchens—because of the risk of water-induced electrical shorts.

A GFI outlet.

Batteries

Most motorhomes have two sets of batteries. One set—the chassis batteries—supplies power to start the engine, and the other set serves as the coach, or house, batteries. Coach batteries are usually 12-volt, deep-cycle batteries, although a couple of new types of batteries are coming on the market.

Coach batteries make it possible for you to boondock—to live more or less comfortably without external electric input—but they don't support all the systems in your rig. Basically, coach batteries can operate interior lights, some fans, the water pump, and the refrigerator. Just remember that your microwave, TV, and air conditioner are not available without external electric power.

If you've purchased a newer luxury coach, you may have an absorbed glass mat (AGM) battery, which is maintenance-free, sealed so it never leaks, and never needs to have water added. These batteries are expensive and require regulated charging with a smart charger (discussed later in this section). The other new type of battery is a gel battery, also maintenance-free, but it too needs regulated charging and is expensive. Most likely your RV will have either four 6-volt or two 12-volt deep-cycle, wet-cell type batteries.

A motor-home battery compartment, showing the house and chassis batteries.

Incidentally, a 12-volt battery does not actually have a 12-volt charge, unless it's dead or dying. A fully charged battery should read around 13.5 volts when you check it under no-load conditions.

To maintain the coach and chassis batteries, check the water level in the cells from time to time. If you need to add water, use only distilled water. Regular water can damage the delicate electrolyte balance in the battery cells. Corrosion of the battery terminals can be cleaned off with a weak baking soda-and-water solution, but never permit baking soda to contact the interior of the battery. Baking soda will neutralize the acid electrolyte and your battery will stop working. Some people also coat the terminals with petroleum jelly or silicone dielectric to prevent corrosion.

If you store your coach, disconnect the batteries at that time or turn off an electrical master switch isolating the batteries from the coach.

SMART CHARGER You can also extend the life of your batteries by using a smart charger. The smart charger regulates the charge in your battery in three separate stages called bulk, absorption, and float cycle charge. The bulk charge comes first; it's a quick charge to restore the battery. The absorption cycle begins after the battery is completely charged and gradually diminishes the charging current. The float cycle supplies current to things connected to the battery. Using a smart charger can reduce the amount of sulfation your battery experiences. Sulfation is a process of deterioration that eventually causes batteries to fail. Xantrex, Go Power, and Samlex America are three well-known brands of smart chargers. If you don't have a smart charger, you may want to consider a battery monitor, which will disconnect the charging source if your battery is in danger of overcharging. Most modern RVs have smart chargers that perform this function automatically.

INVERTER As previously mentioned, an inverter is a device that can tap into your coach batteries' stored 12-volt DC power to run appliances in your coach that use 110-volt AC power. This is useful if you're boondocking or dry-camping. In many dry-camping situations (for example, at a rally with hundreds of other rigs nearby), you're not supposed to run your generator after 10:00 P.M. This is common courtesy, as generators are noisy and people around you may be trying to sleep. So if you want to watch the late-night news on TV or pop some microwave popcorn, you turn on your inverter. An inverter may come preinstalled in your coach or you can buy one as an aftermarket item. Depending on

the load, you may be able to get several hours of power out of an inverter. An inverter will not run an air conditioner and should be used only sparingly with a microwave.

Solar Power

People who spend a lot of time dry-camping in the wilderness often opt to power their rigs with solar power. House batteries run down after extended use, fifth wheels and trailers typically do not have generators, and it's just too bad to have the length of your stay dictated by the capacity of your batteries. Even if you plan on generator power, your generator, too, will stop functioning when your fuel tank gets low.

Solar power is often referred to as PV, short for photo-voltaic (photo meaning light and voltaic meaning electricity). Solar power was first developed by the U.S. government for use in the space program.

All you need to know is that solar power is an alternative source for charging your RV's batteries. A solar panel brings in energy from the sun and stores that energy in your batteries. The size and number of solar panels you need depend on several factors, including your battery bank and your energy requirements. During the day, while the sun shines, your battery bank is being charged by the solar panels. If you have the right solar equipment, every night you should have a 100-percent charge. You need a solar digital charge regulator as part of your equipment, and the readout will tell you the amount of charge and discharge. Ideally, you should limit the evening's use of power such that you do not deplete your batteries by more than half. If your batteries discharge more than 50 percent, you need more batteries. If they don't charge up 100 percent during the day, you need more or larger solar panels.

Be warned that solar does not come cheap—but if you're an avid boondocker, it could be the way to go. To calculate how many solar panels you need, you figure how many amps your batteries hold, how many of those amps each of your appliances uses, and over what period of time the usage occurs. Then you need to convert amps to watts because solar panels are rated in watts. Remember, amps equal watts divided by volts, so to convert from amps to watts you would multiply amps by volts. A solar panel that is rated to produce 50 watts of electricity would store enough energy in a battery to light a 50-watt bulb for an hour. Obviously, you need a solar panel to do more than that. Solar panels come rated up

120 watts. Estimate how many watts you use each day and match that usage to the number of solar panels you need to produce that much electric power. Be aware that the output of a solar cell depends on how much sunlight it sees. If you're camping in gloom and rain, your solar panels may not provide the energy you need.

Fortunately, you don't have to do all those calculations by yourself. There are companies whose business it is to supply solar panels to RVers and they'll take down all your information and fit you with solar panels, for a price.

Awnings

An awning is a useful addition to an RV. It defines an outdoor patio area where you can relax in shaded comfort, barbecue your dinner, or visit with friends. Most RVs come with at least a patio awning, and some have awnings over every window. Like the other RV components discussed in this section, your awning requires a little TLC to preserve its life.

It's important to remember that your patio awning when rolled up still protrudes a little from the side of the coach. Consider this when parking or turning, because a side of the RV can come too close to a wall or other hard surface.

Caring for Your Awning

The canvas part of an awning is expensive to replace and can be maintained by following two simple tips:

- Keep it clean.
- Keep it dry.

If you've had your awning extended for a few days or longer, clean it off with a brush before rolling it up. Allow it to dry completely before rolling.

Sometimes this isn't possible. You may need to roll it up during a rainstorm. In fact, if there are high winds accompanying a rainstorm, you really should bring in your awning before it blows away. If you've had to roll up your awning while it's wet, extend it as soon as you can and let it dry completely.

If your coach came with hand-operated awnings, you may want to consider upgrading to the automatic kind that extends at the push of a button. An after-market automatic awning can cost around $1,100.

Operating the Awning

It's actually best if someone shows you how to extend and retract your awning There's nothing like being walked through the procedure. When you buy your rig, or when you buy an awning for it, ask the owner or dealer to show you the process. If you are putting out your awning for the first time all by yourself, don't panic. Just follow the directions in your owner's manual. It's not rocket science, just a little complicated.

Set the Awning at an Angle

You should set your awning at a slight angle.If it's a little lower on one side than on the other, rainwater will roll off your awning rather than collect in a weighty pool that might tear the fabric from the frame.

Make sure your awning is at an angle, so that water doesn't pool on top and cause the awning to tear.

Making Sure the Awning Stays in Place

Deflappers are small brackets that fasten to the awning frame to hold the canvas tightly in place and prevent it from flapping in high wind. They make it less likely that your whole awning will tear off. These inexpensive devices are easy to install as you're putting up your awning, and they contribute greatly to your peace of mind. You may need a step ladder to set them in place—two to three on each side depending on the size of the awning.

You can also anchor your awning by installing *load binders*—sturdy ropes that go from the end of the awning to stakes that are hammered or screwed into the ground. You can purchase a pair of these for about $15 from Harbor Freight Tools or Costco.

Problems with Awnings

Problems with awnings usually involve the roller tube. You should feel free to replace smaller parts on your own, but the powerful spring-loaded roller tube can be dangerous. If the awning doesn't roll up securely or evenly, or if you can't unroll it, you need to see an expert.

Roof

Maintaining the roof of your rig is crucial because no matter how hard you try to always stay in the perfect climate, some rain will inevitably come your way, and the last thing you want—the very last thing—is a leaky roof. Mildewed clothes, ugly spots in the interior ceiling, and other unpleasant consequences of moisture are all things you want to avoid. Take care of your roof and it will reward you with a comfortable, worry-free living space.

Rubber roofs cover many rigs. They're impermeable and long-lasting but they require some care. Be sure you never clean your rubber roof with a petroleum-based solvent, which can penetrate the membrane and dissolve the adhesive underneath. With rubber roofs, you also want to avoid abrasives or citric-based cleaners. Wash the roof with a mild dishwashing detergent using a brush with a medium bristle or a sponge, then rinse.

If you have a fiberglass roof, maintain it like you would any other fiberglass component: wash and wax it twice a year.

All types of roofs should be inspected as recommended by the manufacturer to check if seams and the penetration points of fasteners require recaulking.

Floors

You have a lot of money invested in your RV, and you want to keep it in good condition. Most RVs come with a combination of carpet and some type of floor tile or linoleum.

The first thing you should do when it comes to protecting your floors is to think Japanese: Take off your shoes off as you enter the RV. You may never have done this in your house, but in an RV, where the space is confined and every square inch sees a lot of traffic, you'll keep your floors in much better condition by walking in bare feet or socks.

I find that even though the area is small, the carpet in our motor home gets dirtier faster than any similar area in a fixed dwelling. Vacuuming frequently seems to be essential. I've always had a vacuum cleaner in my motor homes. In the first two, we had a central system, but I hated wrestling the snake-like hose from one end of the RV to the other, and because of that, I found myself putting off vacuuming as long as possible. In our current motor home, we opted to buy a small bagless upright, the handle of which can be shortened so the whole thing is only about 3 feet tall when not in use. I use this vacuum a lot more, but even so, my carpet always looks dirty. I could spend an hour a day just cleaning up little spots that seem to spring up from nowhere. Some people become so frustrated with their RV carpets that they replace them with tile or hardwood floors.

Unless doing extensive housework on your hands and knees is part of your freewheeling lifestyle, I recommend periodically cleaning your RV carpet either with a carpet-cleaning machine such as the Little Green Clean Machine by Bissell (small enough and portable enough for most RVs), or having it cleaned by a professional carpet cleaner. Professional rug cleaning services will come to your RV and clean it for a reasonable fee. I much prefer that method, but that's because I try to do as little housework as possible!

Changing the carpet or floor material in your RV can be very difficult unless you have a lot of experience at this kind of work. It's probably best to have a professional do it. A number of companies specialize in RV redecoration. One that we've used in Southern California is the Recovery Room (www.recoveryroomrv.com). To find a similar service in your area, try the Internet or the advertising pages of one of the RV magazines.

8

Engine, Tires, Suspension, Brakes, and Transmission

Some automotive maintenance and troubleshooting tasks can be performed by a motivated and knowledgeable RVer. Other tasks are best left to the experts. Here's how to tell the difference.

Light Maintenance and Tune Ups

Basic maintenance of your motor home or large truck engine is similar to what you would do with your car or light truck. Always follow the advice in your owner's manual as to service interval and procedures. Lube and oil-change intervals are greater on a diesel than on a gas-powered vehicle, which is a good thing because of the work involved and the amount of oil to change—measured in gallons, not quarts.

UNLOCKING VAPOR LOCK

Vapor lock occurs in gasoline engines in hot weather when the gasoline is vaporized before it reaches the fuel pump, or between pump and engine. Because the fuel pump is designed to pump liquid not vapor, it won't do its job until the gasoline liquefies. The best solution is to pull over and patiently wait for the vaporized fuel to condense.

Modern gas engines have few ignition problems, but a defective plug or loose spark plug wire can cause misfiring and rough running. Check the wires to be sure they're attached to the appropriate spark plugs. Gradual loss of power in a gas engine can be a sign of a clogged air filter or fuel filter. You can remove the air filter and run without it, at least for short distances, and you should have a spare fuel filter on board—and know how to change it.

Changing the Oil

The process of chassis lubrication and oil change is basically the same for diesel and gas vehicles. The difference between changing the oil in a large diesel engine and changing it in your car is mostly one of size. You need about 24 quarts of replacement oil for the large engine, and a container large enough to hold about 24 quarts of spent oil. Consult the owner's manual for the recommended oil filter replacement.

Disposing of used oil can be a problem, but often the store where you buy the oil will accept your container of used oil. Another problem specific to changing the oil in an RV is that most campgrounds will not permit you to do it on their premises. Instead, you should plan to change your oil on your own property or that of a close friend or relative. A third problem specific to diesel motor homes is the location of the oil drain and filters. Top-of-the-line motor homes often have an easy-to-reach compartment that houses all of their filters, but this is not the case with a majority of motor homes. Filters in these rigs have been placed in whatever location is most convenient for the engineers, not the owners. The filters are tough to get at, in areas with restrictive space for manipulating a wrench.

A possible solution to these difficulties, of

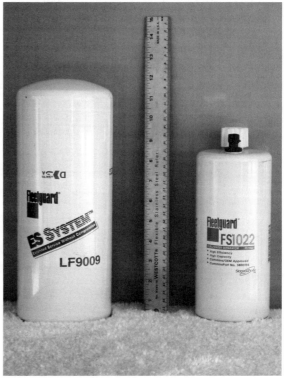

A typical oil filter (left) and fuel filter.

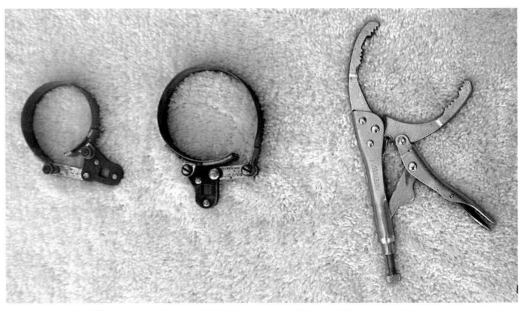

Compare the filter wrenches needed for a 2003 Hyundai car, a 1997 gas-powered Dolphin motor home, and a 2003 diesel-powered Monaco Diplomat (from left).

course, is to have the work done by a professional. That said, having a lube and oil change on a large diesel rig is expensive. As full-timers on the road, we were far from home when the time to change the oil rolled around. We paid about $295 for a package deal, which included oil, filters, and inspection services recommended by the manufacturer. The good news was that the first lube and oil change didn't have to be done until we had driven 15,000 miles.

If you decide to change the oil yourself, here are the steps. Note that unlike a car's oil filter, you'll need to fill the much larger-capacity filter for your RV engine with oil before you install it. Before you start to change the oil, be sure that you've purchased an appropriate filter wrench and have the right size combination wrench to loosen the drain plug.

1. Run the engine until the water temperature gauge indicates normal operating temperature, then shut off the engine.
2. Be sure you have a container that will hold at least 24 quarts of oil. Place this container under the oil pan.
3. Clean the area surrounding the drain plug before removing it.

4. Remove the oil drain plug from the bottom of the oil pan. Beware of hot oil splashing out. You could get burned.

5. Remove the filter. (**Note:** The filter is a cylinder about 4 inches in diameter and 12 inches in length. Don't confuse the oil filter with the fuel filter(s)—they can look quite similar.) Be sure the o-ring comes off with the filter—sometimes they stick to the engine. If it sticks, remove it so that it doesn't prevent proper seating of the replacement filter.

5. Fill the new filter with clean oil.

6. Cover the surface of the sealing gasket with a little fresh oil before installing the filter.

7. Install the new filter as directed by the engine manufacturer's manual.

8. Insert the drain plug, first making sure the plug threads are clean and free from contaminants.

9. Fill the engine with the manufacturer's recommended oil to the proper level.

10. Run the engine, check the oil pressure gauge, and make sure there are no leaks.

11. Recheck the oil level after allowing sufficient time for the oil to fully drain into the crankcase.

Replacing the Fuel Filter

At the same time you change the oil, you may also need to change the fuel filter. If so, follow your manufacturer's directions for this process but most important: you must fill the new filter(s) with diesel fuel before installation. Failure to do so will cause starting problems because the engine cannot start on the relatively small amount of fuel that is in the lines between the filter and the injection pump.

Some diesel engines have a reusable *water-in-fuel sensor,* a part that sends a signal to the display panel in the cockpit if water is in your fuel. Remove that sensor from the old fuel filter, inspect it for cracks or damage, and if it's intact, install it in the new fuel filter before you place the new filter in the engine. Your new fuel filter may come with this sensor already built in, in which case you can just dispose of your old one.

If you're having a problem with your diesel fuel filter, you may notice the problem first when your diesel engine is going uphill. It loses power and goes slower and slower, like the little engine that could. Later, it may actually quit on you.

Sometimes, problems like this are caused by contamination in the fuel filter. You may get a warning light on your panel. If you carry a spare fuel filter and a wrench to fit it, you'll be able to change it yourself and continue on your way without calling your emergency road service to tow you to a shop, but as mentioned earlier, you must make sure that you fill the new filter with diesel fuel before installing it. A diesel engine, because of the reduced volatility of the fuel and the fine tolerance in the injectors, is more affected by fuel contamination than a gas engine, which can suck up minor water contamination and keep running.

Checking the Cooling System

The cooling system should be checked at the same time that the oil and fuel filters are changed.

Check the level of coolant and the concentration of antifreeze. Too strong a concentration can damage the engine. Use a mixture of 50 percent water and 50 percent ethylene glycol to protect the engine to approximately –33 degrees Fahrenheit year-round. Even if you travel in a strictly mild climate all the time, you need to monitor your antifreeze because antifreeze extends the cooling efficiency of your engine. Also, its corrosion inhibitors protect the entire system. To test the coolant concentration, use a test kit recommended by the manufacturer. If you determine that you need to change the antifreeze, you must also change the coolant filter.

Some diesel engines use an additional coolant additive (ACA) that needs to be checked annually. This requires a device that most people don't have in their toolboxes. Given the specialized nature of many diesel service procedures, you may want to have the whole process done by a trained technician.

Be sure to observe the long-term maintenance requirements such as a 60,000-mile inspection. Use manufacturer-recommended or top-quality aftermarket products in your engine. You get what you pay for.

Making Emergency Roadside Repairs

In order to perform emergency roadside repairs, you need to own the appropriate tools and, usually, some essential replacement parts. If you're towing a car, you can always drive to a nearby town and purchase a tool or a part, but you shouldn't leave home without these items:

SCREWDRIVERS
- multi-driver with assorted bits in the handle (common, phillips, torx, square, etc.)
- individual screwdrivers in the above types, in various lengths. The multi-driver may be too short or too fat to reach some areas.

PLIERS
- needle-nose
- diagonal cutter
- common (assorted sizes)
- channel-lock (assorted sizes)

COMBINATION WRENCHES
- basic set, $\frac{1}{4}''$ to $\frac{3}{4}''$
- individual wrenches in sizes greater than 1″ for wheel bearings and suspension parts

SOCKET SET (Six-point preferred to avoid damaging nuts. Use a fine-tooth ratchet in restricted space. Choose metric if you have a foreign vehicle.) Your socket set, at a minimum, should include these pieces:

socket drives
- $\frac{1}{4}''$ fine tooth
- $\frac{1}{2}''$ fine tooth
- $\frac{3}{8}''$ fine tooth, if desired
- appropriate spark plug wrench (for gasoline engines)

socket extensions
- $\frac{1}{4}''$ and $\frac{1}{2}''$ ($+ \frac{3}{8}''$ if desired)
- $\frac{1}{2}''$ to $\frac{1}{4}''$ or $\frac{1}{2}''$ to $\frac{3}{8}''$ drive adapter may be useful if you have to use several extensions in series

hex drive (Allen wrenches)
- set of common sizes

ELECTRICAL
- digital multimeter
- wire stripper
- DC circuit checker

- AC polarity tester
- "F" connector crimping tool/spare connectors.
- fuse puller
- spare fuses (one or more for each size needed)

TIRE TOOLS

- compact portable air compressor (preferably AC powered)
- "truck type" tire gauge that will access dual tires
- tire thumper

MISCELLANEOUS

- assorted filter wrenches in appropriate sizes for your vehicle
- pry bar (Useful if tow bar is jammed due to uneven surface. Also useful for replacing belts or pulling up awning stakes.)
- spark plug gauge (for gasoline engines)

These tools will fit nicely into two small toolboxes stored in the RV lockers. It's better to have two small toolboxes than one large. Try to store each one near the place it will most likely be used. Don't bury them under other items—you'll have enough to worry about without having to completely unload a locker to get to your tools.

Be careful what repairs you attempt on the side of the road. It's easy to get in over your head by taking off too many parts that are hard to replace. Be sure to think through what must be done and be sure you have everything needed to complete the project, including the manual that tells you how to do it. Lacking these, you'll have to call emergency road service each time you have a problem.

The check-engine light is a warning that something is wrong with your RV's engine. Even if everything seems okay, you need to have the problem checked out by a professional using an external computer to access the RV's built-in computer diagnostic systems. These modern diagnostic systems are so sophisticated that in many cases they will shut the engine down or reduce power before any engine or transmission damage can occur. Never ignore a warning light.

Tires

There are ways to extend the life of your tires, and ways to make sure they're ready to take you safely down the road.

The single most important factor in caring for your tires is proper inflation. Your owner's manual will give the recommended tire pressure, but those numbers should be fine-tuned. You should have your coach weighed, and get the individual loads on each wheel, not just the total load on each axle. The only way to do this is to weigh each wheel position separately by placing a separate scale under each one.

Tire inflation should be adjusted according to the tire manufacturer's inflation

WHAT TO DO IF YOUR RV OVERHEATS

Overheating can be due to several different causes, such as fan clutch failure, loss of coolant, and excessive demand on the cooling system. Your first indication will be a warning light or a high temperature indicated on the display panel. Sometimes you can smell hot antifreeze. Pull over as soon as you can, and see if the problem is fixable.

If you've been driving uphill on a hot day with your air conditioner running, first turn off the air. Try turning on the heater (if you can stand it). The heater acts as an additional radiating area, drawing heat away from the engine and reducing the load on the radiator.

The problem may be decreased airflow through the radiator due to a broken fan belt, or obstructed radiator fins.

If the fan belt has snapped, the sudden activation of the alternator light will be the first clue (unless of course the alternator is driven by a separate belt). Carrying spare belts of the appropriate size will enable you to replace them with hand tools. There are universal replacement belts of adjustable sizes, but it makes more sense to carry the exact replacement you need.

If the problem is obstructed airflow through the radiator, carefully remove the obstruction.

A failed radiator hose or a leak in the water jacket or within the engine can also cause overheating. If this happens to you, you'll need to be towed to a shop. If you have a leaky radiator hose, duct tape is a possible emergency solution that might enable you to drive to the nearest mechanic. If your radiator hose appears intact, it still may have restricted flow due to an internal obstruction and need to be replaced.

A defective radiator cap can be another cause of loss of coolant. If you observe any signs of leakage at the cap, like steam or liquid escaping, replace the radiator cap. Remember that a hot radiator is under tremendous pressure. Make sure the radiator has cooled down before you remove the cap. If not, you could suffer very serious burns.

table for the size and load of the tire. However, if you have two different loads on the same axle, tires should be inflated to the recommended pressure for the tire carrying the heaviest load.

Many truck stops have weighing stations, and for a small fee (about $8 the last time we weighed our coach), they'll weigh each axle separately and also weigh the tow car. You can weigh each wheel at some of these, but the process is complicated, and many scales are not designed for it. A rally is another good place to get your rig weighed. The RV Safety Education Foundation conducts seminars at rallies, and provides scales and the opportunity to weigh your rig, and for a nominal fee you can get everything done, including separate weighing of each wheel.

Check the cold tire pressure before starting the rig, each time you travel. You can buy a *tire thumper*—something like a billy club—at a truck stop, and thump the tires for a quick review of their inflation status before taking to the road. An underinflated tire makes a different sound than a properly inflated one. Of course, you can also take the time to check tire pressure with a tire gauge.

Underinflation can cause tires to heat up and, eventually, fail. A tire that is 10 percent underinflated is way too close to being a flat tire, and 10 percent is often less than 10 pounds of air pressure. On the other hand, overinflation can cause a hard ride and abnormal wear patterns.

Many people carry 12-volt compressors with cigarette-lighter adapters in the event they must reinflate a tire. Motor home tires run at 80 pounds per square inch (psi) or more, and trying to inflate them with a light-duty compressor may take a very long time. Vehicles with air brakes have a compressor on the engine and often the RV will come equipped with an air coupler to which you can attach a length of hose. Sears offers a compact 1.5-horsepower compressor that produces 125 psi—adequate volume and pressure to inflate a motor home tire. This compressor must be attached to AC power, but if you have a generator, you can use it for roadside repairs.

Replacing Old Tires

A good rule of thumb is that tires on an RV should be replaced every five to seven years (or earlier if they've gone many miles). A lot of useful information about a tire is printed right on the sidewall. In some cases, this may be on the inside wall, facing away so that you can't possibly see it unless you crawl under the RV. In addition to the tire size and maximum inflation, the date the tire was manufactured is also imprinted on the tire, after the letters *DOT* and two groups of four letters. On our 2003 Monaco, the tires read "DOT MC6Y HHEW 4802." The 48 stands for the 48th week of the year, probably late November, and the 02 is the year of manufacture, 2002. So our tires were actually five months old when we bought the coach in April 2003. Even if you only drive your rig for a couple of weeks each year, you still need to replace the tires after seven years because rubber deteriorates with age.

A tire protector is a simple and effective way to prolong the life of your tires.

If you want your tires to last five to seven years, keep them properly inflated. If you find the tires are relatively old when you're purchasing a new rig, insist that the dealer put newer ones on before you take delivery.

Protecting Tires from Damage

One more caution: If you park for a long time in the same spot, your tires may suffer sun damage such as cracking. A good way to prevent this is to buy tire protectors—cloth covers to put on each tire when the rig is stationary for more than a few days. You can get fitted tire covers at most RV stores.

Also, do not try to make your tires look pretty by using tire dressings, particularly those with petroleum-based derivatives. These chemicals can deteriorate the rubber.

PROTECTING YOUR DRIVEWAY FROM DAMAGE

When parked for a long time, such as when you store your RV, put boards or blocks under the tires to distribute the load. The board or block must be large enough to cover the tire's footprint, especially when dual wheels are involved. This will help prevent dents from forming in your driveway.

Suspension

The axle is attached to a vehicle's frame by a system of springs and shock absorbers. This is known as the suspension system. The vehicle's suspension is either an air system or a mechanical system.

The air system uses rubber bladders located along the frame, a compressor, and a sensor that raises and lowers the corners of the vehicle to keep it level. Most luxury motor homes have full-air suspensions which provide a smooth, comfortable ride.

The spring system uses either coil- or leaf-type springs. Coil springs are made of round spring steel in the form of a vertical coil, and are placed between the axle and the frame. Leaf springs are a number of long, narrow layers of spring steel that form arches between the frame and axels. Coil springs have less internal friction and may provide a smoother ride, but many motor-home suspensions use an all-leaf spring suspension with additional inserts between the leaves to reduce friction.

Shock absorbers are a part of the suspension system designed to stabilize the ride by preventing excessive bounce.

Replace shocks if they leak or do not adequately control rebound. Check shock absorbers for oil leaks. Be aware that some shock absorbers have seals that permit a small amount of oil to seep out past the seals and lubricate the shaft. This is normal. Lubricate suspension components as specified in your owner's manual. With air-suspension systems, consult the manufacturer's manual to learn about ride height and how to inspect components.

Brakes

Brakes are of two types, disc or drum, and operated either by air or hydraulic pressure, sometimes with vacuum assist. A third type, electric brakes, are found in trailers. These brakes use electromagnets to actuate the trailer brakes via a separate electric controller in the truck cockpit.

Drum Brakes

Drum brakes have been used from the early days of automobile manufacture, and consist of a rotating drum that turns with the wheel, and brake shoes that are mounted on a backing plate attached to the axle. When the driver applies pressure

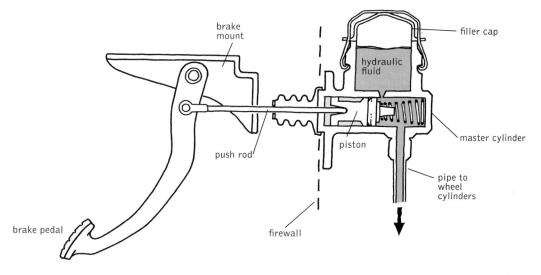

The interaction between the brake pedal and master cylinder.

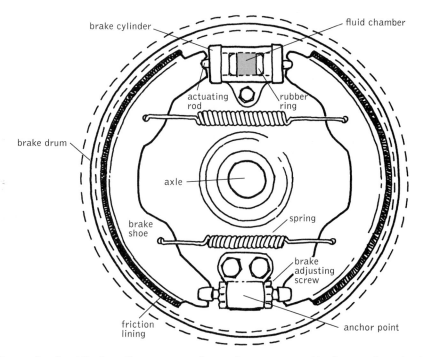

Drum brake. Hydraulic pressure from the master cylinder pushes the brake shoe against the drum, causing the vehicle to stop. Note that as the drum heats up and expands, braking efficacy is reduced.

to the brake pedal, the master cylinder generates hydraulic pressure. This pressure in turn presses the brake shoes against the drum. The resultant friction slows the rotation of the wheel. This process generates heat. If heat causes the drum to expand excessively, it becomes a less effective braking device, and can overheat and even boil the hydraulic fluid in the cylinder. This process is called "brake fade."

Disc Brakes

Disc brakes use a different system. A *rotor*—a rotating metal disc—is attached to the axle. This disc is placed between the jaws of a hydraulic device called a *brake caliper*. The caliper contains hydraulic cylinders, which press against brake pads located on each side of the rotating disc. Compared with a brake drum which expands as it heats and loses contact, the disc is more thermally stable. Disc brakes radiate friction heat more effectively, cooling in the air as they rotate. Disc brakes are, therefore, less subject to brake fade due to overheating. They're also somewhat more efficient than drum brakes.

Air Brakes

Air brakes work by means of air pressure delivered to a rubber bladder, rather than by hydraulic fluid delivered to a hydraulic cylinder. In case of emergency,

ENGINE BRAKES

Many large trucks and motor homes come equipped with engine brakes, sometimes referred to as Jake brakes (derived from the name of the manufacturer, Jacobsen). A Jake brake is actually not a brake at all, but rather an exhaust retarder.

Anyone who has driven an automobile with a standard transmission knows that the car slows if you take your foot off the gas, even if you don't touch the brakes. This is due to engine compression. A diesel vehicle will not slow down from compression the same way a gas vehicle does. The Jake brake solves this problem by restricting the outflow of exhaust gas from the engine.

Jake brakes are standard on some large diesel vehicles and they're a popular aftermarket upgrade. The brake is located in the exhaust pipe and it's noisy when used. Many municipalities restrict the use of Jake brakes within the city limits because of noise.

The Jake brake is generally activated by either a hand or foot switch. Jake brakes should be used when descending steep grades. Check your owner's manual for the proper procedure.

brakes on the rear wheels are automatically applied by springs when air pressure is lost. Additional safety features include one-way valves and dual air tanks to deal with loss of air pressure. Dual air tanks provide separate air sources for front and rear brakes. Built-in safety features permit either tank to brake both axles. Air brakes are the most common system for heavy-duty vehicles.

Brake Inspections

Brake inspection is complicated and should be left to the pros. Be sure to have your brakes inspected if they seem less effective than usual, if they're making unusual noises, or if they're pulling unevenly when applied. Because of the size of the vehicle, RV brakes should be serviced by a brake shop that deals with heavy-duty vehicles. If your vehicle is equipped with hydraulic brakes, monitor the brake fluid level.

Transmission

Maintaining the proper temperature in the transmission fluid is important to the life of your transmission. High temperatures can damage the transmission. The normal operating temperature is between 160 and 200 degrees Fahrenheit. The lubricating qualities of the transmission fluid are diminished by excessive heat and can pose a major threat to the transmission. Be sure to monitor the transmission temperature gauge, especially when going uphill or on a hot day. If your vehicle doesn't have a transmission temperature gauge, get one.

Transmission fluid leaks are a frequent cause of transmission failures. Consult your owner's manual for the proper level of transmission fluid. Usually you should check transmission fluid levels while the engine is running and the transmission is in neutral or park. Many transmissions have a separate level markings for hot and cold readings. Take a look at the color of the fluid while you're checking its level. It should be red and odorless. If you notice a burned smell, you may need to change either the transmission fluid or the filter, and have the transmission checked to determine the cause of the problem.

9

Finding Places to Stay

Traveling every day is not my idea of the perfect RV experience. I get tired of packing up everything every morning, putting bars across the refrigerator shelves, bringing in the slideouts, pulling up the levelers, hooking up the car, and then reversing all these procedures every night when we stop. However, sometimes you have to reach a destination by a certain date, especially if you plan to attend some function like a rally, conference, or festival.

Every afternoon, as the sun gets low and the driver gets tired you'll need to look for a place to spend the night. There are many organizations and publications to help make this task a simple one.

For starters, you should purchase a good general campground directory, either *Trailer Life* or *Woodall's*. These camping guides will tell you exactly what accommodations each park has, provide precise directions for getting there, and give instructions on how to make reservations.

Next, explore cost-saving measures. You can purchase a discount card from the KOA chain of campgrounds. Organizations like Resort Parks International (RPI) or Coast to Coast allow members to camp in selected parks for about $10 per night, but to join either one of these you must be affiliated with some kind of membership campground. If you belong to an RVers club like Good Sam, membership entitles you to a discount at a large number of parks designated "Good Sam Parks." The full-timers organization, Escapees, has a network of campgrounds where you can stay for about $11 per night; it's also affiliated with other parks that offer discounts to Escapees members.

Another good option is a $45 membership in Passport America, which offers half-price stays at all the campgrounds in their guidebook. With all these options, you will rarely need to pay full price for your stop at a campground.

RV parks come in a rich variety. Each one is unique in some special way. One in central California brought a daily newspaper to our doorstep in the morning. Another provided a continental breakfast in the campground office: fresh sweet rolls, juice, and coffee.

As you travel, many considerations will dictate your choice of where to stop. You may want a place that's comfortable, with a playground and swimming pool and even a hot tub. You may want some social activities, or the chance to pick up a few groceries without having to detach your car. Or you may want to stay in the least expensive place on your route. If you're on the road and you just want to stop for dinner and sleep, a pull-through site can be important.

When you've selected a campground, calling ahead to make sure there's room for your rig is a good idea. Occasionally, RV caravans will occupy all the spaces in a park and leave you scrambling for a second choice.

Of course, if you really want to camp someplace inexpensive, you can boondock in most Wal-Mart parking areas. The locations aren't exactly scenic, but the price is right. For a complete list of Wal-Marts, you can buy a directory for $19.95 called *Wal-Mart Locator*, which lists every Wal-Mart and Sam's Club store in the country, with driving directions to each from the nearest major highway or interstate. The guidebook also includes state maps showing store locations and zip codes for easy TV satellite tuning. To obtain the directory, go to the website listed under "Wal-Mart locator book" in the Appendix. Or, to use the opposite approach, for $3.95 from the same website you can download a list of Wal-Marts that do *not* allow overnight parking, and assume that all the others will. One good hint if you park at a mall or a Wal-Mart: Park with your main door facing the cars, the people, and the security cameras.

Other shopping malls may also allow you to stay overnight, but if you aren't sure, it's best to ask permission from someone in charge of the mall area. We've spent the night in the parking lot in front of a Camping World store occasionally, which seems to be okay with that RV-oriented store. Many truck stops and travel centers welcome overnighters, both truckers and RVers. Truck stops like Flying J and TA have a lot of amenities for a traveler. In addition to the opportunity to gas up, most of them have restaurants, mini-marts, and easy-access telephones, and some have Internet access. Quite a few even offer showers.

If you're retired or active-duty military, you can stay at military campgrounds, which offer camping space with hookups in "Fam Camps." These are well-cared-for campgrounds close to military bases or more frequently actually on the base. The fees are really low, averaging $13 to $16, and sometimes the locations can be spectacular. If you have any military affiliation, pick up a copy of *Military, RV, Camping and Outdoor Recreation around the World* at your nearest military exchange.

If you're going to stay a week or more at your destination, pick your campground carefully. Make sure it's far enough off the highway to be quiet, and close enough to the area's attractions.

There are a wide variety of places to stay out there, and with just a little forethought and prioritizing, you can snuggle that RV into a site that feels like home.

County, State, and National Parks

We started full-timing in 1994. At the time, most state parks were not what I would call RV-friendly. Site listings in my *Trailer Life* camping guide often looked like this: "150 tent sites, gravel, no slideouts, back-ins (15 by 29)." In other words, this campground has no electric, water, or sewer facilities, and the largest site is 29 feet long and not wide enough for a slideout. Because we've always driven at least a 35-foot motor home, this is one park we would have to skip, even if we're willing to dry-camp as a tradeoff for the scenery. After repeatedly finding similar listings for other state parks, I more or less crossed them off my list of places to stay—until recently, when I discovered that a lot of state parks are improving their images and facilities in an effort to attract larger RVs. For example, Golden Age Passports, which are designed to provide discounts to National Parks for folks 62 and older, are honored by all Louisiana *state* parks for half-price admission. This is great because state parks are usually in the most interesting, most scenic parts of every state.

You'll probably find a state welcome center near the border of each state you enter. There, you can find out what events are coming up and learn about important highway information—such as whether any of the tunnels in the state have rules prohibiting a rig with propane. In Texas, be sure to get the big *Guide to Texas* book. It has everything you want to know about this diverse and interesting state, in an easy-to-read format. Many other states publish similar guides, but Texas, in its typical fashion, does it grander and in more detail than most.

If you have access, the Internet is a quick and easy way to locate state parks.

The National Association of State Park Directors website (http://naspd.ind state.edu/stateparks.html) provides links to all the state parks in the United States. Their home page displays a map of the United States. Click on the state you're interested in. You'll be taken either to that state's park website or to another state government web page. For Louisiana, for example, you have to carefully scan the page that comes up, and down near the bottom, you'll find the state park link.

The U.S. National Park Service manages land set aside for its special significance. National Parks and National Forests are found in almost every state (except Louisiana, which is why they honor the Golden Age Passport in their state parks). If your journeys are taking you toward a National Park, a little planning ahead is a good idea, as the most popular ones fill up fast. For example, the Yosemite summer camping schedule, from May through August, is generally filled by May and the best you might hope for is a cancellation. Other, less famous parks, are apt to have more room. The typical national park has sites that fit an RV no longer than 25 feet, but some parks can accommodate RVs of up to 40 feet.

You can research a National Park by going to the website of the National Park Service, found at www.nps.gov. There you can select one of several ways to search the site. If you select by activity, you can then choose camping as the activity, and you'll see a list of only those parks that have camping. Campsites are not described in any detail, but if you go to the individual park's website, you'll get information about hookups, or the lack thereof, but not about maximum size for an RV. For that info, you'll have to call; phone numbers are listed at each park's site. At any park's website, click on "Plan Your Visit" to obtain information about campgrounds.

To make a reservation by telephone at one of the National Parks, check the website for contact information. Be warned that on the 5th, 15th, and 25th of the month they receive many calls and may be backed up. This is because reservations are organized in a series of "booking windows." For example, if you call on January 5, you can book reservations for January 6 through June 4 in most of the national park campgrounds. Then on February 5, the booking dates will extend to July 4. However, if you want to visit Yosemite, the booking dates begin on the 15th of the month—January 16 through June 14, for example. On the 25th, the window opens for tour reservations. It's a good idea to skip those three dates in any month if you want to make a phone reservation. To visit one of two reservation websites, look up the addresses in the Appendix. At the website for

Reserve USA, you can make reservations 24 hours a day. At the official National Parks reservation website, reservations are only taken between 10:00 A.M. and 10:00 P.M. Eastern time.

Membership Campgrounds

There are several large chains of membership campgrounds, and all of them offer about the same amenities. You pay a fee to join the group; after that, you pay an annual membership fee. As a member, you have the privilege of camping a fixed number of nights for free at campgrounds in the chain.

Just to give you an idea of what you can expect: we're allowed 50 free nights per year for the dues we pay to Thousand Trails, and if we use those up, additional camping costs about $8 per night. Most membership campgrounds seem to have a "two weeks in, one week out" rule. That is, the longest you can stay in one particular campground for free is two weeks. After that, you have to be out of the campground for one week before returning. With Thousand Trails, you can spend that week at another Thousand Trails site, but not all membership campground groups allow that. Some require you to remain out of their system for that week.

If you want to stay longer than two weeks, you can do so by paying a certain amount per extra night or extra week. Many campgrounds in the Thousand Trails system offer a monthly rate. And many have storage facilities where you can store your RV while you travel away from it, at a very reasonable fee.

I don't think membership campgrounds are worth the money if you're just an occasional or summer camper, but for a full-timer or snowbird (half-timer) they can be economical as well as a safe and pleasant experience. Most have gated security with guards during the day and after-hours entry codes issued only to members staying at the park. Most if not all membership campgrounds have facilities such as pools, miniature golf, tennis and basketball courts.

For example, Thousand Trails has about 50 campgrounds scattered across the country, mainly on the West Coast, the East Coast, and in Texas. The campgrounds are well maintained and most of them have large sites with full hookups.

Thousand Trails campgrounds offer a variety of activities, many of them family-oriented. There is usually a swimming pool, sometimes two—one for adults only and another for families—plus miniature golf, tennis courts, basketball, and two lodges: a family lodge and an adult lodge. The adult lodge is where

Families enjoy the pool at a Thousand Trails preserve.

adults go to play card games or pool. Internet access is available in most locations. Meals are served on weekends in one of the lodges. Dance bands and other performing groups entertain on Saturday nights. There is always something to do.

If you decide to join, you'll need to buy a membership. Do not—I repeat, do *not*—buy your membership directly from the association. You will pay far too much, maybe thousands of dollars too much. Instead, purchase a membership from someone who is giving it up, or from a broker. Memberships for sale are listed in the back of many RV magazines, including *Highways* (the Good Sam magazine), *Family Motor Coaching*, and *Escapees* magazine. You'll see that they cost a fraction of what the organization itself will try to get you to pay, but they come with all the same benefits. You may have to pay a transfer fee in addition to what the member sells the membership for, but even so, you'll come out ahead.

A typical membership campground will offer you a free stay for a few nights in return for listening to their sales pitch. If you're first asked to sign a statement that says that if you don't accept what is offered that day, you can't join the membership campground for a year, be careful. The salesman at a membership campground may tell you that you're getting a special one-time offer, one that other members have not had. For several thousand dollars, you can get the best possible membership, but this offer is only good the day it's made and you're excluded from joining for the next year if you don't join now. Don't fall for these high-pressure sales methods. Smile and walk away. If you've signed the "no memberships for a year" document, and there are two of you, remember the name under which you signed. You can buy a membership later on under the other person's name. If that seems dishonest, keep in mind that trying to pressure someone into buying a membership within a narrow time limit is more dishonest.

CAMPGROUND COURTESY

Campgrounds can be cramped with many people living in close quarters. As such, it's important to be a good neighbor. A few basic considerations will make for happy campers all around.

For starters, be sure you take up only your allotted amount of space. Don't try to shoehorn a 40-foot rig into a 35-foot slot. Don't let your RV hang out into the road. After you select a site that is big enough, be sure to pull into the center of your campsite so that your slideouts do not infringe on the neighbor's space. And if you detach your tow car and tow dolly, don't leave them sticking out in the road so no one can get by.

Read the campground rules. Find out whether it's okay to wash your rig at your site. Some areas have severe water shortages, and some campgrounds don't have good drainage for the runoff from washing a large rig. Most areas will not want you to change your oil or do mechanical repairs onsite.

Usually the campground rules will list "quiet hours," from 10 P.M. to 7 A.M. People don't all sleep and rise at the same time, so if you're a night owl, be sure to consider your early-to-bed, early-to-rise neighbors. Keep the TV or music down. Step outside your rig and check the level of sound that's leaking out. Noisy patio parties should end at a reasonable hour as well. Likewise, if you're an early riser, consider your late-sleeping neighbors when you get up. Keep things quiet until a reasonable hour.

If you're staying a while in one spot, you'll probably unpack some things and set them out on your patio (tables, chairs, rugs). Living outside is one of the pleasures of RV travel, but your neighbors will not appreciate it if you drag out cartons and tools

Dry Camping

Dry camping or *boondocking*—camping without hookups—can be a delightful experience. It provides a chance to experience the less civilized, more beautiful wilderness areas—and isn't that really why you have your RV? Also, if you like to attend rallies, many of them offer camping spots in large parking areas without hookups. Whatever your reasons for self-contained camping, a little forethought and planning will help make the experience easy and enjoyable.

Boondocking means keeping a careful balance of how much water you have, and how much of that comes into your gray- and black-water tanks during your stay. Be sure you arrive with adequate water, and be careful how you use it. Running out of water isn't as great a problem as ensuring that too much of that water doesn't go into your gray- and black-water tanks, because when those tanks are full, you have to find a dump station.

CAMPGROUND COURTESY (continued)

and small machines and leave them lying all over the campsite. Maintaining an aesthetically pleasing site will keep everyone happy.

Picking up after your pets is probably second nature to you if you're traveling with a dog, but sometimes accidents do happen. Your dog may relieve himself on your neighbor's patio before you can stop him. Should this happen, apologize and clean it up. Most people will understand that it was unintentional. Of course you will have a baggie along to pick up whatever "deposits" your dog makes. Walking your dog on a leash gives you better control over the entire situation and makes an accident less likely.

One more thing about pets: don't leave your dog behind in a cage or in your rig while you go off somewhere for the day. You really have no idea whether your dog will whine and cry while you're gone, yip constantly, or bark furiously at passersby. There is no quicker way to make enemies with an entire campground than by leaving a noisy dog behind. Also, unless you've left the air-conditioning on, there is a danger that your trailer or motor home will heat up and be a dangerous environment for your pet.

Finally, be patient. If your neighbor plays loud music, doesn't pick up dog droppings, or does anything else that grates on your nerves, see if you can find a polite way to suggest a change in behavior. And by all means, talk it over with the neighbor rather than complain to the campground office. If the behavior doesn't improve, take solace in knowing that RVers rarely stay in one place for very long. Your situation will likely improve soon. In the meantime, we RVers should get along with our neighbors the best we can.

Some people extend their stay by purchasing a blue plastic tank on wheels into which they can dump waste water. The tank can then be towed or wheeled to the nearest dump station while the RV remains in place. Tanks come in several capacities and cost between $40 and $200.

When dry camping, we try to use disposable dishes and utensils whenever possible. Of course, you'll still have some cooking and serving dishes to wash. Spray each item with liquid cleaner, scrub, and then rinse carefully. This saves filling the sink with soapy water. However, don't skimp on the rinse water—it's important to rinse everything thoroughly because detergent residue can make you sick. If you're camping in an area that allows you to discard water outside, consider doing dishes in the great outdoors in an old-fashioned dishpan. Just be sure to use a biodegradable detergent.

When brushing teeth, wet the brush, turn off the water, apply the toothpaste, and brush. Then turn on the water to rinse, or rinse with water from a glass. As for showering, we usually use campground showers if they're available. But if you need to use your own RV shower, do it "Navy style." Run the water just long enough to wet yourself, turn off the water, soap and scrub, then turn the water back on for a quick rinse.

As for sewer conservation, simply heed the old rhyme from the California drought: "If it's yellow, let it mellow. If it's brown, flush it down."

In addition to water conservation, you may need to conserve electricity. Use of the lights, fans, and other equipment in your RV should be contingent on battery condition and how much current those items draw. You can make rough calculations by adding up the power consumption of items run by battery and checking that against the battery's capacity. The power required by each item is generally listed on the manufacturer's label in either watts or amps. Some coaches have a power-conservation panel that shows how much current is being drawn on the DC system. We keep a close eye on the battery condition indicator on our utility panel.

If your batteries get low, and you have a generator, run it for a while so that the rig's DC converter will charge them. Without some alternate source of electric power such as a generator, you're limited to camping only as long as your coach batteries last. If you're going to be self-contained on a regular or frequent basis, you may want to consider solar panels for your rig (see Chapter 7).

If your rig has a generator, it can provide electricity for just about anything: appliances, TV, VCR, and so on. Many RVs also come equipped with an inverter that draws DC power from the coach batteries and converts it to AC . The inverter does not produce enough power to run air conditioning, though, so if the night (or day) is hot, you may need to resort to open windows and battery-operated fans. The main advantage of the inverter is that it's completely silent. The drawback is that the inverter relies on the house batteries for a source of power, so when it draws down the batteries, they must be recharged by the generator or by plugging in to a source of electric power.

In a motor home, the generator draws its fuel directly from the gas tank or from the diesel fuel tank, so it's a good idea to have a full tank if you plan extended generator use. Generators are designed so they'll never empty your tank and leave you stranded. They usually draw fuel from the top half of the tank only; this way you should have enough fuel to get home or to a filling station. If your trailer or fifth wheel has a generator, it is most likely fueled by the propane tanks; you may want to bring along an extra propane tank when dry camping.

Generators are noisy, and campground courtesy dictates that you shouldn't run them before 8:00 or 9:00 A.M. or after 9:00 P.M. in the evening. Some avid boondockers believe that you should never intrude into the beauty and silence of the wilderness by running a noisy generator, and they rely on a number of ways to do without it—mainly, solar power.

If you're camping someplace without a sewer dump site, be sure to have a plan for when and where to dump. Planning ahead for what's going to fill up, and what you're likely to run out of, will make your boondocking vacation a worry-free adventure.

10

Preventing and Responding to Disasters

When Dan and I embarked on the full-time RV lifestyle, we tried to anticipate and prepare for all eventualities. Of course, a few events occurred that we hadn't imagined in our wildest dreams, but, fortunately, we were more or less prepared for surprises.

Dealing with Roadside Mishaps

You need three things when something goes wrong with your RV:

- A phone
- Emergency road service insurance
- A way to find a reliable repair shop

Carry a Phone with You at All Times

You can never foresee all the possible disasters that may occur, but you can be prepared to deal with them by having a phone. I strongly recommend a cell phone for peace of mind and safety in case something happens in an isolated area. However, keep in mind that although cell service areas are growing rapidly, not all areas are covered. In some remote places, you may be out of cellular range. Search for a cellular phone company with the widest possible national coverage.

If a cell phone's somewhat spotty coverage isn't enough, you may want to invest in a satellite phone. A sat phone offers virtually complete coverage throughout the United States, Canada, and Mexico. This will add greatly to your peace of mind but at the same time it will greatly diminish your cash flow. A satellite phone can cost more than $1,000, and the phone service rates are a minimum of $1.20 per minute of usage. For example, the Iridium satellite phone offered by InfoSat

BEING FLEXIBLE: PART OF BEING AN RVER

So what can you do when a mechanical failure or blown tire spoils your carefully laid plans? First of all, be flexible. Go with the flow. If you must get to a certain destination to attend a particular event, consider an alternate way of traveling. Perhaps you have a tow car, or maybe you can take a bus, train, or plane. If your needs are not tied to time, you can find ways of enjoying your unexpected stay in a new community.

Flexibility is the key to turning a potential disaster into an enjoyable experience. You have to be able to let go of whatever your anticipation was for this day or days, and substitute whatever's at hand. Any community large enough to have a repair facility for your rig probably has some interesting or historic places to visit.

A visit to the Chamber of Commerce is a good way to start. There you can get maps and brochures of interesting places to see—old houses made into museums, vineyards for wine-tasting, and the like. You can find out about internet cafes, movie theaters, and shops. If the community is large enough, I like to hang out at one of those big discount bookstores. Usually, they have a coffee shop attached where you can get snacks and coffee. They also have plenty of tables and chairs where you can relax and just hang out all day if you want to. Generally you can find an electric outlet for a laptop.

Believe it or not, a town cemetery makes an interesting diversion. Grave markers and headstones provide fascinating insight into a community's history. Were many people killed in a local disaster, or one of the wars? Are there numerous headstones from the flu epidemic of 1918?

Go in and out of the town's shops, sample the local restaurant fare, walk the residential neighborhoods, or picnic in the park. Visit with the locals and ask about their town. You may be intrigued and enchanted by what you find.

Sometimes you may have to stay overnight or even for several days while your vehicle is repaired. Most RV repair shops have at the least an electric outlet you can plug into for electricity. Failing that, you can boondock. Or, because you'll likely have fewer neighbors in the locked repair yard than a campground, you can run your generator as late as you want if, like us, you want to watch the eleven o'clock news or the *Tonight Show* afterward. Cooking breakfast or lunch can be a little problematic, because the mechanics usually want you out of the coach while they're working on it, but people in the office can probably point you in the direction of a good café.

is priced at $1,495. In addition, you need a subscriber identity module (SIM) card for $50. You must also pay a one-time activation fee of $60, and a monthly access fee of $29.95 which includes call forwarding, message service, and an e-mail address. Beyond that, you pay for your minutes of usage at a base rate of $1.39 per minute. Keep your eye on these rates, though. It wasn't that long ago when cellular phones were impossibly priced; sat phones, too, will become more affordable in the coming years.

Joining an Emergency Road Service

There are a number of reliable emergency road service policies designed for RVers. We have one with Roadcare, affiliated with Camping World, which has proven reliable during the many years we've depended on them. The Family Motor Coach Association also offers emergency road service for its members, as do other RV organizations (see Appendix).

Whatever kind of emergency road service you have, check that it will properly cover your RV before you leave home. By obtaining a policy designed for RV coverage, you'll be guaranteed towing should the RV need it, something generally not covered by automobile clubs like AAA.

Finding a Reliable Repair Shop

A warning: I've heard many stories about RVers who have been ripped off at various unscrupulous repair places, so be cautious, especially if the service finds additional "problems" beyond the one you've consulted them about.

One way to find a good mechanic is to call your RV's manufacturer or the manufacturer of the part that has failed. Generally, they maintain a list of authorized repair services.

Another way to find reliable service is to ask your emergency road service when they arrive. These are local people and they can direct you, or tow you, to the best facility in town.

If you belong to the Family Motor Coach Association, you can take advantage of their annual directory, which lists the names and phone numbers of participants in a countrywide network of volunteers who will help a traveler find repair services.

Personal Safety

Certain routine precautions that you use at home are equally important on the road. Lock the RV when you leave it, and lock it from the inside before you go to sleep. If you're camped in a campground, you'll probably feel comfortable leaving some items outside overnight or while you go sightseeing. Such things as tables, chairs, and barbecue grills are probably safe to leave.

One advantage of membership campgrounds is that they provide a high level of security. You must identify yourself when entering, or enter a code into the gate at night. We've always enjoyed peace of mind in these gated, secure places.

WHAT TO DO IF YOUR WALLET IS STOLEN

My wallet was stolen one summer, probably while we were on the ferry from Orcas Island, in the San Juans, to Anacortes, Washington. The experience was decidedly unpleasant. I didn't discover the loss until we got back to our motor home, a few miles from Anacortes. After a frantic search of the RV and our car, we went to the nearest pay phone to make a dozen calls to banks and credit-card issuers.

The worst part was that we had to cancel two debit cards, which were our only source of cash. I'd had about $35 in my wallet, and Dan was left with only $6 in his, so getting cash became our priority the next morning. In the small Washington town where we were camped, the only bank charged us $6 to cash a check, and the manager made it clear he was doing us a favor to cash an out-of-state check—a favor he would not repeat.

Other than that, replacement of our cards was relatively painless. Our debit cards arrived within three days by FedEx, and other replacement materials fairly soon after. I replaced my military ID with a visit to nearby Whidbey Island Naval Air Station, and we made Oregon our next destination, a trip of about 100 miles, so I could obtain a duplicate driver's license, which requires a photo.

Whether you're traveling by RV, train, or plane, you can take certain steps that may not prevent your wallet from being stolen but will definitely make recovering what you lost a bit easier. Write down all your credit card numbers, along with the name of the card (for example, United Airlines Mileage Plus Visa), and the toll-free number to call if your card is stolen. Then store that information in a secure place. You might, for example, leave it with a trusted family member or friend you can call if something happens. Do the same with your passport number if you're leaving the country. That way, you don't have to deal with calling directory assistance to try to remember the name of your credit cards, and you don't have to rely on memory to make sure you cancel all the cards in your wallet. A quick way to do this is to photograph your cards, license and passport, and put the photos safely away.

In contrast, camping alone, say, in a vacant parking lot or by the side of the road, poses a certain hazard. No one may be around to hear your cry for help if someone threatens you in the dark. If you choose to camp in parking lots or at rest stops, you run a risk, however slight, of being vulnerable to predatory passersby.

No matter where you're camped, but especially if you're camped in an isolated area, don't open the door to just anyone who knocks. Ask who's there and what he or she wants. Even if the person seems legitimate, you may want to step outside to speak with him or her rather than invite a stranger inside your RV, where you're more vulnerable and less visible to neighbors.

Along those same lines, if you have one of those attractive little signs on the front of your rig with your names on it, you run the risk that a scam artist may use it for his own benefit. "Hi, Bob," he'll say, implying that he knows you. Or he might use your name to gain the confidence of your neighbors ("I've just talked to Bob and Darlene next door, and they said . . .").

In order to feel secure while traveling, some people carry a gun in their rigs, and they may even advertise the fact with a bumper sticker that warns, "Insured by Smith and Wesson." Carrying a gun is a personal decision. Some people feel safer knowing they have a means of protection. Others fear a weapon could be turned against them in a struggle, and many people just have a personal aversion to guns. This is a personal choice. Also note that state laws concerning firearms vary. To check the law in a state you plan to visit, go to the website listed in the Appendix. (Also, be sure to read Chapter 16 before you take any firearms across the border into Mexico or Canada.)

In general, keeping yourself safe on the road is mostly a matter of common sense. Avoid places and situations where you instinctively feel unsafe. Trust your instincts in dealing with strangers. If a situation doesn't feel right, get out of it. Ensure your own safety, even if it involves apparent rudeness to a stranger. Always take routine precautions when leaving your coach and your car. The goal is to travel with peace of mind.

Fire Safety

Each year, there are 20,000 fires in RVs in the United States. To avoid becoming one of these statistics, you must eliminate the fire hazards in your rig. Most RVs are equipped with appliances that use a flame, usually fed by propane, such as heaters, stoves, water heaters, and even the refrigerator when you aren't plugged into electricity. The electrical systems, both AC and DC, provide another potential fire hazard, as do the fuel systems, gasoline, diesel, and propane. You need to be sure that all these systems are working as they should, without leaks.

Fire needs three components: heat, air, and combustible material. The correct method to extinguish a fire depends on what material is burning. For example, if you have a grease fire on your stove, you can't put it out with water. You need to smother it, dump baking soda on it, or spray it with a chemical extinguisher.

In our motor home, we have two fire extinguishers. One is located near the front door and the other is in the bathroom, in the middle part of the coach. Printed on these extinguishers are instructions for how to use them. Familiarize yourself with your extinguishers *before* any emergency. That way you won't be reading the instructions while your RV is burning around you.

Combustible materials are generally classified in three basic groups. Class A combustibles are materials that leave ash when they burn, like draperies, cabinetry, clothing, and carpet. Class B combustibles are liquids you may well have on board your RV, such as gasoline, propane, diesel fuel, and motor oil. Class C combustibles are electrical, such as wiring, fuse boxes, TVs, and appliances. Check the fire extinguishers that you purchase to make sure they are appropriate for all the combustible materials in your RV.

To prevent fires, it's important to have as few flammable materials inside the RV as possible. For example, we store the propane bottles we use for our barbecue grill in an outside locker.

From time to time you should inspect your propane lines, electrical outlets, wiring, furnace, stove, and other appliances. Be sure your RV has all three types of detectors: smoke, propane (see next section), and carbon monoxide. Carbon monoxide is a particularly insidious gas because it's colorless and odorless. Test your smoke, carbon monoxide, and propane detectors to make sure they're working. A smoke detector can be annoying if it goes off when you're just making toast, but it provides an invaluable warning in case of a real fire.

Knowing you've made your unit as free from fire hazards as possible will bring peace of mind, but fires do still happen. Most newer RVs have a window designed for emergency exit. Ours is right over the bed, a good place, because if we were in the bedroom and a fire broke out elsewhere in the coach, we would have no way to get to the door. Be sure that you know how to open that breakaway window so you don't have to figure it out in an emergency. It's a good idea to practice squeezing through the window at least once, so you're familiar with the process.

An emergency exit like this provides a way to get out if fire breaks out in the front part of your RV. Note the handle on the right.

In case of a fire, the important thing to do is get out as quickly as you can. Don't stop to take any important documents or any treasures with you. Things can be replaced, but you can't. If the coach is filled with smoke, drop below the smoke and crawl. Inhaling smoke can be deadly.

Propane Safety

Propane is probably the heart of the heating and cooking systems in your RV. If your RV is a trailer, the propane tanks are located on the tongue. In a fifth wheel or motor home, they're in a vented compartment outside. Regulators reduce the pressure in the tank to an acceptable level for use in your RV and should be located in a protected area of the RV.

To get the fuel flowing to your appliances, you must turn it on at the main tank. Then light the pilot light. If your appliances don't stay lit, have the tank checked—it may have air inside, which can be purged. Most propane systems are equipped with a shutdown valve designed to close if an abnormal flow is detected.

When you first open your service valve, this system may operate for a few seconds before allowing the propane to flow through, so don't be alarmed if it doesn't work immediately.

When you're on the road, if you have a two- or three-way refrigerator system, your refrigerator is likely to be running on propane. This alarms some people, who fear what might happen if the main tank is open during a crash. This is understandable. Propane is an explosive gas. Some experts recommend that you turn the propane off while traveling. Your refrigerator will stay cold for 8 to 12 hours if you don't open the door. If you travel with the propane on, be sure to turn off your refrigerator when you stop for fuel. Whether you travel with propane on is a decision you need to make for yourself. The arguments against it are fairly strong. Propane lines can fail or break while you're traveling. Sometimes propane lines are routed around wheel wells. This means that if your tire blows, it may cut into the propane line, causing a dangerous leak if the propane is turned on. Weigh this information and the likelihood of these events against the inconvenience of turning off the tank outside your rig and turning it back on at your destination.

A word of warning: Some states and/or cities are fussy about rigs containing propane driving through their tunnels. This is the kind of information you can find out at a welcome center when you first enter a state.

If your rig doesn't have a propane detector already, you should definitely have one installed. In the event that the propane alarm goes off, you may have a propane leak from your stove, furnace, or refrigerator. The first thing to do is shut off your main propane tank at the source. Put out all open flames such as the stove pilot light. The slightest spark can set it off. For that reason, don't operate an electrical switch if your propane alarm has sounded. Don't even use a telephone. Propane is heavier than air and tends to pool near the floor, so be sure to open all doors in addition to all windows. Then go outside. Have the propane system checked before you occupy the RV again.

Preparing for Medical Emergencies

After you've obtained the best medical coverage you can afford, another way you can take charge of your personal health is by preparing for a medical emergency. For example, take a first aid class so you can learn to cope with the treatment of burns, sprains, cuts, and more serious procedures like CPR or the Heimlich maneuver. With any luck, you'll never need to use this knowledge, but the training will add to your peace of mind. Check with the local Red Cross or fire department for classes.

Be sure you travel with a first-aid kit that includes a variety of bandages and over-the-counter medications to deal with accidents on the road. Bring along a book on general medical care. Because you may be far from a doctor or pharmacy, you want to be sure that the first-aid kit you have in your RV is well stocked. Here are some suggestions:

- Bandages in a variety of shapes and sizes
- Adhesive tape
- Gauze pads
- Cotton balls
- Acetaminophen, ibuprofen, or aspirin to relieve pain and fever
- Antihistamine to relieve allergies and inflammation
- Antibiotic ointment to prevent infection
- Hydrocortisone cream to relieve skin irritation
- Hydrogen peroxide to disinfect and clean wounds
- Antidiarrheal medication
- Upset-stomach remedy
- Bee-sting kit (essential if you or people you travel with are allergic)
- Antiseptic wipes
- Scissors
- Tweezers
- Cotton swabs
- Thermometer
- Flashlight and extra batteries (in case you need a close look at a wound or injury)
- Safety pins for fastening splints and bandages
- Disposable gloves
- Sunscreen with SPF 15 or higher

Carry a list of your medications with you in your wallet, so it's always available. Due to the possibility of harmful drug interactions, a doctor will want to know what drugs you're currently taking before prescribing any new ones. In addition, it's a good idea to carry a document listing your medical history, any allergies, the names and addresses of your current healthcare providers and medical insurance provider, and emergency contact information. This way, a doctor can contact your primary physician or specialist in an emergency. Any doctor you see will give you a copy of your record, if you ask; then you can take this record back to the doctor you normally see, so it will be added to your complete health history.

The final way you can remain in control of your health is through prevention. Get an annual flu shot and see a doctor for regular checkups. Use sunscreen when outdoors. Be sure that you exercise every day, even if it's just walking around the RV park where you're staying. When traveling for a long day, take frequent breaks, and get out and walk around for awhile. Sitting too long can cause blood clots to form in your legs. These clots could potentially travel elsewhere in your body and cause life-threatening health problems. Besides, walking will provide a nice break from the road. Finally, eat a healthy diet. Remember, the better your health, the more you'll enjoy your travels.

11

Leaving Your RV

In a letter to the editor published in *Family Motor Coaching*, Pat Darger made the case for taking trips away from one's RV. She said that she used her motor home to transport her to an area, but when she got there, she often liked to explore places where, as she put it, "big mama just don't fit."

Occasionally, it simply isn't practical to take your home on wheels when you want to visit a particular spot. You may be camped too far away, or you may just opt for a trip involving a hotel stay, tent camping, or backpacking. You may also leave the big RV behind when the road to your destination is impassable for a large vehicle.

If you plan to leave your RV behind at a campground longer than overnight, let campground personnel know, so they can keep an eye on your rig. Nothing should go wrong if you leave it a few days—but it's best to be prepared.

As full-timers, the world is ours for the taking. We aren't limited by where the RV can go, only by where we ourselves want to travel. Sometimes we need to go to those intriguing places where "big mama just don't fit."

Choosing the Right Storage Location

Your RV's health is at its best when you're on the road because you constantly check and maintain it, and charge the batteries while plugged in overnight. However, we all need to store our rigs every now and again.

Most mini-storage lots have places where you can park and store an RV. Check that the place has good security and is located in a reasonably safe part of town.

Sometimes you don't have any choice about where to store your RV, but if you do, the climate where it's stored is an important factor. Extremes of heat, cold, dampness, or dryness can adversely affect various parts of the complex mechanism that is your home away from home. The ideal storage location is probably someplace with a mild climate, not too dry and not too damp, not too hot and not too cold.

Preparing Your RV for Storage

Preparing your RV for storage takes some thought. Naturally, if you're going to be away any length of time, you have to empty out your refrigerator and dispose of everything in it. It's hard to plan ahead far enough to avoid tossing out sacks full of food—and feeling guilty about the waste—but sometimes that's your only option.

If you're going to be gone only a week or two, you might try letting your refrigerator run on propane while you're gone (assuming it has this capability), but RV refrigerators are not 100 percent reliable when running on propane, so you risk finding a fridge full of spoiled food on your return. Plan on a large refrigerator using about a gallon of propane per day. If your propane tank and refrigerator are both large, you may be able to let it run for a month, assuming that the coach batteries that light the propane keep running that long.

Personally, I wouldn't chance it. Give the perishable food away, or beg someone to store it for you. A campground manager may have a corner in the office refrigerator where you can tuck your most important items.

Some RVs have openings underneath that are big enough to admit small critters like mice or ground squirrels. There isn't any way to keep them out except to select the storage location thoughtfully, and you can't always do that.

Just to be sure, store your food in "mouseproof" containers. Put cereal, flour, sugar, and similar foods in securely fastened plastic bags, or better yet, in sturdy plastic containers.

Before you leave your RV, check the batteries' electrolyte level, and make sure that the batteries are fully charged. Then disconnect the terminals so the batteries won't discharge. Next, be sure that the tires are properly inflated, and cover the wheels with tire covers to prevent sun damage. In a motor home, leave the dash air vent open to prevent condensation inside the coach.

Finally, check that the trash cans are empty, and make sure all curtains and

PARK YOUR STORED RV CAREFULLY

It began with a tiny stutter in the engine as the motor home climbed a hill. Then it escalated to a definite miss. And pretty soon, the engine wasn't running.

After a while, with the help of some knowledgeable mechanics, we diagnosed the problem as "fuel starvation" due to a clogged fuel filter. We replaced the filter and examined the old one. It was filled with rusty sludge from a fuel tank full of very fine rust particles.

We lived with the problem for a while, replacing the fuel filters whenever the motor started to sputter. On one occasion, we were terrified when the engine climbed a 6 percent grade in spurts. Eventually, we had to spring for an expensive repair: having the gas tank removed and cleaned. Our mechanic said the tank was the biggest and dirtiest he'd ever seen. In fact, it had to be cleaned twice before all the rust was removed.

Naturally, we wondered how that had happened, and came to the conclusion that we'd made a couple of mistakes about a year before. We stored the motor home for several months at the California coast, and we stored it with the fuel tank nearly empty. Water condenses in an empty tank, and water leads to rust.

That error was really mine. We had a hundred-gallon fuel tank, and I didn't want to spend a lot of money filling it up just before we parked it for several months. In retrospect, I wish I hadn't been so stingy, and I also wish I hadn't selected such a damp storage location.

The next time we stored the motor home for a few months, it was in a completely different environment: the dry desert near Tucson, Arizona. This time, all the coach batteries dried out and were completely dead, and we had to buy five new deep-cycle marine batteries to get the coach on the road. Apparently, a dry climate can be just as harmful over time as a moist one.

The moral of this story? Consider climate when selecting a storage area for your RV. A mild, not-too-wet and not-too-dry location is best. Avoid coastal and desert locations, if possible.

blinds are tightly closed. External sunshades over a motor-home window will protect the dash better than drapes. With some forethought, you'll find your RV waiting in good condition when you're ready to resume your travels.

PART THREE

The Joys of the Open Road

12
Loading the RV and Preparing to Leave

Even though RVing is a freewheeling lifestyle, you can't just pick up and go without doing a little preparatory work.

There are three things to consider when loading your RV: balance, convenience, and breakage protection. Your RV will level better and travel better if the heavier items are distributed equally among lockers on both sides, with some in front lockers and some in the rear. This is especially important if your RV is a travel trailer. An evenly balanced trailer is less subject to loss of control on the road.

Getting It All In

"On a long journey, even a straw weighs heavy." —Old Chinese proverb

When I was a sloppy teenager I kept my room in a permanent state of disaster. My mother used to plead with me to have "a place for everything, and everything in its place." I hated that phrase. Today, as an RVer, I understand it.

For the sake of your own sanity, everything in the spatially-limited environment of an RV must be stowed when moving, and kept tidy while camping. Carefully planned storage will make this easier.

As part of planning a trip in your RV, make a list of what you want to take along. Think about food, clothing, emergencies, and entertainment (books, games, puzzles, DVDs, and so on). Just to be sure, have plenty to do if the weather turns sour and you're more or less trapped inside. Then load the RV and check off items as you do.

If you find you've forgotten a vital item, don't panic. You're not leaving civilization completely behind, and even if you are, you can pick up the missing item on your way. The point is to have enough stuff along so you don't feel deprived but not so much that you keep tripping over things and have no place to put them. A short shakedown trip is often a good idea to help you discover what things you absolutely need and which things you'll never miss if you leave them behind.

You may be surprised at how many things you can get into the compact space of your RV. Whenever Dan and I go shopping for food, he winces as I fill the shopping cart with meat, fruits, vegetables, milk and other things that have to be refrigerated. "You'll never get all that in," he warns, but I always do. I have a one-word secret: *decant.*

Things you buy in the supermarket come packaged in bulky cartons and containers that take up a lot of room. Remove the items, put them in resealable plastic bags, and you'll be surprised how much a refrigerator or cupboard can hold. Even if you've placed the food in a plastic bag provided by the store, when you get home, put it into a resealable plastic bag. It will take up less room. Large bottles of juice can be decanted into plastic quart-size bottles to fit better in the fridge. Before freezing meat or fish, bag it in portion sizes.

The same idea works for your cupboards. For example, a huge box of cereal from Costco or Sam's Club can be repackaged into a resealable bag that will fit much better. To cut down on possible confusion, cut out the product's box top and any instructions for preparation, and put them in the baggie, too.

Stacking items will help you get the most out of your cabinet space. However, before you take the RV on the road, be sure you've arranged items in your cupboards so they won't fall over or crash into each other and then fall out the door when you open it at your destination.

To protect breakables, cut up some non-slip plastic "Line-it" from Camping World or elsewhere ($2.50 a roll), and put a square of it between plates, bowls and other breakable dishes. You can also wrap a strip around each glass and tape the ends together. Plastic bubble wrap works, too. It's a tedious task but prevents glasses breaking as the RV rattles over an unexpected rough patch of road. Alternatively, don't bring glasses at all. Substitute plastic instead.

Refrigerator bars help prevent food from sliding out of your refrigerator.

A slideout tray can be a real help when you're loading and unloading your storage lockers.

And, of course, be sure your cupboard doors and refrigerator doors are latched before you take off. On one of our first trips, the fridge door flew open as we went around a curve, and out spilled a dreadful mixture of eggs, salad dressing, and leftover lasagna. It was no fun to clean up. Your RV will get back at you for every little lapse in memory, sad to say.

Something that may avert a disaster like that is a set of refrigerator bars, which you can buy at an RV store. Usually, they come three to a set, one for each shelf in your RV refrigerator. These round metal bars come in two joined sections that slide apart or together to fit exactly against the refrigerator's walls and act as a barrier to anything falling out when you open the door.

The inner face of cupboard doors can be fitted with racks to hold additional items, using the "empty" space inside the doors. The microwave oven provides another good storage area for such things as bread and rolls. Storing baked goods in the microwave helps keep them fresh, because the door seals tightly.

If you're an avid reader, book storage can create a problem. Try to limit purchases to paperbacks, which are cheaper and easier to store; you can stack them in double rows in RV cupboards. Recipe books are a special case. If you've used a cookbook for a while, you probably have favorite recipes and others you know you'll never use. Photocopying or tearing out those favorites and placing them in a notebook or photo album saves the space the entire cookbook would require. For this purpose, I use a photo album with each sticky page covered by a plastic sheet. Spilled food wipes right off the plastic sheets, leaving the recipe intact—an added benefit if you're a sloppy cook like me.

You'll be tempted to bring some cooking utensils from your home kitchen into your RV but use common sense. Enormous cookie tins and big pizza pans, for example, won't fit into a smaller convection oven. Take stock of your current supplies and, wherever possible, shop for something smaller.

Departure Checklist

Pilots and astronauts use them, surgeons use them, and RVers should use them, too. This important safety device is a checklist. When breaking camp in your RV, a single missed step (such as forgetting to unplug your electric cord, or towing your car with the brake set) can spell disaster.

Your checklist should include both interior and exterior areas, and be

MAKE A LIST; CHECK IT TWICE

Dan and I were enjoying a late breakfast one morning at a membership park in Washington state when a large Class C drove past. Dan suddenly pointed at the vehicle.

"Look, his locker is open!" he exclaimed. "And he's dragging his power cord, and the plug is missing."

Just then another man came running over. "Do you have a CB?" he asked us breathlessly. "That rig just tore the water pipe from its site and there's water gushing everywhere. Someone needs to call the ranger."

Dan got on our CB and called in. Then we ran across the street to survey the damage. It was considerable. When the rig drove off still plugged in, the power cord looped around the wooden post that held both water pipe and electric box, and ripped the whole thing out. The water pipe was torn apart underground, and water gushed up and out through the electric box.

Water and electricity had to be shut off in that section of the park, and eventually a backhoe was brought in to dig out the soggy mess and a pump was brought in to remove a small lake of water. It took hours for the repair crew to fix the damage.

The accidental culprits were extremely dismayed. "Don't blame me. I don't touch the outside of the coach," said the wife. The husband had no comment.

Accidents like this can be avoided if you use a written checklist and double-check that you've done everything you need to do before you start your motor.

customized to your individual situation. Organize it to fit the way you walk around your rig, inside and outside. Think about where you want to start, and which direction you'll move in, then write down the tasks in that order.

Here's a sample checklist you can start with, and customize to fit your needs. Our list is for a motor home, but you can easily modify it for a fifth wheel or trailer.

Inside the coach:

- ❏ Raise rear blinds so the driver can see through the rear of the coach (if you have a rear window).
- ❏ Open other blinds and fasten them so they won't rattle.
- ❏ Fasten back the front curtains.
- ❏ Close the windows, so they're quiet while traveling.
- ❏ Clear off the countertop and put away all dishes.
- ❏ Stow small appliances in cupboards.
- ❏ Lower the roof antenna.
- ❏ Stow items in the refrigerator, so they won't leak or fall over, and check that all lids are fastened tightly.
- ❏ Latch the refrigerator door.
- ❏ Close and secure all cupboard and closet doors and drawers.
- ❏ Clear off the bathroom countertop.
- ❏ Empty the shower of anything that could fall over or spill.
- ❏ Turn off the furnace.
- ❏ Turn off the water pump.
- ❏ Clear off the bedside tables.
- ❏ Stow knickknacks in cupboards.

Outside the coach:

- ❏ Fill your coach's water tanks about one-third full.
- ❏ Detach and stow electric cords, water hoses, and sewer hoses. (Be sure to include the pressure regulator. It's easy to accidentally leave it attached to the faucet.)
- ❏ Roll up and secure the awning.
- ❏ Stow items such as grass mats, tablecloths, folding chairs, and portable barbecues.

❑ Visually inspect to be sure the antenna has been retracted.

❑ Dismantle and stow the satellite dish.

❑ Detach and stow the TV cable.

❑ Retract the hydraulic jacks; if you've used boards to help level your rig, remove and stow them.

❑ Remove and stow wheel covers.

❑ Close and latch outside lockers.

❑ Check oil and water levels, as well as windshield washer fluid.

❑ Check tire inflation.

❑ Hook up your tow car, and ensure that it's in neutral, with the key in the "accessory" position, the steering wheel unlocked, and the emergency brake, radio, heating, air conditioning, and fan off.

❑ Check turn signals, brake lights, and headlights on your RV or tow vehicle, and on your trailer or toad if you have one.

❑ Retract the electric step.

This checklist works for us, and even when we're itching to get on the road, we try to remain patient enough to work through all of it.

Signs are helpful, too. For instance, you can buy a sign that says "Antenna Up" and attach it somewhere conspicuous immediately after you've raised the antenna. If the sign is hung over, say, the instrument panel, it's unlikely that you'd drive off without lowering the antenna. You might consider making signs for other easily overlooked tasks as well, such as removing the "booties" from the coach's wheels.

13

Arranging to Be Gone

S o you've purchased and loaded your RV and now you're ready to set off on your first adventure. Of course, you'll do the usual things everyone does when going on vacation: stop the paper, have mail held, arrange for someone to watch the house and perhaps care for the garden. However, you may not be planning the typical American two-week vacation this time. In your RV, you have an opportunity to be gone for as long as you like—months or even years—and if you're setting forth on that kind of journey, here are a few additional things to consider.

Mail Services

If you're only going to travel for a month or two, you may be content with just having the post office hold your mail, but if you're going to be gone a considerable time, you probably need to receive and pay your bills. There are a couple of ways to do this. One is to have your mail forwarded to a family member. The drawback is that it's a lot to ask, even of a close and willing relative. Your relative must separate your mail from their own, find a secure place to store it, and have large envelopes ready to enclose it all when you call with a forwarding address. Then he or she must find time to take your package to the post office or the FedEx drop box.

Instead, consider signing up with a mail-forwarding service. For a fee, you have your mail diverted to one of these companies. When you're ready to have it forwarded, you call in or e-mail them with your present address. Some offer 24-hour service, and many have a toll-free phone number, a website, and/or an e-mail address you can use to contact them. Good Sam Club, Family Motor Coaching, and Escapees offer mail-forwarding service for their members. Mail services are listed in many RV magazines under the "Services" heading. (*Family Motor Coaching* lists them under "Miscellaneous.")

A few things to keep in mind: general-delivery mail is held for 30 days. If you impulsively decide to change your travel plans (one of the sheer delights of the RV lifestyle), and will not be able to pick up your mail as planned, you can send a change-of-address form requesting your mail to be sent to another post office. Keeping a supply of these forms on hand is a good idea. Also, keep a picture ID handy when picking up general-delivery mail.

Certain kinds of mail cannot be sent to general delivery. Most Internet and mail-order stores ship either by UPS or FedEx, both of which require a street address for delivery. The good news: your slot at an RV park can constitute such an address. You'll need to check with the RV park office about how such deliveries should be addressed. Sometimes delivering to the office is recommended, especially if you're an active sightseer and seldom found at your site. If you know you're going to be gone and you're expecting a delivery, you can put a note on your door directing delivery to the campground office.

Getting Cash

Years ago, a long trip away from your home town meant carrying cash, traveler's checks, or lots of ID to produce in banks (which were reluctant to cash checks for non-members). In those days, supermarkets dealt only in cash, and banks preferred to cash checks from their own branches, or at least within their own state. It was a problem.

Thanks to ATMs, it's a problem no more. However, even those apparently efficient ATM machines can break down or run out of cash just when you hope to make a withdrawal.

You can diminish the risk of being unable to get cash by having two bank accounts, each with a debit card. It's unlikely that both your banks will experience difficulties simultaneously, but it's very possible that one will. For instance, a friend of ours traveling in Mexico found one day that ATMs would not accept her card. Unbeknownst to her (because she wasn't receiving her mail), her bank had issued new cards to all clients after she left on her trip. Her old card was no longer valid.

While you're traveling, your bank might also develop difficulties with its computers. Hurricanes or other disasters can incapacitate your bank's server, leaving you unable to withdraw funds from that account. If you have half your money in another account with another bank, you'll be okay.

Also be aware that ATM machines can attract more than just computer troubles. Withdrawing cash from an outdoor ATM can put you in a vulnerable position. You need to be alert. A new tool for crooks is the picture-capable cell phone. Someone who appears to be having a conversation while waiting behind you might actually be taking a picture of your credit card and the buttons you push for your PIN. True, that person will have only your PIN and card number—not the card itself. However, these days that's not a problem. You can use those numbers to order by phone or Internet without anyone even seeing the plastic.

If your card is lost or stolen, phone your bank as quickly as you can. They will cancel your card and arrange to send you a new one. If you've divided your funds into two accounts, you'll be okay until the new card arrives.

If you share a joint account, the bank will issue a card and a separate PIN to each person. In this case, you can continue to withdraw funds with the remaining card.

You don't have to use an ATM machine that is located right out in the open, where anyone can approach you. Walk around town a little and find a bank with a glassed-in ATM machine where you must swipe your card to enter. Some banks in Mexico have an armed guard beside their ATMs, adding to your sense of security.

Trips to the supermarket can also be a way to get cash. This method has the advantage of avoiding the fees some banks charge for using their ATMs. Just about all supermarkets these days accept ATM cards and will give you cash back when you pay for your groceries. Some, however, limit cash back to $25 or $50.

From time to time, an ATM may reject your card for its own reasons. Perhaps it's out of cash, its phone line is out of service, or its computer is down. In this case, be sure to make a note of the time, place, name of the bank, and the amount you attempted to withdraw before you search for another bank. Next time you check your account, make sure you haven't been charged for money you didn't receive. If you don't receive any money, you'll have a hard time proving that. If the machine doesn't give you any money, it probably won't give you a receipt either.

Internet Banking

Internet banking seems as though it was designed specifically for the RV traveler. A particularly useful feature is the option to have your bills paid automatically each month. Bills that recur in the same amount every month can be set up so that the bank sends out the payments on the dates you specify.

Bills that vary every month can be handled in a few different ways: You can wait until the bill is received and then write and mail a paper check for it, you can direct your bank at that time to make a one-time payment, or you can have those accounts billed to your credit card. You can then go online near the end of the month, view the credit card balance, and direct your bank to send that amount to the credit card. This makes for one transaction instead of several. Among the bills that can be paid by credit card are cellular phone, Internet, and TV satellite services. The amounts on all these statements typically vary, so it's just easier to pay them this way.

Of course, this system isn't foolproof. Your phone company or TV service may decide to change its accounting system and temporarily suspend all billings to credit cards. You may be the last to know because they may notify you by snail mail. If you're on the road and relying on Internet banking and automatic bill pay, check your balances frequently to make sure that some unpaid bill is not hanging out there. If it is, contact the company right away.

Some banks will charge a small monthly fee for Internet bill-paying functions and some do not charge at all. You may want to shop around for the best deal.

Another bill-paying option is to use the services of MyCheckFree.com. This free bill-paying web service receives your bills, then it e-mails you to let you know when they're due and how much you owe, and sends payments to the billers that you select. The list of companies that MyCheckFree.com serves is extensive and includes local utilities, banks, finance companies, credit card companies, phone companies and many more.

Cellular Phone Service

An early ad for cellular service boasted, "This can be your only phone." This was music to RVers' ears. With a cellphone, you're never far from your family no matter where you are in the United States.

You can get a phone number in any part of the country you'd like. If possible, choose a number that is local for most of your family. That way they can call you wherever you are, and they'll pay only for a local call even if you're in New York and they're in California. If you get a calling plan with national coverage, you'll pay only for the minutes you use while talking to them, no matter how far away you are.

When signing up for phone service that you want to use all across the United States, there are a couple of factors to consider. One is the coverage that the company has. You can research the coverage provided by different cellphone carriers online. Check out CNET.com and *Consumer Reports* for ratings of different companies.

Internet connection is another factor. Right now, many RVers are customers of Verizon Wireless because this cellular provider does not charge extra if you use your Verizon minutes for Internet connection. However, some Verizon plans do not have good national coverage—so make sure you're aware of exactly what your plan includes.

Another factor to consider when signing up for cellular service is the phone itself. Find out whether the phone you're considering is both analog and digital. You need digital if you want to use your cell phone to connect a laptop computer to the Internet, as many RVers do. In remote areas, where the only service you receive is analog, you are able to use your phone for calling but not for the Internet. Also, find out if the cellular company offers laptop Internet connection (not just the option to connect the cell phone directly to Internet), and whether or not they charge extra for this service. You may also want to check out other features like speaker phone, or plans that will let each member of your family have a phone.

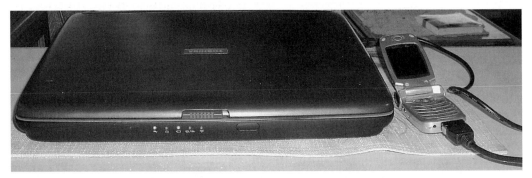

Depending on your cellular service plan, you may be able to connect to the Internet via your cellphone.

Connecting to the Internet using a cell phone is not my first choice, but it is an emergency backup capability I want to have. And I do not want to be charged extra for "data" minutes.

Medical Care

Even if you're just going to travel a short time, you need to be sure that your medical insurance covers you while you're gone. Many HMOs do not cover their customers outside the local area. Some require you not travel more than a certain number of miles from home, or that you not be gone more than a certain number of days. If you're in a PPO type of arrangement, you may be traveling where there are no "preferred" physicians available. Find out how your insurance company handles this. Some simply charge extra, while others will not reimburse you if you use a doctor or hospital not in the system.

With the high cost of medical care these days, don't leave home without medical insurance. Your out-of-pocket medical costs could change if you travel outside of your provider's network. Be sure to check with your insurer to learn the details of your coverage. Be prepared to supplement your insurance with short-term medical insurance for travelers. Traveler's medical insurance is expensive, but the peace of mind is worth it on a relatively short trip. If you're traveling outside the United States, Medicare will not cover you at all when you leave the country.

Finding Doctors and Clinics on the Road

If you become a full-timer or travel for several months in your RV, you'll probably find yourself taking more responsibility for your health than you used to. It's hard to consult with your regular doctor when you're in an RV park hundreds of miles from familiar territory. But sometimes you have to see a doctor or visit the emergency room in a town you're unfamiliar with, and you'll need to have some way to find a doctor.

The Internet offers one way to do this. Go to a search engine such as Google, and enter "urgent care clinics" and the name of the city and state (for example, you might type " 'urgent care clinics' Jacksonville Florida"), and you should be able to turn up a clinic not too far from you. If you need a specialist, such as a dermatologist, enter that into Google as well, and you'll usually find a list of board-certified specialists in the area.

Another option is to ask at the office of the campground where you're staying. Often the people there, or the campground host, will know of a good medical facility.

Making Sure of Medical Coverage

Just having good medical insurance won't guarantee a worry-free journey, but it will give you some peace of mind. Things happen, and all you can do is try to make sure you have made the best possible provision for unforeseen events.

A number of HMOs offer attractive rates to Medicare patients because the government gives these HMOs a Medicare subsidy on a per capita basis. In California, some HMOs don't charge Medicare patients anything, which is great except that this coverage, like most HMO coverages, is regional. According to rules set by Medicare, you have to remain within the region to continue your HMO coverage. Some exceptions to these rules do exist, but you probably don't want to rely on becoming an "exceptional case."

Getting medical treatment on the road isn't just a financial matter, though. There are some practical drawbacks to having a rotating series of doctors. If you see the same doctor on a regular basis, he or she becomes familiar with your particular situation and may have a better idea of what treatment would be best for you.

One solution to this dilemma is to make a regular visit to the city where most of your medical records reside. When you visit doctors and clinics on the road, be sure they fax or send a record of your treatment to your "regular" doctor.

As we travel, we've noticed that medical coverage is a hot topic with most full-timers. People we've met have gotten around the problem in a variety of creative ways. Many just never tell their HMO they're gone. They keep a mailing address in the area of their medical coverage, and plan to fly back there if a serious health problem develops.

One RVer we know told us that if he hadn't stayed with his HMO in his original home state, his insurance costs would have been $1,000 per month. He pays the HMO about $250. Although his coverage is strictly regional, and he can receive only emergency care outside his HMO's region, he and his wife decided they could make a lot of trips home each year for regular checkups before they'd spend an additional $9,000. He maintains a mailing address in that state in order to keep this coverage. The risk to this type of deception is that if the HMO finds out you haven't been truthful, they can deny coverage.

Traveling to Mexico, Canada, or any foreign country presents a different concern. Medicare doesn't cover anyone outside the country, and your HMO may not either, but you can get traveler's insurance although it is fairly costly. Some Medicare-supplement policies will pay for medical expenses for the first 90 days outside the country, usually with a deductible. Be sure to check on this if you're planning an international trip.

Too Young for Medicare? Check Out Your Options

People under the age of 65 are likely to have the most trouble getting medical insurance while on the road. After 65, Medicare will cover you. If you're not yet eligible for Medicare, and you don't have insurance through your past or present employer, you'll need to find an individual policy. These policies can be very expensive, particularly if you want coast-to-coast coverage.

Many full-timers opt to get a medical insurance policy with a large deductible that will cover them just for major medical emergencies. A deductible of $5,000 is most common. The deductible you select should be an amount you know you can pay if you have to, even if you have to put it on a credit card. With that kind of deductible, your monthly fees become more reasonable, but, depending on the plan, you may not be covered for those smaller medical events that send you to an urgent care clinic, like an intestinal virus or a sprained ankle. For those you'll have to pay cash. Five thousand dollars may sound like a lot of money, but consider the fact that medical attention for a heart attack, stroke, or injuries sustained in an accident could cost as much as half a million dollars.

Medical insurance companies offer three types of coverage: HMOs, PPOs, and indemnity policies. HMOs (or health maintenance organizations) are regional in their organization and generally don't offer practical coverage for perpetual travelers. PPO stands for *preferred provider option.* This means that you must choose your doctor from a list of physician members supplied by the insurance company. In some cases, this can be a national list. Some insurance companies will charge you one co-pay amount when you visit a preferred provider, but allow you, for a higher fee, to visit other doctors if you choose. An indemnity policy allows you to visit any doctor anywhere in the country whenever you like, usually without needing a referral, but this kind of policy is hard to find and can cost around $1,500 per month.

All insurance policies are issued within a state to the residents of that state, even if the residents are rarely there. Insurance regulations vary from state to state, as do the tables insurers use to calculate their probable expenses. For these reasons, the same Blue Shield policy may cost more in Texas or Florida than in Idaho or Oregon. This is a factor to consider when choosing a domicile state (see Chapter 18). When we moved our domicile from Oregon to Texas, the monthly fee went up on our Medicare supplement policy.

Plans without any prescription coverage are less expensive, but you have to assess whether the difference in monthly rates is made up for by your out-of-pocket costs for medications.

On their website, AARP offers a guide to help you select medical insurance. *Your Personal Guide to Buying Health Insurance, What Everyone 50 to 64 Should Know* walks you through the process of choosing and applying for medical insurance. Intended for the general public, its points seem to apply quite specifically to the needs of RVers. Here is a brief summary of the main points, but I recommend that you get this publication and read it yourself.

- **Look-back periods:** The amount of past medical history the insurance company will review to decide whether to accept you. A short look-back period is usually desirable so that you won't be penalized for a medical problem you had years ago and now no longer have.
- **Waivers for preexisting conditions:** If you've had a serious medical condition in the recent past, your insurance may exclude treatment for any recurrence of that condition.
- **Entry age rating*:** Whatever age you are when you enroll, you will pay the rate for that age as long as you have coverage.
- **Attained age rating*:** Each year, as you age, your rates go up. Your rates may also rise because of an increase in medical rates in your state.

Don't overlook company or union retirement plans; affiliation groups like FMCA, AARP, Escapees; fraternal and veterans' organizations; and Medicare for your medical options.

---

*You will be enrolled by an insurance company in one of these two ways: attained age is the most common; entry age is the most desirable. Attained age ratings can be in spans of years (e.g., 50–54), meaning that your coverage costs the same for each five-year period, and then goes up.

Filling Prescriptions

Another concern of RVers is keeping up with medications. The older you get, it seems, the more pills you need. How and where can you get prescriptions filled—and refilled somewhere else in 90 days?

Some national pharmacies (Wal-Mart and RiteAid, for example) record prescriptions in their computers, so you can get refills anywhere in the country where the pharmacy chain exists. However, this is not entirely necessary. I took a pill bottle for refill to a pharmacy in Delaware, which simply telephoned the independent pharmacy in Utah where I'd initially had the prescription filled. No problem.

Transferring a prescription from one pharmacy to another in a different state is subject to the laws of the state to which the transfer is being made. Controlled substances may be restricted to only one transfer, while in most cases an ordinary prescription for what are called "legend drugs" (blood-pressure medications and the like) can be transferred several times as long as a valid refill is available.

Another option is the AARP pharmacy mail service, which offers competitive pricing and good service. With AARP, you won't have to mail in your prescriptions to get them filled. AARP will call your doctors and ship your pills to your current location. As of June 1, 2004, any Medicare-eligible person who does not have prescription coverage through another provider can get a Medicare prescription benefit card.

14

Traveling with Kids and Pets

Children and pets can make RVing even more fun than it is on your own. But both situations require a little planning and consideration. Here are some ways to ensure that your RVing adventure with kids and pets is a great one.

On the Road with Pets

If you have a four-footed member of the family, you'll most likely want to include your cat or dog in your RV adventures.

A cat is an easy pet for a small environment like a motor home. Your cat's litter box can be placed in several convenient spots: up front, under the table, in the tub, or in the kitchen nook. She doesn't require much attention—just occasional cuddling—and you can feel comfortable leaving her alone during the day when you want to sightsee.

Dogs take up more space, are more energetic, require more exercise, and may bark when left alone, but dog owners can and do find ways to deal with all these problems. There are a variety of ways to provide exercise for your dog. I've seen small dogs enclosed outside an RV in a large wire cage. I frequently meet people walking dogs of all sizes around RV parks.

On the road, you may want to stop occasionally to give your dog a chance to walk around outside. Most rest areas have sections designated for walking dogs on leashes. I don't have to tell you about bringing along a bag to pick up droppings.

You may not know whether your dog yips or whines when you leave him alone, but it's important to find out before you do so. It isn't fair to inflict that noise on your fellow travelers. If your dog barks excessively, consider training him to behave differently. Consistent rewards for appropriate behavior work with animals just as with children.

Although most RV travelers keep their dogs confined inside their rigs, in an outside cage, or on a leash, some people let their cats out to roam freely, and occasionally some get lost. Imagine the panic of being ready to leave a campground and being unable to locate your pet. Get a nametag for your pet before embarking on a trip, and watch closely when you take her outside. You can have the license number of your rig engraved on the pet name tag, or your cellphone number, or both. People who make pet nametags can be found at craft fairs and also in many large shopping malls. Some malls even have robotic vending machines that will engrave tags while you watch. The Good Sam club provides a pet-tag service for its members. The tags contain the Good Sam member's number and the toll-free phone number for the Good Sam club. Members are notified if their lost pet is located.

Of course, you want your pet to have the proper shots, so he isn't at risk and doesn't risk infecting other animals. Vaccinations and a recent physical exam are required to take an animal into Canada or Mexico. To find a veterinary clinic when you need one, ask at campgrounds or ask other pet owners. You may have luck with the Yellow Pages.

The hazards of the RV life are slight for a cat or dog. However, if your pet is allowed to roam, accidental poisoning is always possible. If you can, take the animal immediately to a vet. The National Animal Poison Control Center operates a 24-hour hotline at 800-548-2423 and charges $25 for its services. The fee can be paid with a credit card.

If you don't have a pet but want one, consider matching the pet to the RV lifestyle. Get a small quiet dog, a cat, or even a bird.

Deciding whether to take your pet with you on a long trip is a personal decision, involving factors of the animal's size and temperament, the length of your trip, costs of boarding, the adaptability of your pet, and your own feelings about the situation. On the whole, you and the pet will probably be happier if you're together in the RV.

RVing with Kids

When traveling with kids, there are three factors to consider: destination, interests, and food. If you're bringing a child on a special trip in your RV, you'll probably select a kid-oriented destination such as a theme park or scenic wonderland. What you do at your destination when traveling with kids is probably not the same as what you would do on your own, although there is definitely some overlap. You want to tailor your touring to child-oriented activities like hiking, swimming, visiting petting zoos, and so on.

TEACH YOUR CHILDREN WELL

You'd be surprised at how cheerfully parents will let you borrow their kids. School systems, on the other hand, will place certain demands on you. As retired teachers, Dan and I were ready for the challenge of teaching our grandchildren on the road. And along the way, we realized that an RV can provide an educational experience unmatched by a classroom.

A few years ago, we took our granddaughter Jenny—an eighth grader—on a two-month journey. Before the trip, we met with all her teachers and received assignments to be completed while traveling. In those days, e-mail access was more limited, so every Friday we mailed her assignments to her school. In addition to the classwork, Jenny visited destinations that included Baja California; the Date Festival in Indio, California; and her pick, the Arabian Horse Show in Phoenix, Arizona.

More recently we took our granddaughter Brittany, age 12, on a three-week trip to Baja. We got assignments from her teachers and set aside a homework period each day. Brittany had the time of her life discovering Baja. We took her on an adventurous drive high into the mountains to see 11,000-year-old cave paintings, and to the beautiful bays that dot the long Baja coastline. An animal-lover, Brittany was thrilled by sightings of the indigenous creatures in each area we visited. While kayaking in Bahia de los Angeles, she met some giant sea turtles. Later she swam in Bahia Concepcion among dolphins and pelicans. Everywhere we went, she made friends with dogs—and there were lots of them. At one RV park, she befriended the resident parrot. Making friends with pets was an entry to making friends with their owners, despite the language barrier. Along the way, she developed an interest in learning Spanish. Everyone she met became her teacher, and she didn't hesitate to try out her small but growing vocabulary. The whole trip was an educational experience for her—and a bonding experience for all of us.

When traveling with children, you may need to adjust your palate to take in some kid-friendly meals. Stock up on macaroni and cheese, a good supply of juice and milk, and hot dogs to be barbecued on the grill or over a campfire. Don't forget the marshmallows and s'mores fixings! Teens seem to go through a vegetarian phase, which can be easier to deal with than the junk-food tastes of younger children. Plenty of fresh fruits and vegetables, peanut butter, and some staples like pasta will satisfy your growing vegetarian and keep him or her healthy.

Don't forget to locate the seatbelts on your motor-home couch, or wherever kids will sit while the RV is on the road, to keep them safely belted in. Make sure they have something along to entertain themselves: books, drawing paper and crayons, headphones and CD players, or handheld games. You may want to arrange some kind of lap board so kids can play games or draw pictures as they travel. Encourage them, too, to look out the windows at the passing scenery.

Traveling in an RV with kids requires giving up a little of your independence and a lot of your space. You (and they) have to be willing to yield at least partially to someone else's TV choices and eating habits, but you'll find that the trade-off is well worth the effort.

15

Taking Long Trips

"Oh, the places you'll go!" —Dr. Seuss

"We used to be full-timers," a woman told me, "but we gave it up after nine months." She shook her head. "The towns we visited began to seem all the same to me, and the local museums were interchangeable."

"Then you were right to end it," I agreed, but I went away puzzled. After several years, I'm still excited when we pull in somewhere I've never been. RV travel can remain a constant fascination, if you pursue it in the right way—slowly.

The Advantages of a Long Stay

It's true that many communities are outwardly alike. Drive down the main streets, and you'll find similar small shops, banks, perhaps a city park in the center of town, perhaps a historic museum with artifacts of the town's past. But if you dig a little deeper, scratch the veneer, every community is unique. Who settled this area initially, and why? What industries drove this town in the past, and what others drive it today? The town may have flourished as a buggy-whip manufacturing center 150 years ago and now features a thriving automotive parts factory. Has the population increased or decreased, and why? What are the wonders of nature close to this area, deserving of a short or long visit? What's the best time of year to be here? What are the passionate issues in the local community—schooling, the environment, planned or departing businesses?

Discovering the answers to these questions takes time—time I believe is worth spending. A question I didn't ask the woman who gave up full-timing was how long she spent in those towns that began to seem identical to her. I suspect it wasn't long. Perhaps she was touring the country in an "It's Tuesday—it must be Belgium" fashion, and never stayed anywhere long enough to get a real feel for what makes that place unique. As full-timers, we have all the time we want to spend in an area, so why move on before we've truly savored it?

A long stay need not be expensive. State and National Parks are extremely reasonable, although they may limit your visit to 7 or 14 days. Most commercial RV parks have weekly and monthly rates, and the monthly hookup fees generally are in the $300 to $400 vicinity. Not bad rent, utilities included. Some campgrounds, because of the high cost of electricity, will charge you a fixed fee per month plus an additional charge based on how much electricity you use. The electric post you plug into will be wired to a meter.

Winter is an especially good time to hole up somewhere warm and attractive. Mexico is a wonderful choice. Within the United States, Arizona is probably the most popular winter destination, although all of the southern states make good winter spots.

Climate isn't the only reason for spending a long time in one place. You may decide to take a class at a local college, or participate in some community activity. Or you may just want to explore the area in depth. In big cities like San Antonio, Texas, or Savannah, Georgia, you can start with a guided tour. A one- or two-hour tour hits the high spots of a community and helps you decide where to return for more leisurely exploration.

One of the advantages of full-timing lies in the opportunity to travel through life at your own speed, to take time to savor each new adventure, to explore a locality in depth if you desire. And to always stay warm.

Becoming a Snowbird

Depending on their interests, full-timers may be found anywhere, year-round. A separate group of RVers—called "snowbirds"—migrate seasonally, south to warm climates in the winter and then back home to northern climates in the summer. In RV parks in the southern United States and Mexico, you'll find a lively mix of people who've fled from cold climates. Many Americans come from Alaska, Minnesota, New York, and other places where no one in his right mind would want to spend the winter. Canadians, too, fly south.

The three favorite "snowbird" locations in the U.S. are Florida, Arizona, and

California. Many people enjoy Arizona in the winter, so it's hard to pass through Yuma in January and find a place to stay overnight—all the parks are full. Tight-fisted RVers like to boondock at Quartzite, where you can camp out on Bureau of Land Management land for free. Rockhounds are in gem-hunters' paradise there, and in the winter, a little city of RVs grows up across the desert. So many people gather there that enterprising businesses have sprung up offering "honey wagon" service to drain sewer tanks, and freshwater delivery, so you don't have to leave your site to take care of these essential items.

If you're retired military, be sure and check out the Family Camps, which offer affordable camping with hookups at many military bases. Many of these are located in snowbirds' favorite places, including Tucson, San Antonio, and several near San Diego.

If you're still working, you may not be able to go away for a whole season, but you may have a couple of months' vacation time accumulated. Or perhaps you can arrange to telecommute. At our favorite park in Mexico, we met one couple who run a seasonal business in the summer, another pair who have a reliable person to run their business in their absence, and others who telecommute. With a little planning and foresight, you never have to endure a cold winter again.

Give it some thought.

16

Crossing Borders: Taking Your RV to Canada or Mexico

Both Canada and Mexico are wonderful places to visit in your RV, and there's no reason why your travels should be limited to the United States. Canada offers beautiful scenery and numerous historic sites. Mexico offers a visit to a very different, fascinating world with a rich history and culture. Getting to either country, however, requires a little planning. Even though the RV lifestyle can often be wonderfully impromptu, you need some preparation before you cross the border. You can't just point your rig north or south and hope for the best.

Both Canada and Mexico forbid bringing in firearms. If you travel with a handgun—and many RVers feel safer knowing they have this kind of protection—you must find a place to leave it behind. Leave it with a family member, or consider renting a safe deposit box for the period you'll be gone. Be sure that if you leave your handgun behind, you also leave the ammunition. If an inspector finds cartridges in your rig, he'll tear it apart looking for the gun, no matter how much you try to explain.

The most famous site in eastern Canada, Niagara Falls.

Visiting Canada

Before going to Canada, you should ask your insurance company to issue you a Canada insurance card that verifies you're covered for travel there. Also, you need good identification: a passport or birth certificate, and a driver's license.

Check out how much alcohol and other substances you're permitted to bring into the country. Guidebooks for Canada by either Lonely Planet or Moon can give you this information, or you can find it on the Internet.

After you arrive in Canada, you'll be delighted to find that some things are different there. The exchange rate for Canadian dollars has been favorable to U.S. visitors for several years. That means that your money may go a little farther while you're visiting Canada.

The bills and coins also take some getting used to. The smallest Canadian bill is a five-dollar bill. Lesser denominations are all coins. The $1 coin, a big brass thing about the size of old U.S. silver dollars, is called a "loonie," and the $2 coin (which you'll never confuse with the $1 coin because it's silver with a brass center) is called a "toonie." Loonies and toonies have nothing to do with crazy people or Looney Tunes cartoons. The one-dollar loonie gets its name because the face of the coin bears the image of a loon—a northern water bird. The two-dollar toonie is Canadian slang for "two loonies."

A visit to the gas station is another surprise. Gasoline is sold by the liter, which makes the price on the gas station sound really cheap until you calculate 3.78 liters to the gallon.

Of course, after you enter the country and see a speed limit of 100 on the freeway, don't think those Canadians are speed demons. Speeds are given in kilometers per hour, not miles. To calculate the difference, multiply the kilometers by 0.6. So 100 is actually a fairly sedate 60 miles per hour. Most newer cars and RVs have the speedometer graduated in both miles and kilometers.

And then there's the weather forecast. If the local TV weatherman announces with a smile that it's supposed to reach a high of 20 today and a low of 16 tonight, we would be shivering, wearing our heavy parkas and sweaters, right? Not exactly. Canadian temperatures, like those in most of the world, are given in degrees centigrade. To convert from centigrade to Fahrenheit, you have to multiply the centigrade temperature by $\frac{9}{5}$ (or 1.8) and then add 32. For instance, $\frac{9}{5}$ of 20 is 36. Add 32, and you see that the high of 20 is a near-balmy 68 degrees.

You'll find another difference between things Canadian and things American in the grocery store: $1.96 seemed like a high price for apples, and $16 seemed

PROHIBITED FOODSTUFFS

On our first trip back to the United States across the border from Mexico, I was quite shocked to find I couldn't bring a lot of ordinary food into the United States. My guidebook said that "certain meats, fruits, and vegetables" were not allowed, but it didn't specify which ones. I made one last visit to the vegetable market because I just couldn't help myself, loading up on avocados at 40 cents each and tomatoes for even less. As it turned out, that didn't create a problem. I didn't buy any fruits or vegetables that I couldn't bring into the United States except for potatoes. (That was then. In 2004, my single Mexican avocado was confiscated.)

Here's a list of food the agricultural inspector confiscated on that first return to the United States:

uncooked eggs
frozen pork
frozen chicken
frozen sausage (that we had brought into Mexico from the United States and hadn't eaten)
a sack of potatoes

I had no idea why these items and not others had been removed, so I wrote an e-mail to the USDA.

I received a prompt and complete response from Anna L. Cherry of the Agriculture and Public Health Information Service (APHIS) department of the USDA. It said, in part:

The things that were taken from you were not allowed into the United States from Mexico due to the fact that they could harbor plant or animal pests or diseases. Not all diseases are killed by freezing. . . . Even items for personal consumption—the risk those items pose comes from what may be thrown out as waste. Waste can move into the animal food chain; pigs are fed garbage. Also, if you throw away a pit or peel of something, that could spread the disease to U.S. crops and livestock. Mexico is considered free of foot-and-mouth disease and has never had a case of mad cow disease, so the steaks you mentioned were allowed entry. The poultry and swine products however, were not, due to several diseases that we do not want to accidentally spread here. Please check our website for more details.

When I checked the website (www.aphis.usda.gov), I found a complete listing of what you can and can't bring back. I discovered that I could have cooked the potatoes and eggs and made a giant potato salad. And that is exactly what I did on the next trip.

Returning to the United States from Canada is less restrictive. We were only asked about beef products, of which we had none. Entering Canada three weeks before, we were asked by the Canadian agricultural inspector about fruit. I had a peach and was allowed to keep it provided I removed the pit before entering Canada. So I did, and ate the peach as we drove into the country.

incredibly high for a pound of steak, until I realized that all those prices were per kilogram. A kilogram is 2.2 pounds, so the actual prices per pound, especially when you consider they're in Canadian dollars, turn out to be quite reasonable. In the larger grocery stores, items are often priced in both pounds and kilos.

After a while, you'll probably find that doing all that math on a regular basis is way too much trouble. Just get a fistful of Canadian money from an ATM, and go out and spend it. Trust that the prices are close to or less than those at home. Contribute to the Canadian economy, enjoy the novelties of a foreign country, and relax.

Mail forwarding is another thing to plan for before you leave for Canada. (For details on mail forwarding options, see Chapter 13). We normally have our mail service forward our mail weekly to wherever we are. However, when we discussed forwarding our mail to Canada, our service pointed out that large packets of mail go through Canadian Customs and could be held there for as long as ten days. The mail that normally reaches us in two to three days could take two weeks. Because we hadn't planned to stop in any one place that long, we just had our mail held until we returned to the United States.

Check to see if your cellular service covers calls originating in Canada, or has a plan whereby you can add Canada for just a few dollars for the time you will be there. Caution: When checking on cellular plans for Canada, make sure they cover areas where you plan to travel. Some are valid only in major cities.

Another option is to use a prepaid phone card, but again you'll need to check about international usage of that card. You may need a special number to access your phone card provider. The numbers printed on your card are not necessarily good in Canada.

On the plus side, many pay phones in Canada have a dataport where you can connect a phone line to your computer and get on the Internet using the pay phone. Contact your Internet service provider for details on how to do this.

With all those mundane problems taken care of, you can feel free to appreciate some of the most spectacular scenery in the world.

Adventuring in Mexico

If you've been spending winters shoveling the white stuff off your driveway, if you have to scrape frost from your windshield every winter morning, and if you pay an astronomical heating bill from November through February, consider this:

there are places in the world where the weather in January is almost too warm for comfort. One of these places is a long strip of coast in mainland Mexico that runs from the Sea of Cortez in the north, near Mazatlan, to the Pacific Coastal area in the south, near Puerto Vallarta. This is our favorite winter retreat.

Before you set out to travel anywhere in an RV in Mexico, purchase the excellent campground guide called *The Traveler's Guide to Mexican Camping* by Mike and Terri Church. This book lists all the campgrounds in Mexico and Baja California, with complete directions on how to find each one. The first chapter deals with crossing the border. It includes diagrams and directions for most border crossing points. Visit their website (www.rollinghomes.com) and browse the updated information about places you plan to visit.

Crossing the border in a big rig can present some problems. At some border crossings, you should use a truck crossing rather than the one designed for passenger cars. The problem lies not with the Mexican side of the border, but with the American side. After September 11, 2001, U.S. Customs deliberately narrowed the passageway through its border checkpoints, and the newer, wide-body RVs can have a problem scraping through the portals. The Churches' *Traveler's Guide to Mexican Camping* will point you toward the best gate to use with a big RV.

When you bring your rig to Mexico, you have to buy Mexican insurance, which costs us about $700 for a year, covering both our motor home and our tow car. Mexican law requires you to be insured by a Mexican company. If you have an accident there and you're uninsured, you could go to jail.

You must also bring proof of citizenship, the title and registration documents for your vehicles, and either a credit card (not a debit card) or about $200 in cash to post as a bond. You need written permission from the lienholder if you do not own your vehicle outright. This can be obtained more easily than you might expect by means of a phone call to your bank or lienholder. Call the department that handles your vehicle loan. Allow a week or two to receive the letter, and call again if necessary. Actually, we have never been asked to show this document in many border crossings, but we always obtain it because it is required.

A few miles after you cross the border into Mexico, you'll come upon a vehicle inspection station, where you obtain a tourist permit and a temporary import permit for your vehicle. You have to jump through several hoops to accomplish this, so be prepared to be patient. At the final window you must present a credit card or pay around $200 in bond. Your credit card is charged about $30 for your vehicle permit, but if you don't leave the country within your allotted tourist paper time, usually 180 days, daily fines could be assessed on that card until you leave. The bureaucratic hassles are due to black-market demand for illegally imported American cars—a practice the Mexican government is determined to stop.

One more caution about vehicles. Each person may bring in just one vehicle to Mexico, so if, like us, you're driving a motor home and towing a car, be sure you have a companion. Dan brings in the motor home and I bring in the car. In the case of a truck towing a fifth wheel or trailer, only the truck is a vehicle, so a solo driver will not have a problem.

After receiving your papers, you must pass a Customs inspection of your rig. The important thing to remember here is, as I said earlier, not to attempt to bring guns or ammunition into Mexico. Possession of either one can land you in jail. Otherwise, bringing in ordinary household goods—a TV/VCR/DVD, a microwave, and so on—is not a problem unless the Customs officer thinks you're bringing things in to sell. It's not a good idea to have five brand-new microwaves, for instance.

Your pet will need a recent health certificate from a veterinarian (within 30 days) and proof of inoculation against rabies and distemper. It's easy to bring your pet into Mexico; bringing your pet home may be more difficult. Check with U.S. Customs for rules about returning. If your pet has been out of the country more than 30 days, he may need to be revaccinated before you return to the United States.

After these details are completed, stow your papers in a safe (and memorable!) location for reentry into the United States. Then kick back and enjoy your visit to Mexico. The coastal sunsets are incredible, the ocean is warm, the beaches are clean, and the fishing is spectacular. Also, a nice bonus: the Mexican people are friendly and cheerful.

We appreciate the fact that the 1,000-plus mile trip from Nogales, Arizona, to Puerto Vallarta and beyond is along one of the best highways in Mexico, making the trip a pleasant drive rather than a white-knuckles experience such as you may have in Baja California. Most of the distance is over toll roads, but they aren't cheap. The tolls from Nogales to Puerto Vallarta add up to about $150 for motor home plus tow car (they rate the motor home the same as a bus, and charge separately for the car), but the four-lane divided highway is worth the cost. Many other Mexican highways are two-lane winding roads that seem to be bumper-to-bumper with giant Mexican trucks, many of which are seriously underpowered and climb hills at 15 miles per hour, not pleasant driving for a big rig.

The drawback of the three- or four-day drive to Mazatlan, Puerto Vallarta, or one of the charming little towns between is a shortage of RV parks. You'll find only a handful listed in *The Traveler's Guide to Mexican Camping*. The good news is that you can camp for a nominal fee at one of the many Pemex gas stations spaced along the road. Just ask permission and pull in next to the commercial trucks that also park there at night.

As everyone knows, don't drink the tap water in Mexico. Depending on the length of your stay, you may want to fill your water tanks before you come, and drink your own water while there, but bottled water is available and cheap. You can have a 5-gallon bottle of water delivered to your rig for about $1.

You can also bring your own food, but you'll need to buy local fruits and vegetables, which are plentiful and delicious. Some American "box stores" have come to Mexico. These stores will supply you with all the comforts of home, but for a real treat, try shopping in a Mexican market, sometimes called a *tianguis*. Almost every town has a market day when local farmers bring in their produce, and local craftspeople bring in their wares to sell. Prices are good, and the experience is unique.

If you travel with a satellite TV system, read the part of Chapter 17 that deals with using your satellite dish in foreign countries. You may want to get Canadian service if you're traveling either to Canada or to Mexico, as explained in Chapter 17. People can receive Dish and DirecTV signals in some locations of Mexico by using a very large dish. The farther south you go, the bigger the dish you'll need. A meter dish will work in Mazatlan, but in Puerto Vallarta you need one twice that diameter. Much smaller Canadian Star Choice dishes, around ¾ meter, work just fine if you're subscribed to that service.

A final caution about Mexico: Although most shopkeepers and store clerks are scrupulously honest, it's only common sense to know what change you should receive when paying for something. Do the math in your head and make sure the clerk has not made a mistake with your change. Also, be careful about trying to pay with a large bill. For some reason, no store in Mexico except the very large supermarkets seems to have any change of more than a few pesos. If you can pay with exact change or small bills, you'll save yourself the wait while the storekeeper tries to get change from a store down the block.

The only place we've encountered any effort to cheat us in Mexico has been in the Pemex gas stations. Pemex stations are run by the government and the cost per liter of gas or diesel is uniform throughout the country, so you don't have to hunt for the best price. That's the upside. The downside is that, frequently, the attendant who pumps your gas (no self-service here) will try to cheat you. Be sure the pump is set to zero before the attendant starts to fuel. Be sure you're looking at the pump he's actually using. It's easy for him to charge you the larger amount registered on an adjacent pump. And be very careful with your change.

I like to pay with a 500-peso note in Pemex stations because they're one of the few places that can change a bill that large. Five-hundred-peso notes are what you generally get from an ATM machine. They're worth about $50, and changing them is a challenge. Toll booths and Pemexes are good opportunities to break up the big bills. Tollbooth operators universally give correct change, but attendants at Pemexes sometimes do not. The 500-peso note may disappear into the attendant's pocket to be replaced by a 50-peso note, which is almost the same color. The attendant will then try to tell you that you gave him 50 and owe him more. You have two alternatives in this case. One is to ask for the *gerente,* the manager. The other is to simply insist on your change and say you aren't coming up with any more money. Usually, one or the other of these tactics will cause the attendant to back down and give you correct change. Take it and leave. There is no point in trying to make a formal complaint.

17

Technology for the Traveler

Your RV is like a home away from home, but there are obvious differences. Technology that is familiar to you in your home may be quite different on an RV. In this chapter, you'll find all the information you need on everything from television to the Internet, digital cameras to GPS.

Television

Before you set out on a long journey in your RV, think about what you're going to do for entertainment at night while you're stopped. If you enjoy TV—whether you watch it only occasionally, or you're helplessly addicted—you don't have to give it up. You have several options.

Your RV probably came with a TV set or two, as well as a roof-mounted antenna. With the antenna you can receive a handful of local broadcast channels if you're near a fairly large community. This is the simplest TV option, but the least reliable due to the uncertainty of reception.

Many, but by no means all, campgrounds offer cable TV, sometimes for an extra charge and sometimes included with the camping fee. Hooking up to local cable is a little like Russian roulette: you never know exactly what you're going to get, or how many channels. Viewing local cable channels will provide a good opportunity to view the regional news and find out what is important in a particular community (and perhaps more than you want to know about the local high-school football team).

If you're taking a long trip and planning to travel in rural or remote areas, the

This dedicated, high-tech tent camper and TV watcher had to bring along a generator to power his receiver and TV set.

best option and the one used by most full-time RVers is to bring along a TV satellite dish. Dishes can be set up almost anywhere, as long as there aren't any trees or tall buildings in the way. Setting up a dish is not difficult, but it can take some practice.

In the United States, there are two satellite TV systems, DirecTV and Dish. Technically, the two systems are very similar, but setting them up is slightly different. Both systems give about the same package of programs for about the same cost. Both systems offer pay-per-view special events and movies. Both companies used to include PBS in their lineup of networks broadcast to travelers, but in the past few years, both have eliminated PBS. DirecTV does not offer it at all, but you can now get it as part of Dish TV's network bundle.

If you're a DirecTV or Dish customer in a major service area, you probably receive your local commercial channels spot-beamed to you. If you put your receiver and satellite dish in your RV and drive away with them, you'll soon drive out of the reception area for those channels. You'll receive everything else that Dish or DirecTV offers, but not your local channels or any other commercial network channels.

To get the major networks in your RV (CBS, NBC, ABC, and Fox) you have to sign a waiver stating that your dish is not being used in a fixed location. This frees you from the obligation to be continuously connected to a phone line, which both DirecTV and Dish require of their customers in fixed locations.

When you sign an RV waiver, the company will allow you to receive two sets of commercial networks, one from New York and one from Los Angeles. This arrangement has a lot of advantages. For example, if you have two favorite programs that come on at the same time, you can watch one on California time and the other on New York time, three hours later. You will receive these two networks wherever you travel in the United States. The DirecTV satellite signal doesn't quite reach Canada or Mexico, although with a very large dish you may be able to receive some or all channels in those countries. Dish subscribers seem to have better luck getting a usable signal in Mexico.

Dish customers generally feel that the Dish system is more user-friendly and that they receive better treatment from customer service. DirecTV customers rarely, if ever, make that claim. DirecTV doesn't go out of its way to attract RVers as customers.

After you've signed up with a satellite TV service, you'll need to purchase three components that are usually sold together: a receiver box, a remote control, and the dish itself. Sometimes DirecTV and Dish run specials to encourage customers to sign up, and they offer this equipment at a bargain price or even free. You may want to also purchase some kind of tripod to set the dish on, and devise a way to secure the tripod so it won't move after you aim the dish. Many people hang weights like sandbags or gallon bottles of water to provide this stability. If you are setting up on bare ground, you can also anchor the tripod with tent stakes.

To set up DirecTV, you have to aim the dish for elevation and *azimuth*. Elevation is the dish's angle in the vertical plane (i.e., up and down), and azimuth is its horizontal angle or compass reading (i.e., back and forth). When setting up for service through the

If you don't have a large rock, you can use a one-gallon bottle filled with water.

Dish antenna, you have to aim the dish for elevation, azimuth, and a third factor called skew, or polarization. (Dish uses two satellites so the dish must be skewed to optimize the signal.)

To determine how to aim the dish, go to the antenna-pointing screen using the menu function of your receiver box. Once there, you'll be prompted to enter the zip code of your current location. (DirecTV subscribers with a GPS receiver can enter latitude and longitude. This is particularly helpful if you're traveling outside of the United States.) The screen will then give you values for azimuth, elevation, and—if you're a Dish subscriber—polarization. Write down these numbers, go outside, and aim your dish.

To make it easy to find the satellite when setting up a dish in a campground, most RVers buy a satellite finder. Lacking a meter, you must either have someone

A satellite finder can makes dish setup easier.

inside monitoring the setup screen on the TV and calling out your signal strength, or you have to keep running inside to check it. But with a meter, you'll have instant feedback within arms' reach. Connect this meter to the dish's output cable and consult the gauge to achieve the best signal. (A separate cable can be run from the meter to your receiver. This allows you to leave the meter "in stream" between the dish and TV.) A signal strength of 35 or 40 units will work, but you want to try for the strongest possible signal to avoid interruptions. Signal strengths of 60 or higher are ideal.

What about receiving satellite TV outside the United States? U.S. satellite TV providers, especially DirecTV, do not want you to take the equipment to Mexico or Canada. I don't know why, but people who have called DirecTV for help from Mexico, and admitted where they were, have had their service terminated. In addition, DirecTV doesn't work well in either country unless you have a very large (and cumbersome) dish—about a meter or more in diameter. Dish subscribers tend to receive better signals in Mexico than DirecTV customers, but reception is still spotty.

An easier option for travelers to Canada or Mexico is to subscribe to Canadian TV. Star Choice—one of two major Canadian satellite TV providers—uses a satellite that provides coverage to the entire continent, from northern Canada to southern Mexico.

The Internet provides a gray-market solution for Americans who want to subscribe to Canadian TV. Due to restrictions placed on their operating licenses from the Canadian government, Canadian satellite TV providers are not allowed to knowingly sell services outside of Canada. In reality, as long as you're registered with a legitimate address within Canada, they'll be happy to do business. If you aren't a resident of Canada, you'll find that use of a programming broker is the most practical solution to this problem. You won't be breaking any laws if you subscribe to Canadian TV services, but in the unlikely event that the provider discovers that your address is bogus, you will lose the service.

When you buy the needed equipment for Star Choice or Bell Express (two major Canadian satellite TV providers) from a reputable dealer like Mike Kohl at global-cm (see Appendix), the vendor will direct you to a broker. The broker—for a fee of $50 to $100 per year—will give you a Canadian address and sign you up. Star Choice or Bell Express will then charge its monthly fees directly to your credit card. Depending on your subscription package, Canadian TV generally costs less than its American counterparts.

Star Choice, the company most commonly used by American RVers, carries many American channels. It carries all four major U.S. networks and you can arrange to get two affiliates from each network—one from the Pacific Time Zone (Seattle or Spokane) and one from the Eastern Time Zone (Buffalo or Detroit). PBS is included in the package. You can also receive U.S. "cable" networks like CNN, A&E, ESPN and more. Star Choice also carries local channels from across the whole of Canada.

Audio Entertainment

Satellite Radio

Everyone has experienced the frustration of losing radio reception just as a really good song comes on or right in the middle of an enthralling news story. Now there's a solution. A new concept has made it possible to listen to the radio without it ever fading: subscription satellite radio. There are at least three satellite radio providers, Sirius, WorldSpace, and XM Radio. All offer a large variety of programming, each with a slightly different focus.

To use satellite radio, you need some special equipment: a radio capable of satellite reception, a tuner, and a satellite antenna. The radio costs between $100 and $120. The cost of the tuner and antenna is about $100, and the cost of the basic monthly service ranges from $9.99 to $12.99.

WorldSpace satellite radio has more of an international focus than the other two. WorldSpace was initially founded to provide radio service to military people overseas, and has three satellites that cover the planet. Depending on where you live, you can subscribe to AmeriStar, AfriStar, or AsiaStar.

XM radio claims on its website that it is the most popular satellite radio provider, with over 2 million customers. Its slogan is "Radio to the power of X." In addition to offering a large variety of music channels, XM offers college football, news, and talk shows.

The third major satellite radio station, Sirius, offers country, jazz, rock, and classical music channels. Sirius programming includes NPR, the National Football League, Court TV, and BBC World Service News.

Sirius broadcasts to most of Mexico and Canada, although you cannot buy its equipment in those countries. Sirius makes several plug-and-play radios that allow you to play a radio through your RV sound system, and then easily move it and play it through your car or home stereo system or a boombox. Each location requires a docking station that comes with a power supply and antenna. You don't need a separate subscription for each sound system because you're using just one radio receiver.

Audio Books

Audio books offer another way to be entertained on tedious drives. One audio book on five CDs lasts just about a day's driving (five or six hours). Audio CDs are a bit expensive, however, costing around $20 each. For a while we bought from the meager selections at Costco (roughly $17.95 each) and used bookstores (when we were shopping on-the-cheap).

Then we discovered Audible.com. Audible.com is a book listener's paradise. They have a huge selection of the latest books on CD, and for a monthly fee of $21.95, you can download two books each month, just about cutting in half the cost of audio books. When you download their software, you also get a free Roxio CD burning program so you can easily turn your downloads into CDs.

Internet Access

The Internet keeps you in touch with everything as you travel: your bank, favorite stores, the news, and your family. You'll want to find a way of accessing the Internet that works for you. Fortunately, there are many ways to do this.

Phone and DSL Lines

More and more campgrounds are offering some kind of Internet access to their customers. This can vary from a slow phone line to the most up-to date DSL or cable connection. Some campgrounds are even offering wireless connections. In January 2005, the State of California announced that it was offering wireless connectivity at 85 state parks, at a cost of $7.95 per day to campers who use it.

The whole process is getting easier, but it's far from perfect. For one thing, it's not universal and you're never sure, pulling into a campground, what kind of Internet connection, if any, it will have. For the past few years, *Trailer Life Campground Directory* has included this information, placing the words *modem hu* (modem hookup) as part of a campground's information, but of course there is no indication of what kind of hookup this may be. You may have to share a single phone line with other campers and staff. Relying on a campground is not a dependable option, but sometimes it's the only option. Some campgrounds offer DSL—a faster and more reliable connection. However, not every DSL line is compatible with every laptop computer.

Cell Phones

A more reliable way to connect to the Internet while on the road is by cell phone. Cingular, Verizon, and Sprint, to name a few carriers, all offer the option of connecting to the Web with their phones. Web-capable phones are a fun novelty, but you really don't want to be reading or writing e-mails using the tiny screen and keypad on a cell phone. Before purchasing a new phone or a new provider, make sure you can connect the cell phone directly to your computer and get online that way.

Be advised that connecting to the Internet through your cell phone can eat up your monthly minutes like you wouldn't believe, especially if the connection is slow. However, the technology is improving all the time, and newer cell phones offer faster connection speeds.

Some full-timers sign up for a national no-roaming, no-long-distance plan (meaning no additional charges for long distance or roaming) that also includes free nighttime and weekend minutes. They wait until 9:00 P.M. on a weeknight or until the weekend to go online, and stay online as long as they like, for free. However, the service they've signed up for may not include rural areas.

If you're a full-timer or an RVer who likes to travel to remote places, check the national "footprint" of your wireless phone company before you sign up for services like these. Will they cover you in Nevada or North Dakota, or is coverage limited to urban areas? To get online with your cell phone, you need to be in a digital service area. Even if the company offers nationwide phone service, that coverage consists of both digital and analog signals, depending on the area. In areas of analog service, you can make calls but you can't connect to the Internet.

The good news, according to a Verizon representative, is that the FCC has mandated that all areas be digital by 2007.

Pocketmail

A number of RVers I know use Pocketmail to get their e-mail from a pay telephone. Pocketmail is a little device that you connect to a telephone to send or receive e-mail. Pocketmail recipients cannot connect to the Web, nor can they receive graphics, photos, attachments, or e-cards. Nonetheless, a number of RVers find this service fits their needs perfectly. Pocketmail is very affordable. The monthly charge is about $10, and the gadget itself costs about $100. You can purchase the unit from RV stores and at RV rallies. Recently the company announced that it's selling its devices in Canada at Radio Shacks.

The device is about 8 inches by 4 inches, and fits into a large pocket or a medium purse. It has a small keyboard and display screen. Pocketmail provides two toll-free numbers to connect to their service. If you're out of the country where toll-free numbers don't work, there is a third number (not toll-free but accessible as a long-distance call). Once you're connected, place your device up to the phone's receiver, press a button, and send and receive e-mail messages. Our friends who use Pocketmail like the portability. They always carry the device with them, and can always find a pay phone to use it—at least at the present time. Phone companies are scrapping many of their pay phones as the use of cell phones increases, and they may become extinct someday soon. Pocketmail messages can be up to 6,000 characters. The device has an inbox, an outbox, and an address book. If you have problems using the miniature keyboard, you can compose your message on a computer and transfer it to the Pocketmail device for sending. You can check it out at their website, listed in the Appendix.

Wireless

Wireless fidelity (Wi-Fi) is a technology that allows you to access the Internet without plugging into anything. With wireless Internet access, you don't need a wire, a USB cord or a DSL line. It's like receiving a radio signal. However, you need to be in range of the signal, you need certain equipment on your computer, and in many but not all cases you need to sign up for Wi-Fi service.

If your computer doesn't have built-in wireless technology, you can buy a PCMCIA card at any electronics store for around $50. This card will allow you to access Wi-Fi. If you're buying a new computer, look for 802.11g wireless capability.

Signing up for service is a bit more complicated. If you sign up with one company, you may find that the Wi-Fi *hotspot*—wireless reception area—at your next destination is offered by someone else, and your service is useless there. The solution is to pay a daily fee at each campground you visit, but that can get expensive. Many campgrounds charge $6.95 or $7.95 per day, although some offer wireless as a free service.

An article in the May 2004 issue of *Highways* likens this situation to the early days of cellular service when, if you traveled out of your provider's area and into another's, you had to pay a lot of money to use your phone. Eventually the cellular companies began to honor each other's territories. That is hopefully what will happen with wireless technology. In the meantime, Wi-Fi may remain a convenient yet costly option if you travel a lot in your RV. Fee-based wireless hotspots work through an encryption system. When you sign up, you are given a code or password to use to access the wireless network. Other wireless networks, like those offered by some campgrounds, are free and not encrypted. Be aware that using these "open" networks exposes you to some privacy risks.

Direcway, to name one provider, is hoping to sell Wi-Fi by satellite to campgrounds across the United States. And Starband recently put out a press release indicating that it, too, is hoping to snag the campground market with what it calls the "Anywhere Hotspot."

Information about which campgrounds offer Wi-Fi access can be found through a link on my favorite RVing e-zine, *Chuck Woodbury's RV Travel*—delivered to subscribers every Sunday via e-mail. (Go to www.rvtravel.com/wifi.html.)

In addition to campgrounds, companies like Verizon and T-Mobile are installing wireless access points at a variety of hot spots across the country, in public locations like airports, coffee shops, copy centers, and hotels. Through partnerships with T-Mobile, Kinko's and Starbucks offer wireless Internet service in many of their stores.

Verizon offers a similar hot-spot service in hotels and airports. Additionally, Verizon is now offering a plan called Wireless Broadband. With a Verizon wireless PC card installed in your computer and a monthly fee of $79.99, you can access the Broadband network wherever Verizon broadcasts it (which it claims is nationwide). Though it's intended mainly for businesses, the plan is well suited to the RV lifestyle.

EarthLink is offering a similar wireless PC-card service for a comparable price. The Earthlink program is new, and at the moment is offered to subscribers in only a few cities. Check Earthlink's website for complete information: click on Internet Access and then go to Wireless Laptop Cellular Service. Be sure to look at the coverage map for this service; although Earthlink touts the accessibility, the current map on their website shows availability to be restricted mainly to major cities. Earthlink charges $299 for the "air card" inserted in your laptop; monthly fees begin at $19.95 and depend on the minutes used.

If you are not ready to go wireless, you may find other commercial establishments that will lend access to a phone or DSL line. Not everyone will, but some places will allow you to use their computers. Public libraries are a good bet, as are some chambers of commerce.

All full-serve Kinko's offer Internet access on self-serve rental computers, and many also offer free DSL lines to which you can connect your laptop. Internet cafes also rent similar services.

Satellite

A cellphone provides one way to connect to the Internet from the comfort of your own RV, but there are some drawbacks to cellular Internet access. Sometimes it just doesn't work, and you may need to revert to sharing the use of a campground phone line with many other campers or go for days without being able to check your e-mail.

The almost perfect way for an RVer to connect to the Internet is by satellite dish. The technology for doing this has been around for a while, but neither of the companies that own the technology (Hughes and Starband) were willing to allow their equipment to be moved around and set up repeatedly by RVers. These companies overlooked the fact that we RVers represent the most logical set of customers for satellite Internet service, and also disregarded the fact that setting up an Internet satellite dish is only slightly more complicated than setting up a TV dish. There are about a million of us, and we have more need to be in contact with friends and family via the Internet and e-mail than people who live in a regular house and can easily use a phone line. Among the reasons postulated for their unwillingness, two seem plausible: perhaps the companies do not want to be bombarded with requests for help by mobile users who are having trouble, and/or they did not wish tripod-mounted dishes to compete with the more expensive roof mounts that they do offer for RVs.

The manual for setting up DirecPC, Hughes's satellite Internet system, warned the user that professional installation of a two-way satellite dish is required by the Federal Communications Commission. The same statement appeared on Starband's website. The FCC, however, informed me that they have no such regulation. Whatever the reason, Hughes and Starband for years would not knowingly offer service to anyone planning to drive their satellite dish around in an RV, with the single exception of the roof-mounted antenna system that sells for around $5,000. The result was a lively gray market of RVers who managed to get the service anyway. All this is changing, thank goodness.

Starband is leading the way in changing their attitude. Now you can purchase an Internet satellite dish from Starband and transport the dish with Starband's blessing. The only requirement unique to RVers is that you'll need to be trained to set up the dish. StarBand uses satellites in a fixed orbit to provide Internet access via a 3-×-2-foot antenna (dish) from any location in the continental United States that has unobstructed line-of-sight to the satellite. The service is also offered in Alaska, Hawaii, Puerto Rico, and the U.S. Virgin Islands via a larger 1.2-meter antenna. For the latest information and where and how to purchase a Starband satellite dish, visit Starband's website (www.starband.com). Starband charges about $700 for the equipment and home installation, and roughly $55 per month for their service. The equipment prices may be different for RV users, because you'll probably need a signal meter and a tripod for dish setup. The first Starband-authorized installer of tripod-mounted dishes is Ron Brundage of RV-Sat-Link in Gila Bend, Arizona. Ron has sold hundreds of Starbands to RVers and is installing more every day. The package he offers includes a short certification program during which you'll learn how to set up your dish. This certification is recommended by the FCC and has sparked Starband's new willingness to offer its product to RVers. To contact Ron Brundage, go to his website (www.2waysatlink.com). Ron charges $1,350, which includes installation of the standard equipment, plus a tripod, signal meter, and the certification.

At roughly $50 per month, Starband's monthly fee is $10 less than Direcway's (and Direcway Internet service for your RV remains in the gray market). The Starband satellite footprint covers all of the United States, about 200 miles into Canada on the north and about 200 miles into Mexico on the south, as

A Direcway Internet satellite dish. This dish is set to receive TV signals as well. A separate "bird on a wire," or TV LNB, is visible to the left of the satellite's arm.

well as the state of Alaska. Starband can be connected to a router for wireless access. If you're interested but have no plans to be near Gila Bend, contact Ron Brundage for his itinerary. He travels frequently to RV shows and may be coming somewhere near you.

Direcway satellite dishes, installed at your house—they generally won't install them at your RV—cost about $750 to $800, a little less if you don't get the pointing equipment. One of the nice features of these satellite dishes is that if you purchase a bracket to hold an additional TV LNB (a low noise blocking converter, also known as a "bird on the wire") you can receive satellite Internet *and* satellite TV from the same dish. With Direcway's service, you can receive DirecTV. With Starband's service, you get Dish TV. In either case, you pay separately for the TV service. Whether you go for Starband or Direcway service may depend on which satellite TV service you may already have. If you're starting from scratch, I recommend Starband/Dish as the more user-friendly of the two.

Another factor to check out is the "footprint" of each company's array of satellites. Some Direcway satellites do not transmit a good signal to the Pacific Northwest. Others work well in the Northwest but the signal fades in the Southeast. The person from whom you purchase your equipment can see that you are assigned to the satellite that will best fit your needs and travel plans.

If you're considering satellite Internet service, be aware that aiming an Internet satellite dish is a precise and somewhat difficult procedure. It requires a much higher degree of precision than setting up your dish for TV. With DirecTV, you're aiming at something the size of a basketball. With an Internet satellite dish, you're aiming at something the size of a pop can. In addition, there are three elements that must be precisely aligned: azimuth, elevation, and polarization. It's also important that your mounting bracket be absolutely vertical in two planes so that the polarization and elevation angles set into the bracket are accurate.

Nevertheless, the steps to follow in setting up and aiming an Internet satellite dish are not rocket science. It can be done over and over across the country in about half an hour, and has been accomplished on a daily basis for the past several years by more than 700 RVers nationwide who, lacking any "legal" way to get an Internet satellite, purchased Direcway dishes and service through a gray market.

The information you need to find the satellite is in the software installed on your computer when you buy the dish. That software has a component called *antenna pointing.* When you open the program, you can enter your zip code, or, better yet, the latitude and longitude of your current location, and the software will tell you exactly what numbers to use to set the azimuth, elevation, and polarization of your dish.

Starband and Direcway dishes are much larger than the 18-inch Hughes or Dish TV dishes. They're approximately 39 inches wide and 23 inches tall, and butterfly shaped. The TV LNB is large, too. Each time you set up, you have to assemble everything, and be very precise about the numbers, but once that's done—voila!—you can be on the Internet as long as you want, and at speeds purported to be faster than DSL. What a luxury! The TV reception is good, too.

As of this writing, Direcway is happy to provide their dish to those RVers who care to pay for the Moto-Sat or Optistream automatic pointing roof installation, at a cost of approximately $5,000, but it has no plan to offer its satellite dish to RVers who want to install and use the dish on a tripod. Direcway's position is that the FCC requires that all installation must be made by certified installers, and that every time an RVer sets his or her dish up on a tripod in a new location, that act is a new installation. Actually, the FCC *suggests* but does not mandate that dish installers be certified. One other note: The FCC does not grant those certifications, or issue any licenses to installers. Certification is a process entirely run by Direcway or Starband. The FCC has no regulations that prohibit moving or aiming an Internet satellite dish.

While researching Direcway for RVers, I came across several installers who will sell you the equipment, including a tripod and aiming device, and show you how to set it up in your RV. Some did not want to be listed here. One who did, Art at RV Anywhere (www.rv-anywhere.org), charges $2,765 for the complete DW 6000 Direcway system. This installation includes an elevation tool for aiming the dish, signal meter, OPI (optical pointing instrument) for fine-tuning, tripod mount, cable (with cable carrier), activation of your Direcway account, and instruction in dish aiming—in short, everything you need for traveling with Direcway in your RV. Art says that he is the only dealer providing full support for customers, and affirms the FCC's position that a professional is not required for day-to-day installations. If you have any kind of problem, you can call him and he'll help. You don't have to travel to where he is; he'll ship the equipment anywhere in the continent, and talk you through the process over the phone while you learn how to use it.

As mentioned above, it is possible to get a Direcway Internet satellite connection for your RV with Direcway's blessing. The gray market company is called Moto-Sat and for about $5,000 they will install their system on the roof of your motor home or fifth wheel. The system consists of a Direcway dish and some automatic aiming equipment that eliminates the need for installation certification. The $100 monthly fee for the mobile service is a bit pricey compared to roughly $60 for fix-mounted home service. (Of course, if you can swing the $5,000 installation you can probably afford the monthly fee.) Keep in mind that with the steeper fees comes quicker download times.

On the Internet you can find several companies that provide satellite Internet access at the corporate level (to TV network news vans, for example). At least one company, VSAT, offers mobile Internet service for monthly access fees beginning at $119 per month. These are the large dishes you see on mobile TV news vans. Television reception is not associated with these business installations, but they are quite willing to install their dishes on your RV.

Digital Cameras

One of the pleasures of travel is recording one's memories through photography. In our motor home, I used to have a growing collection of photo albums that I had no place for, as well as notebooks full of slides that I took for travel articles I wrote. One thing you must constantly remember in an RV: space is limited. Each time you add something, like another bulky photo album, you should, ideally, throw something about the same size away. It isn't always possible to do that, and at one point we were drowning in albums and running out of places to store them.

There ought to be a solution—and there is: the digital camera. Digital cameras have so many advantages over film cameras that, once you get one, you'll be hooked. First, you save a bundle on the cost of film and the time spent getting your pictures developed and printed. You can review each picture you take, immediately. If you don't like the photo, you just delete that picture and take another. You won't have the problem of finding out until weeks and many miles have passed that a spectacular sunset shot was out of focus.

Digital images are stored on a memory card, and when the card is full, you download the images to your computer or insert the card into your printer and print them out directly. You can purchase additional or larger capacity memory cards in case you're away from your computer when your card fills up. The cost of memory cards depends on storage capacity, but prices are generally around $40.

When downloaded into your computer, your photos can be e-mailed, printed out, or simply stored. You can look at your pictures full-size on your computer screen or even connect your computer to your TV for a dramatic slide show.

With a good photo-editing program such as Microsoft Picture It or Adobe Photoshop, you can improve on your photography. You can adjust the color, zoom in on desirable parts of the photo and eliminate the bad ones. You can also print out your photos on photo paper and put them in an album or send them as greeting cards. The possibilities are virtually limitless.

A digital camera fits the RV lifestyle well. You can keep your family and friends up to date on your travels, and maybe even tempt them to join you.

If you're thinking of getting a digital camera, it pays to shop around for the features you want at the price you're willing to pay. The Internet is one good resource for comparing prices and technology. Most digital camera makers have websites featuring their products. Retailers on the Internet offer competitive pricing.

The one drawback of digital cameras is storage. No, they don't take up room in drawers and cupboards. The images you shoot with them take up room on your computer. A computer's hard drive has a finite amount of space, so you may want to copy your pictures onto CDs for long-term storage.

Using GPS: Never Get Lost Again

Every full-timer can tell a story about getting lost. Depending on the size of your rig, this story may or may not be funny. Not so funny is when you've driven your 40-foot motor home and dinghy down a narrow, dead-end street.

Wouldn't it be wonderful if you had some device in your rig that would prevent you from ever making that mistake? Well, I won't say never, but at the very least a GPS receiver will let you know within seconds if you've veered off-course, and at best it will guide you reliably to your destination even if you wander off the beaten path.

A GPS plus some mapping software in your computer will keep you on track wherever you travel. If the GPS is near a window (where it can "see" at least three

A GPS receiver attached to a computer with mapping software can keep you from getting lost.

satellites) and connected to your computer, you'll see where you are, where you've been, and where you're going. It can estimate your time of arrival and the remaining miles to your destination. There are several mapping programs. Microsoft makes Streets & Trips. Magellan, which makes the GPS that we use, also makes their own mapping software. Another good mapping software program is made by Rand McNally.

18

Going Full-Time

*F*ull-timing is defined as living in your RV on a permanent basis. It's a loose definition allowing for a lot of different styles. Some full-timers travel every day, while others stay at one or two locations more or less permanently. Some full-timers have sold their homes and given away their possessions, while others rent out their homes and have all their possessions in storage. They're a varied and interesting group of people, independent, curious, and active. I'm proud to be counted among them.

So why do we do it? Many different kinds of experiences prompt people to leave the stationary life behind and take off to explore the world. Perhaps it has been a lifelong dream that you can finally fulfill.

You may or may not be retired when you decide to full-time. John Veach is a full-timer who, with his wife, Libby, took early retirement from their careers with Bell South when they were both close to 50 years old. Their pensions are small, and they stop from time to time to work at jobs that bring in some income, but they're passionate about the rewards of living and traveling on the road. You can visit John and get some full-timing tips at his website (www.The RollingHome.com). Research indicates that many people in John's generation, the Baby Boomers, are doing exactly as he did.

Most people who decide to go full-time have usually traveled in their RVs for some time, grown used to the drawbacks, and appreciate the advantages. Some find that they're spending more and more time on the road, perhaps as much as eight months a year, and the question arises in their minds: "What if we just didn't go home for those measly four months?" It's a scary but thrilling thought.

THE TRADEOFFS OF RVING

I was doing the laundry one evening in an RV park laundry room. Next to me, a woman about my age folded jeans and T-shirts and put them in her basket. We got to talking and she said, "I really miss having my own washer and dryer." I told her that I didn't miss those particular items (maybe because my husband usually does the laundry), but I did admit to missing my garden.

My laundry room companion said that she missed having her own sewing room all set up ready to use. She also said that for the first five years she and her husband were full-timing, she missed the home they had sold.

I felt sad for her. Five years is a long time to grieve over something.

I began to wonder how common her feelings were. From years of casual conversations around RV parks, I've realized that sometimes one partner is more excited about full-timing than the other. One person may go along with the idea out of loyalty or a wish to make the other one happy, and then be miserable. That's not how it should be. If you both don't feel a thrill every time you find yourselves in a new, unexplored part of the country, you should rethink the whole thing. If your rig isn't home enough for you, if it seems physically or emotionally confining, or lacking in things that are really important to you, maybe it's time to give it up.

I took an informal poll on a full-timers' Internet forum, asking "What do you miss while full-timing?" and received some interesting responses.

- Family
- Computer station
- Big-screen TV
- Workshop
- Second car
- A big bathroom
- Hot baths
- A large hot water tank
- Washer/dryer

Several people sent a list of things they *don't* miss:

- House payments
- House insurance
- Electric bill
- Water bill
- Cable bill
- Property taxes
- Corrupt local government
- Out-of-control neighborhood kids
- Having to cut acres of grass, rake leaves, pull weeds, split wood
- House cleaning

THE TRADEOFFS OF RVING (continued)

One full-timer captured the positive aspects of the lifestyle:

I like the companionship I find with other full-timers and travelers passing through. The majority of the people I meet are warm and friendly and very sincere. Before full-timing, it seemed as though nobody (including us) had time for anything more than a casual wave to neighbors. You'd work, come home, lock the door. Nothing more.

Full-timing gives us the freedom to travel anywhere whenever we want, and we now have friends who want to share the travels with us. . . . Overall, there is very little that we miss because we are rewarded by so much. We're glad we made the choice of going full-time RVing.

To which I add a hearty amen.

But, the full-timing lifestyle is clearly not for everyone. You can try finding a tradeoff for whatever you're missing. I get around my desire to garden by having a potted plant or two and buying a lot of cut flowers, and there have been some years when I've had a small portable herb garden. A true tradeoff is that I've become interested in birds instead of plants; I carry two bird books plus a bird feeder and a hummingbird feeder. I've seen some beautiful birds—most recently a brilliant red cardinal, and a great blue heron that I watched for half an hour until it lifted off from the lake and flapped away on its giant wings. I would never have encountered these at home.

Everything in life seems to be a tradeoff. You just need to choose the ones that suit you. For me, it's still the open road.

Dan and I had never traveled in an RV until we bought our first one three months before we went full-time. We listed our house for sale at the same time. This approach to full-timing—the sink-or-swim method—works fine, too. If just reading this book gets you excited about going full-time, give it a try. You don't have to burn any bridges to do it. Keep your house and everything you own, just in case.

Getting Started at Full-timing

The first and most important criterion for going full-time is that if two people are going to do it together, both must want to do it. For many people, the drawback is leaving the house they've lived in for many years. Some come to realize that it's just a house and worth the tradeoff. If one of you can't let go of some cherished part of the stationary life, limit your RV experiences to trips that in time bring you back home.

After you've decided to go full-time, you have to make a lot of nuts-and-bolts decisions. If you don't already have a rig, what kind do you want? What will you do with your home? Sell or rent? (If you decide to rent it, get a reliable property manager who will handle all the repair headaches, screen tenants, and keep your house rented for a percentage of the rent.) What will you do with your possessions? Give them to kids and have a yard sale of items the kids don't want, or store them? How will you get mail, TV, Internet access, and medical help? (See the relevant chapters in this book to help with all of that.) Finally, what are your destinations? Make a list of all the places you've always wanted to go to, and plan a rough itinerary to get you to each one.

If you decide to go for it, welcome to the full-timing lifestyle. I hope you love it as much as we do. To get you started, here is a checklist of things to do before you take off:

- Sell or rent your house, or get a house sitter.
- If you're keeping your house, and your state has a homestead exemption for property taxes, notify the tax office that you'll no longer be eligible for it.
- Store your furniture, have a garage sale, give it to the kids—or do a combination of all of these.
- If you're renting out your house, you'll need a different kind of policy than you had while you lived there. If you sell your house, you still want renter's insurance to cover the things in your RV that you take with you, and anything you put in storage.
- Notify utility companies of the date you're moving out so they can read the meter if someone else is moving in, or shut off utilities if the house will be vacant. Also notify cable companies, telephone companies, and any other services. Provide an address where you can receive your final bills.
- Arrange for a new mailing address, using either a mail-forwarding service, a friend, or a family member. See Chapter 13 for more information about mail services.
- Fill out a change-of-address card at the post office.
- If you don't already have one, get a cellphone, at least for on-the-road emergencies. Consider a national calling plan and whether or not you want your cellphone to serve as your Internet connection. Detailed information is in chapters 13 and 17.

- Decide whether you want satellite TV on the road, and, if so, select a service. Be sure to sign an RV waiver if you want to receive the major networks.
- Consider signing up for Internet banking and Internet bill paying. It saves a lot of worry. Get debit cards if you don't have them. Consider having two bank accounts (see Chapter 13).
- Consider having recurring expenses such as phone service and satellite TV service billed to a credit card. The idea is to cut down on paper transactions, as you may be going weeks or even months without receiving mail.
- Shop around for insurance designed for RVs.
- Sign up for emergency road service that includes towing of a large RV. Camping World and Good Sam offer this insurance, among others.
- You may want to join RV-related organizations like Good Sam, Family Motor coaching, and/or Escapees.
- Get a good campground guide—*Woodall's* or *Trailer Life*—and also get the directory for KOA campgrounds. Consider Passport America for half-price camping (see Chapter 9).
- Think about joining a membership campground. Chapter 9 gives the pros and cons. You may want to defer that decision until you've been on the road a while and discussed it with other full-timers.
- Select medical insurance. See Chapter 13 for detailed suggestions. I can't stress its importance enough.
- Have a first-aid kit in your RV and a book on general medical care. See Chapter 10 for more on first-aid kits.
- Consider a supplemental insurance policy that covers airlift and other emergency evacuations from anywhere in the world. Good Sam and Family Motor Coaching offer these. Good Sam's is at a reasonable rate. Family Motor Coaching emergency evacuation insurance is free to members.
- Decide how you'll get refills of your prescriptions on a regular basis. See Chapter 13.
- Consider carefully what you want to take with you and be sure it will all fit in. See Chapter 12 for some suggestions.
- Load your RV a few days in advance of leaving to make sure you have everything you want and that there is room for all of it. Of course, if you change your mind after you leave, you can revisit your storage locker, or buy the item you mistakenly gave away.

DECIDING WHAT TO BRING

When Dan and I embarked on the full-time RV lifestyle, deciding what to take with us in the motor home involved a compromise between our desires and the amount of space available in the RV.

We were going to be on the road for years, and if we left behind something we later needed, it would have been hard (or expensive) to get that item. We'd have to buy a new one, or wait until we returned to our storage location to retrieve it.

Some items were automatically on the to-take list, including cameras, tripod, both laptop computers (we need a backup), printer, cell phone, TV satellite dish, and some, but by no means all, of Dan's tools. I bought a musical keyboard as a substitute for the full-size electronic organ we put into storage. As it turned out, I took on other hobbies (like writing this book) and seldom used the keyboard, so after a year we returned it to our storage locker. We brought our tennis rackets, and over the years we've used these a lot.

Our enormous book collection was a problem. We donated the Encyclopedia Britannica that had been my mother's to the local library and instead brought along the Britannica CD-ROM. I brought a few professional writers' books, Dan added repair manuals for the car and the motor home, and books about flying and photography. For our regular fiction reading, we decided that we could buy and later give away paperbacks as we traveled, a plan that has worked well. We donate books every few weeks to libraries, RV park book trades, and fellow travelers.

Some kitchen decisions were easy. The good china went into storage; the everyday dishes came with us. The lace tablecloths remained behind; the checkered one came along. The elegant silver-plate remained behind; the everyday knives and forks went into the RV kitchen drawers.

I made two mistakes in selecting kitchen supplies. I left my large, powerful KitchenAid mixer with my daughter, trading for her handheld. The first time I tried to mash potatoes with that little mixer, I knew I was in trouble. I was in even deeper trouble with cookie dough. You can cook anything in your RV's kitchen that you can cook in your kitchen at home, but decent equipment is still important.

My other mistake was in leaving behind our breadmaker. We enjoy homemade bread, and I thought there wasn't room for a breadmaker, but there was. I was happily reunited with mixer and breadmaker a year later, and found places for both of them without difficulty. You don't necessarily have to store kitchen items like this in the kitchen. The breadmaker has been stored under the bed and in the hall closet.

What clothing to bring was an easier decision. The dresses, skirts, and jackets I'd worn to work were obviously unnecessary once I retired, as were Dan's suits. Dan brought one sport coat, one pair of slacks, one white shirt, and a couple of ties. I brought two dresses for churchgoing, special events, concerts, or meals at fancy restaurants.

Otherwise, our wardrobe now consists of T-shirts, jeans, and shorts. One warm jacket, one sweater, two pairs of sandals, a pair of tennies, and a pair of flat shoes

---

completed my list. The rest of our clothing went either to Goodwill or storage. A couple of years later, I gave all the stored clothing to Goodwill.

Every year at Christmas we fly from wherever we are to Portland to spend time with the kids. I keep a supply of winter clothes and Christmas sweaters at my daughter's house. The rest of the time, we do our darndest to avoid cold or rainy weather.

When getting ready to leave, list your possessions in three categories and place items for each category in a separate room:

- Items to take in the RV
- Items to store or give to family
- Items to give to charity

The Frugal Full-Timer

As full-timers, we're blessed more by what we *don't* have to spend. We have no utility bills, yard-care expenses, or costly home repairs. We have the same expenses for food and clothing, of course, but we tend to buy less clothing because we have less storage space. (Besides, we rarely dress up.) We're never tempted to purchase new furniture or large appliances or a bigger TV; our movable home came fully furnished and our TVs are the largest that will fit in the rig's TV spaces.

Alas, there are some big expenses. Fuel and campground fees will pose the two biggest drains on your funds.

Saving on Fuel Costs

If you're traveling on a tight budget, a sharp rise in gasoline or diesel prices can be upsetting. However, you don't have to give up full-timing in the face of increasing costs. You can make adjustments.

For one thing, think about traveling less frequently and stopping for longer periods. After all, camping is as much a part of the RV life as driving. If you travel no more than 5 to 7 days in a month rather than 10 or 15, you'll keep fuel costs to a more acceptable level. There's a lot to be said for a leisurely pace when there is plenty of time to discover and explore the unique flavor and history of each area.

Hunt for the least expensive fuel. Gas stations near freeway exits usually charge the most; drive into a town to find a more reasonable price. It's been my experience that Arco and independent stations usually have the lowest price per gallon, but if you pay by credit or debit card, Arco charges a 35-cent fee. When filling up a big rig, the 35 cents doesn't increase the price per gallon much when spread over 75 gallons, but when you fill up a tow car at Arco, consider paying cash.

Saving on Campground Fees

Campground fees pose the second major expense that full-timers contend with. However, fees can be kept to a minimum by camping at national forests, BLM (Bureau of Land Management) lands, or state or national parks. State or national parks are generally half the cost of commercial campgrounds. Most parks limit your stay to about two weeks. Many of the sites are primitive, with limited hookups, but you can't beat the beauty of the surroundings.

Although commercial campgrounds are generally more expensive, most campgrounds' monthly rates are far more affordable than daily or weekly. If you consider that you won't be consuming any fuel during that month, the savings can be significant.

A monthly stay usually requires some planning. Many campgrounds set aside only a few sites for longer-term campers. Once those sites are occupied, you'll be stuck paying the higher rates regardless of your length of stay. You especially need to reserve a few weeks or even a couple of months ahead for the summer months in some locations like the Pacific Northwest, or for the winter months in such snowbird havens as Arizona and Florida. For example, we reserve in March for a month-long July stay near Portland, Oregon. By April, the park reservations for summer are full.

When you move on after your month's stay, there are still ways to economize on daily campground expenses while traveling. Membership campgrounds, RV club discounts, and Passport America all give discounts on your nightly stays. Read Passport America's directory carefully, though, as each listed campground has its own way of allowing half-price visitors. Some offer the discount only in the off-season, or only on weekdays or only for one night.

Budgeting

Life is short. For that reason, frugal full-timers shouldn't pinch pennies when it comes to the best part of the RV lifestyle: exploration. Bus tours, museums, riverboat trips, concerts, and adventures in regional food are just a few of the reasons you're RVing; therefore, they should be the last items to get cut from your budget. Plan to travel slowly and savor the adventure.

The accompanying table offers a look at some typical budgets for RVers. The first column reflects what Dan and I actually spent for the month of June 2004. The second column shows what an economy budget might have looked like for that same month (with no RV payments). The third column shows a typical annual budget for full-timers with sufficient income who own a fairly large RV and travel frequently.

FULL-TIMER EXPENSES

Item	Monthly		Typical Annual
	Our actual costs for June 2004	Economy	
Campground fees	$751	$400	$4,800
Fuel for two vehicles	$456	$200	$2,800
Sightseeing expenses	$131	$60	$1,200
Books/newspapers	$41	$30	$250
Groceries for two adults	$516	$300	$4,000
Furniture storage	$80	Give away	$1,000
Loan payment for RV	$715	Old RV; own	$4,000
Maintenance/repairs	—	$175	$900
Cellphone services	$135	$40	$840
Internet access	$60	—	—
E-mail service	$18	$10	$240
TV service	$44	—	$480
Insurance: car, RV, renter's	$200	$100	$2,000
Medical insurance	—	—	$4,000
Prescriptions	—	$60	$800
Membership campgrounds	—	—	$475
RV club memberships	—	—	$75
Discount camping clubs	—	—	$45
Totals	$3,227	$1,375	$27,900

During June 2004, Dan and I were actively traveling every few days in the eastern part of the United States and Canada, and our camping fees were higher than normal. No campgrounds in our membership organization were on our route. We did economize by staying at several military parks and some parks affiliated with Passport America, but we found that commercial campground fees in Canada and the northeastern part of the United States were higher than they are in the southern and western states (averaging close to $25 per day compared to about $20 in the south and west). Our fuel expenses were for both vehicles—motor home, and tow car—during a time when gasoline was running about $1.90 per gallon and diesel was running about $1.72.

In our actual budget, you won't see any expenses for medical insurance and

WORKING ON THE ROAD

Increasingly, younger people are becoming full-timers. Some people retire at 50 or 55 on reduced pension or investment income in order to experience the thrill of RVing. If your income is small, you may need to work part-time while you travel. Even if your income is sufficient, you may want to have extra money for luxuries. There are a variety of ways to bring in money while traveling in an RV.

In the TV show *Promised Land*—a fictional story about a family that traveled around the country full-timing in a trailer—the couple always managed to find work wherever they landed. He was a handyman and she was a teacher. She got a job substituting in just about every city.

In the real world, that would probably never happen.

But finding temporary work wherever you go is certainly something you can do. For instance, try signing up at temporary agencies to do clerical work, filling in for receptionists, secretaries, and clerks on vacation.

Survey your skills, experience, and interests; decide what work you can (or want to) do, then see what's available. Start by typing "freelance jobs" into a search engine and see what turns up. There are also many job-search websites (like HotJobs.com or Monster.com) where you can check listings, post your resume, and set up an automatic e-mail service that will alert you when a job listing suits you. Or, you can do things the old-fashioned way and check the local paper for temporary jobs.

Some full-timing couples take a small traveling workshop with them as they go. I've met people towing tool shops on wheels; they set up their mobile repair stations at RV parks and offer a fix-it-all service. In campgrounds, they're the folks who can plane that cabinet door that won't close or stop your dripping faucet. Some people tow materials and equipment to make craft items that they then sell at local craft fairs as they travel.

prescriptions, because Dan and I don't have to pay for them. Dan's military retirement includes free medical coverage and requires a very small copay for prescriptions.

Also, we didn't have any maintenance expenses for the motor home because it was just about a year old. The tradeoff for this is that we do have a high monthly payment. We started out full-timing with an old motor home that we bought for cash, and at that time we didn't have any monthly payments. However, that RV was 11 years old when we bought it, and we did have maintenance expenses of some sort nearly every month.

The economy budget reflects a situation where an older RV is owned outright but has maintenance and repair expenses. To keep expenses down, you can

WORKING ON THE ROAD (continued)

Probably the most common job for full-timers (and one that practically everyone can do) is to serve as campground host for a few months. You help campers resolve small problems, greet new arrivals, and just be there to be helpful. Most of these jobs pay your camping fees for staying at the park. Some also pay a small stipend. You can find these and similar jobs advertised in RV magazines like *Highways* or *Family Motor Coaching*.

An organization called Workampers offers hundreds of jobs tailored to RVers. You have to subscribe to its newsletter for $25 per year to access current job offerings. You can also advertise for work in their Situations Wanted section and post your resume. To check them out, visit www.workamper.com or call them at 800-446-5627.

Another job I've seen advertised frequently is housesitting. You park your rig in front of some vacationing family's house and provide security (maybe water the lawn, collect the mail, and feed the pets) while they're gone. This is a paying job, contracted through an agency that advertises in RV publications.

One full-timer I know stopped traveling for a few months to take a job selling RVs—a subject about which he was definitely an expert. I'm sure his enthusiasm and knowledge helped him be very successful. He commented that this job brought in a lot more money than being a campground host.

An important thing to keep in mind as a working full-timer is that you have certain reasons for your lifestyle. You want to travel and not be tied down. Be sure you look for jobs in places you want to visit. Don't just go there because there's a job. Don't take on too much work, either. It's hard to say no, but sometimes it's important to do so. Leave yourself time for seeing the sights, visiting with friends, and having time to smell the roses along the way.

restrict the amount of travel you do each month, how much you elect to spend for phone service and/or TV, what you eat and where you stay. The annual economy budget adds up to just $16,500. It's very possible to live and travel on that amount.

The Full-Timer's Social Life

When you decide to become a full-timer, you choose to leave behind an entire lifestyle. Much of it you may be glad to be rid of: shaggy lawns to mow, weeds to pull, daily traffic jams, noisy neighbors, and barking dogs.

These are all things we can do without, but doing without contact with friends and family can be a little harder. Maybe you belong to a social group that meets on a regular basis, and now they'll be meeting without you. Don't worry. It is possible for a full-timer to lead a fairly rich social life.

Generally speaking, RVers are a friendly group. Night after night you may find yourself in a campground full of strangers, but chances are you'll have a lot more in common with your new neighbors than you did with the ones you left behind at home. When you arrive at a site, you won't know the names of your new neighbors or the details of their lives, but you'll know that they like to travel and live in the same way you do. That's quite an icebreaker. If you have a couple of extra chairs placed under your awning, you'll have no problem filling them with congenial company. Or take a casual walk around the campground and introduce yourself to people you encounter.

If you stay anywhere for several months, you may find the people at your campground devising their own activities to mark Thanksgiving, Christmas, New Year's, Valentine's Day, and other holidays. Birthdays and anniversaries are often celebrated communally. These occasions offer an opportunity to share your specialties, like deviled eggs, crab dip, or potato salad. Often there is music and impromptu dancing. It's a lot of fun!

Membership campgrounds offer a variety of activities, including card games, potlucks, dancing, and group tours of the area.

Rallies provide another social opportunity for full-timers. Rallies are one part convention and one part country fair. At a rally you can learn about the newest developments in RV travel, view the latest RVs, attend lectures (on subjects like safe driving and fuel conservation), participate in square dancing, line dancing, and a host of other social events. *Webster's* defines a *rally* as "a mass meeting to arouse enthusiasm." Indeed, you'll find rallies to be enthusiastic events. Many

There is no shortage of social interaction in a full-time RVer's life.

rallies are held at fairgrounds because they often draw hundreds of rigs to dry-camp for days.

It may seem like something of a wrench to give up your accustomed social contacts, but don't think for a minute that life on the road has to be the life of a hermit. Your family is as close as a phone call or e-mail. And your friends are camped right next door.

Citizens of Everywhere: Selecting a Domicile

When you're a full-timer, every person you meet will probably ask you, "Where are you from?" Increasingly, it will be hard to answer. Many full-timers answer by naming three states: the state they used to live in, the state where they have mail service, and the state in which they register their vehicles and vote.

Laws in every state require the selection of a legal domicile, a state that you declare to be your legal residence and to which you plan to return when you end your full-timing days. The organization for full-timers, Escapees, publishes a handbook to help its members select a domicile state. One of the major points it makes is that you must move everything to your state of domicile: voter registration, mailing address, vehicle registration and insurance, and driver's license. The booklet warns, "Do not try to get by with mixing states, taking the best of State A and the best of State B. That doesn't demonstrate your intent to choose a new domicile; it demonstrates your intent to defraud State A of the things you have in State B, and vice versa. There is no defense for any claims the states may have against you in that situation."

Your first awareness of the domicile situation may be when your forwarded mail includes a notice that your vehicles need re-registration or your driver's license is about to expire. In some states, you can send a check and receive the new materials by mail, but before you do that, ask yourself if this state is the one you really want to claim as your home state.

The decision can be complicated. You don't actually live anywhere now, but you do need to register your vehicles, obtain a driver's license, and vote as a citizen of some state. The question is, which one?

Finances can help you make this decision. Some states charge a bundle to license an RV, and they charge that bundle every year. Other states have high income taxes. Other states have low vehicle registration fees. Some have no state income tax, and some have no sales tax.

There are 50 choices, and you can find reasons for and against each one. Nevada and Texas seem to be the most popular among the full-timers I know, perhaps because of their lack of a state income tax and the ease of licensing a vehicle there.

Most states issue driver's licenses that are good for four or five years, and most but not all require renewal in person. An Oregon license, good for five years, can be renewed by mail every other time. Only a few states, among them Oregon, Vermont and Arizona, issue licenses on the spot. The other states mail the license to your address, which can't be a post office box, and your license may take up to six weeks to arrive. If the address you give is an RV park, you'll have to have the RV park forward your license to your new location if you've left when it arrives.

Interestingly, Arizona licenses are good from the date of issue until one's 60th birthday. After that, renewals are required every five years. Thirteen other states and the District of Columbia require special examinations for license renewal based on age.

Almost all states require their residents to meet vehicle and driver's license regulations soon after moving to the state. The exception is Hawaii, which accepts a license from any state until its expiration if the driver is over 18. Some states allow a new resident as long as 60 days before obtaining a driver's or vehicle license, but many require a new resident to obtain vehicle and driver's licenses immediately.

All states except for Oregon register vehicles every year, so the renewal problem persists for full-timers on the road. It's a good reason to choose as a domicile state one that will let you renew your licenses by mail. Texas is one such state. Escapees, headquartered in Livingston, Texas, offers mail-forwarding service and a street address to interested members. The street address is legal for vehicle, driver's license, and voter registration, which is not the case in many other states. Also, the cost of registering vehicles in Texas is relatively reasonable—roughly $250 for a large, new motor home. Texas requires that vehicles have an annual inspection, but this can be deferred until you visit the state again. (Did I mention that Texas has no state income tax?)

Rules for residence vary from state to state, but in most cases you need a street address, not a post office box, both to qualify as a resident and to register as a voter. This street address can in some cases be the RV park where you're staying.

A domicile in one state does not entirely free you from paying state income taxes in another state if you own property or earn income there. Seven states do not have a state income tax. These are Texas, Alaska, Florida, Nevada, South Dakota, Washington, and Wyoming. Two other states, New Hampshire and Tennessee, only tax dividend and interest income. Other states to consider are those that have favorable treatment of retirement income. Alabama, Hawaii, Illinois, Mississippi, and Pennsylvania don't tax retirement income from any source—federal, state, or private—including Social Security.

A couple of books can help you make a domicile decision. The American Automobile Association publishes *A Digest of Motor Laws* giving licensing and driving regulations for each of the 50 states. Another useful guide to selecting a state of residence is *Retirement Places Rated* by David Savageau. This publication delves into all factors you might consider when establishing residence in a particular location and includes charts showing taxation and license policies for the 50 states.

Our goal as full-timers is for bureaucratic hassles such as licenses to impinge as little as humanly possible on our carefree lifestyle. We want to fill out the paperwork, pay reasonable fees, and be on our way—citizens of everywhere.

A TESTIMONIAL

(REPRINTED FROM RVTRAVEL.COM)

An idea has been bouncing around in my head lately that living in one place, in one home, isn't as "normal" as it once was. The fact is, every day the number of people who sell their homes to travel full-time by RV grows. Just observe the traffic along a busy highway. Notice the numbers of "big rig" RVs passing by. These folks are not on the way to the Grand Canyon for a week of camping. Many are on their way to yet another temporary home base, where they will stay a week, a month, or maybe a season. Some are following the sun.

Have you been inside a big Class A motor home or fifth-wheel trailer recently? If not, visit an RV dealer and take a look. Check out one of these RVs with its slideouts extended. They're "houses," aren't they? They have virtually all the amenities of a traditional home. They're not made for "camping." They're made for living.

The fact is, if you are the type of person who loves to travel, who gets restless in one place, who doesn't need a lot of "stuff," then you may find that the life of a full-time RVer is incredibly stimulating (and ultimately addictive).

As the baby-boom crowd grows older and retires, it seems to me that full-time RV travel will become even more popular than today. Face it, lawn mowing gets old. And many of us, as we get older, realize that most of our "stuff" isn't important.

I can envision millions and millions of happy, wandering nomads, exploring the nooks and crannies of wherever a road leads. And what do they give up for this life of freedom and exhilaration? Not much. In their rolling houses, they have cellular phones, computers with Internet access, televisions, DVD players, and all the amenities of any home—bedroom, bathroom with shower, heater, coffeemaker, refrigerator and, yes, even a kitchen sink.

Anyone who is possessed with wanderlust who travels by RV even once is in serious danger of catching the travel bug. It gnaws at you. It won't go away. It makes you question why you continue to live in the same place and do the same things over and over. You start to feel like you're rotting. You need to "air out," get away, see something new, have adventures. Life is short. You begin to fear that day by day, week by week, you are letting your life slip away.

Those of us possessed by the travel bug look at a map and go crazy. We see names of towns and rivers and lakes, and we see thin, twisty blue lines that are roads. We want to get on one of those "blue highways" to see where it goes. We want to drop into a roadside cafe to order ham and eggs from a gum-chewing waitress who calls us "Hon." We want to gab with the toothless cowboy on the stool next to us at the counter. "Been here long, pard?"

In Prescott, Arizona, as I dined on ham and eggs in a crowded little cafe, a guy walked in and asked to buy a pack of cigarettes. "We don't sell 'em," the waitress said. "Check across the street at the health food store." Yeah . . . that's what she said. Funny, huh? I could tell you a dozen more stories like this from my RV roadtrips. What

A TESTIMONIAL (continued)

fun! What a life! How utterly opposite from boring! When I think of these stories and my many adventures on the road, I want to drop what I am doing right this moment and run away. Alas, I can only do it part time . . . for now.

   Will there be more people on the road in RVs next year than today? I think so. Maybe one of them will be you.

— Chuck Woodbury, RVTravel.com

Amen.
—Jayne

Start Your Engines

So there you have it. The RVing life is basically simple, and simply wonderful. Traveling in your RV sets you free from many responsibilities and allows you to seize each day. What could be more important, more thrilling than that? You can spend your summers with family, and your winters someplace warm. You can explore all the nooks and crannies of our beautiful country from shore to shore, from north to south, slowly

Jayne and Dan Freeman.

and leisurely at your own pace. You can watch seagulls and blue herons at a remote coastal paradise, or camp near our nation's capitol and spend a few weeks discovering its urban charms. The world lies before you. As for the RV in which you travel, your choices are almost as infinite as the destinations. The choices are yours to make.

   Go for it!

Appendix

Resources for the RVer

Campground Guides

KOA Directory. Published by Meredith Integrated Marketing, Des Moines, IA 50309. Guide to KOA campgrounds throughout the United States with contact details. KOA campgrounds are often close to the highway, good for overnight stays, but can be a bit more expensive than others in the same area.

Passport America. All the 1,200+ campgrounds listed in this guide can be visited for half their posted price. Sometimes excluded on weekends, holidays, or in high season, this organization reimburses its $44 annual fee with two or three overnight stays. Sign up at Camping World stores, call 800-283-7183, or go to www.passport-america.com for more information.

Traveler's Guide to Mexican Camping by Mike and Terri Church. Published by Rolling Homes Press, 161 Rainbow Dr., #6157, Livingston, TX 77399. A comprehensive guide to campsites and border crossings with very precise directions. A goldmine for the traveler in Mexico. Sold at Amazon.com and also on the authors' website, www.rolling homes.com, as well as at rallies and bookstores.

Trailer Life Campground Directory. Published by TL Enterprises, 2575 Vista del Mar Drive, Ventura, CA 93001. This is the campground guide that we have. Covers a large number of campgrounds in the United States, Canada, and Mexico. Updated annually. Get a copy at RV stores like Camping World, or order from www.tldirectory.com. Also comes as a CD-ROM.

Woodall's Campground Directory. Published by Woodall Publications Corp, 13975 West Polo Trail Drive, Lake Forest, IL 60045; 800-323-9076. Similar to *Trailer Life* (see info above). Woodall's directories are also sold at RV stores.

Highway Directories

Next EXIT. Published by *Next EXIT* Corporate, P.O. Box 888, Garden City, UT 84028. A guide to gas, food, lodging, medical services, and retail stores at every interstate highway exit. Updated annually. You can get these at RV stores.

Mountain Directory (East) and *Mountain Directory (West).* Published by R & R Publishing Inc., P. O. Box 941, Baldwin City, KS 66006; 800-594-5999. Available at most RV stores. Locations and descriptions of mountain passes and steep grades in each part of the United States. Gives precise information as to location and percent of grade.

Membership Campground Affiliations

Coast to Coast. Requires other campground affiliation. Members camp for $8 per night, one-week limit. Large number of campgrounds. Obtain materials through membership in other association. Annual fee around $90.

Resort Parks International. Must be affiliated with other membership campground association. Members camp at affiliated campgrounds for $8 per night, one-week limit. Annual fee of $65. Membership materials obtained from the other membership organization (for example, Thousand Trails, Western Horizons, and so on).

Thousand Trails. Membership campground with 50 "preserves" mainly on the West Coast, Texas, and the East Coast of the United States. Two preserves in Florida, one in Las Vegas. Members camp free at any Thousand Trails campground 50 nights per year, but pay an up-front fee to join and an annual membership fee of around $500. Check them out at www.thousandtrails.com.

Western Horizons. Membership campground with 25 parks affiliated with AOR (Adventure Outdoor Resorts) and Coast to Coast. Requires fee to join and annual dues of between $200 and $400. Contact them online at www.whresorts.com, or visit one of their parks and listen to a sales pitch.

Retailer

Camping World. A network of RV stores spread throughout the United States selling everything you might possibly want for your RV. Check them out online at www.campingworld.com to find the store nearest you.

RV Organizations

The Good Sam Club, 2575 Vista Del Mar, Ventura, CA 93001; www.goodsamclub.com. An organization with many benefits for RVers. Affiliated with *Trailer Life* campground guides. Members receive discounts to some campgrounds listed in *Trailer Life*. Members are offered discounts on insurance, both medical and for their RVs, and many other benefits, including mail forwarding. Annual dues of $25. You get a lot for your money here, including a great magazine, *Highways*, offered free to members. The Affinity group also publishes *Trailer Life* magazine and *Motorhome* magazine.

Family Motorcoach Association, 8291 Clough Pike, Cincinnati, OH 45244; www.fmca.com. An organization for people who have motor homes. Many benefits, including insurance, emergency transport, mail service, and a great magazine. Annual dues $45 initially and $35 renewal.

Escapees, 100 Rainbow Drive, Livingston, TX 77351; 888-757-2582; fax: 936-327-4388; www.escapees.com. An RV club for serious RVers. Offers mail service and many other benefits, including a magazine, affordable parks where members can stay for a small nightly fee, and a retirement facility for RVers who hang up their keys. Annual dues $60.

Websites Useful to RVers

Audio Books
www.audible.com

Author's Website
www.completervhandbook.com

Agricultural Inspection at U.S. Border
www.aphis.usda.gov
www.aphis.usda.gov/vs/ncie

Appliances for RVs
www.dometic.com
www.norcold.com
www.splendide.com

Bill Paying Service
www.mycheckfree.com

Campsites
    Big Rigs, Sites for
    www.newrver.com/bigrigbook.html

    Discount RV Parks
    www.passportamerica.com

    State Parks
    naspd.indstate.edu/stateparks.html

National Parks
www.nps.gov. (National Parks)
reservations.nps.gov. (reservations)
www.reserveusa.com (alternate National Park reservations)

Driving Instruction
www.rvschool.com

Dump Stations (U.S. Listings)
www.rvdumps.com

E-mail Access
www.mail2web.com
www.pocketmail.com
www.webmail.earthlink.net

Firearms Laws
www.nraila.org/GunLaws/Default.aspx

Fulltime RVing
www.fulltimerver.com
www.TheRollingHome.com

General RV Information and Forums
www.fulltimerver.com
www.rv.net
www.rvamerica.com
www.rvia.com
www.RVtravel.com

Health Insurance Guide
www.aarp.org

Jobs for RVers
www.workamper.com

Purchasing an RV
www.jheggen@bigsky.net (licensing an RV in Montana)
www.kbb.com (Kelley Blue Book appraisals)
www.nada.com (National Auto Dealers Association)
www.rvs-r-us.com (appraisals)

Redecorating an RV
www.recoveryroomrv.com

Satellite Services
Internet
www.2waysatlink.com (Ron Brundage, Starband dealer, 520-907-2712)
www.c-comsat.com
www.earthlink.net
www.direcway.com
www.groundcontrol.com
www.optistreams.com
www.rv-anywhere.org
www.starband.com

TV
www.directv.com
www.dishnetwork.com
www.global-cm.net

Supplemental Braking Systems
www.aemfg.com
www.brakebuddy.com/800-470-2287
www.brakesafesystems.com
www.rvstuf.com
www.smibrake.com
www.towbrake.com

Towing
Regulations
www.aemfg.com/towingbasics.html
www.dmv.ca.gov/pubs/dl648/dl648pt12.htm

Towables (Information, etc.)
www.fmca.com
www.motorhomemagazine.com

Wal-Mart Locator Book
http://rvtraveler.c.topica.com/maab6Vyaa5IDFbd511sb/

Wireless Internet Sites
www.rvtravel.com/wifi.html

Index

Numbers in **bold** refer to pages with illustrations or diagrams.

AARP, 176–77
acceleration, 71–72
AC voltmeter, 113
air brakes, 136–37
air conditioning, 110–11, 147
Airstream, 33–34
American Automobile Association (AAA), 150, 223
amps, calculating, 116, 119
antenna, satellite, 202–6
antifreeze, 128, 131
appliances, power consumption, 116, 146–47
ATMs, 169–70, 192
audio books, 198
audio entertainment, 197–98
auto transformers, 114
awnings, 50–51, 120–22

backing up
    driving school and, 66, 68
    fifth wheels/trailers, 76–77
    motor homes, 75–76
    with tow car, 87
banking on Internet, 171
bathrooms, **43**–44, 92–94
    "cassette toilet," 31
batteries
    about, **117**–18
    dry-camping and, 119, 146
    electrical system and, 111
    furnace and, 109–10
    inverters and, 114, 118–19
    positioning fifth wheels and, 89–90
    refrigerator and, 104–105
    RV storage and, 159–60
    solar power and, 119
bedrooms, 46–48
Bigfoot truck campers, **14**–15
bill-paying services, 171

black-water holding tank, 22–23, 92–98
books, 164
boondocking. *See* dry-camping
brakes
    about, 134–37
    steep hills and, 74, 136
    stopping/slowing RVs, 70–71, 73
    supplemental for towing, **88**
    towed cars and, 90–91
bridge clearances, 74–75
Brundage, Ron, 203
buying RVs
    evaluating, 55–57
    financing, 58
    making the best deal, 58–60
    motor homes, 15–29, 38
    from private parties, 59, 62
    taxes, registration, insurance, 60–61, 221–23
    towables, **30**–38
    truck campers, **13**–15
    typical prices by class, 11–12
    walk-through, 62–63

cameras, digital, 206–7
campgrounds
    about, 138–40
    cable TV in, 193
    courtesy in, 144–45, 147
    guides, 29, 226
    leaving RVs in, 142, 158
    membership, 142–44, 151, 213, 216, 227
    in Mexico, 191
    military, 140, 184
    saving on fees, 216–19
    in state and national park systems, 140–42
    and Wi-Fi access, 201
Camping World RV stores, 61, 82, 139, 150
Canada, 28, 186–88, 196–97

cars
    towing, 83–88
    towing into Mexico, 189–90
cash, getting, 169–70
cassette toilets, 31
cell phones
    about, 171–73
    in Canada, 188
    emergencies and, 148, 212
    Internet access and, 199–200
Chamber of Commerce, 149, 202
cheater boxes, 114
checklists, departure, 165–67
children, traveling with, 4, 6, 9–10, **180**–81
choosing RVs. *See* buying RVs
circuit checker, **113**
Class A motor homes, 25–29
Class B motor homes, **15**–19
Class C motor homes, **19**–25
Classic Supreme (Class B), 17–**18**
classification system for RVs, 11–12
climate considerations, 159–60, 183–84
Coach House (Class C), **19**–21
Coachmen Freelander (Class C), **23**–24
Coast to Coast, 138
compressors, 132
computers, 171–73, 198–202, 207–8
convection ovens, 40–41
cookbooks, 164–65
cooling system, 128, 131
costs
    diesel *vs.* gasoline engines, 53
    fuel expenses, 215–16
    for full-time RVers, 217–20
    by transportation type, 7–8
credit cards, 151, 189

deflappers, 122
diesel engines
    fuel filters, 127–28

diesel engines *(continued)*
  gas mileage and, 20–21
  gasoline engines *vs.*, 53
  Jake brakes and, 74, 136
  motor homes and, 38
  oil changes, 124
  performance, 26
  steep hills and, 74
digital cameras, 206–7
dinettes, 42, 47
dinghies, 84
disc brakes, 136
documentation, 151, 186, 189
domicile state, 60–61, 221–25
driving basics. *See also* highway
      driving
  driving forward, 66–69
  driving safely, 72–75
  highway driving, 71–72
  parking/leveling, 75–82
  turning, 69–70
driving schools, 66–68
drum brakes, 134–36
dry-camping, 23, 42, 117–20,
      145–47
DSL, 198–99, 202
dump sites, 98–99, 145–47

eating, RVs and, 5–7
electrical considerations
  conservation, 146
  dry-camping and, 146–47
  features in RVs, 48–50
  fire safety and, 152–53
  GFIs, 116–**17**
  heating backup and, 109
  hitching and, 89–91
  power supply/electrical sys-
      tems, 111–20
  propane tanks and, 109, 155
  refrigerator, 104–5
  tools for repairs, 129–30
  towing and, 86–87
  for washer/dryers, 45
  water tank pump and, 100
emergencies
  fire safety, 152–**54**
  medical emergencies, 155–57
  personal safety, 151–52

propane safety, 154–55
roadside repairs, 128–30
vehicle accidents, 148–50
emergency exits, **154**
engine brakes, 136
Escapees
  campgrounds and, 138
  on domicile states, 221–22
  mail-forwarding service, 169,
      223
  memberships for sale, 143
  RV insurance companies, 61

Family Motor Coach
      Association, 83, 150, 169
Family Motor Coaching, 59, 61,
      143
FCC, 203, 205
fifth wheels
  about, 35
  awnings and, 50
  backing, 76–**77**
  engines and, 34, 38, 53
  generators and, 119
  hitching, 88–90
  insurance and, 37
  levelers and, 78–80
  motor homes *vs.*, 37–38
  propane tanks, 154
  stability and, 33
  as towables, 30
50-amp service, **48,** 49, 111, **112,**
      114
filters
  air, 125, 127
  coolant, 128
  fuel, 125, 127–28, 160
  water, 101–2
financing RVs, 58
firearms, 152, 185, 190
fire safety, 152–54
first-aid kits, 156, 213
Fleetwood Destiny, **32**–33
floors, caring for, 123
footpads, 80
freeways. *See* highway driving
freshwater supply, 98–103
  conservation, 146
fuel expenses, 215–16

fuel filters, 125, 127–28, 160
fuel starvation, 160
full-timing
  about, 209–11
  domicile state and, 60,
      221–25
  getting started, 211–15
  insurance and, 61
  medical care and, 173–75
  membership campgrounds,
      142
  savings with, 8, 215–20
  social life, 220–21
furnaces in RVs, 109–10, 153,
      155

gas mileage, 20–21, 53, 100
gasoline engines
  diesel engines *vs.*, 53
  fuel filters and, 128
  gas mileage and, 20–21
  maintenance, 125
  motor homes and, 38
  oil changes, 124–27
  steep hills and, 74
  vapor lock, 124
generators
  compressors and, 132
  dry-camping and, 118,
      146–47
  instruction on, 62
  purpose, **49**–50
  unreliable power sources and,
      114–15
GFI (ground fault interrupter),
      116–**17**
Golden Age Passport, 140
Good Sam Club, 138, 169, 179
GPS, 207–**8**
gray-water holding tank, 22–23,
      95–99

heating. *See* furnaces
heating/cooling RVs, 108–11
highway directories, 227
highway driving
  bridge clearances, 74–75
  entering, exiting, passing,
      71–72

steep hills, 73–74
    weather conditions, 73
    wind and, 72–73
Highways, 59, 61, 67, 143
hills, steep, 73–74
hitching a trailer, 90–**91**
hitching fifth wheels/trailers,
    88–90
holding tanks, 22–23, 92, **95**–99
Holiday Rambler Savoy, **35**–36

icemakers, 43, 54, 107
insurance
    buying RVs and, 60–61
    fifth wheels and, 37
    medical, 173–76, 213
    renter's, 212
    visiting Canada, 186
    visiting Mexico, 189
Internet
    accessing, 198–206
    banking on, 171
    campgrounds and, 143
    Canada and, 188
    comparing RVs on, 59–60
    finding doctors, 173
    phone connection, 172
    state parks, 141
    truck stops and, 139
inverters
    dry-camping and, 146–47
    icemakers and, 106
    purpose, 48, **50**, 118–19
    unreliable power sources and,
        114–15

jacks, **80–81**, 82
Jake brakes, 74, 136
Jayco Escapade (Class C), 21–23

Kelley Blue Book, 56–57
kids, traveling with, 4, 6, 9–10,
    180–81
kitchens in RVs, 39–43

laptops. *See* computers
leveling the RV, 77–82, 91, 105
libraries, 202
license renewals, 222–23

load binders, 122
loading the RV, 162–67

mail-forwarding service, 168–69,
    188, 212
maintenance
    brakes, 134–37
    cooling system, 128
    emergency roadside repairs,
        128–30
    fuel filters, 127–28
    oil changes, 125–27
    suspension, 134
    tires, 131–33
    transmission, 137
medical care
    arranging for, 173–77, 213
    emergency, 155–57
    for pets, 179
Medicare, 173–77
membership campgrounds,
    142–44, 151, 213, 216
metric system conversion, 186,
    188
Mexico, 170, 183, 187–92, 196
microwaves, 40–41, 164
military campgrounds, 140, 184
Minnie Winnie (Class C),
    24–25
mirrors, **68**–69, 75
money, obtaining, 169–71
motor homes
    awnings and, 50
    backing, 75–76
    Class A, 16, **25**–29, 53
    Class B, **15**–19
    Class C, **19**–25, 53
    driving with car in tow, 87–88
    engines in, 38
    fifth wheels *vs.,* 37–38
    inverters in, 50
    leveling, 77–82
    propane tanks, 154
    storage of, 133, 158–60
    typical prices, 12
    wind and, 72
MSRP (manufacturer's suggested
    retail price), 12, 21
MyCheckFree.com, 171

National Automobile Dealers
    Association (NADA), 12,
    55–57
National Parks, 140–42
nonresident corporations, 61
Nuwa Hitchhiker, **36–37**

ohm meters, 106
oil changes, **125**–27
ovens, 40–41
overheating, 131

parking
    Class As and, 28
    driving basics, 75–82
    driving school and, 66
    larger motor homes and, 20
    with tow car, 87
passing safely, 71–72
Passport America, 139, 213, 216
passports, 151
Pemex gas stations, 191–92
personal safety, 151–52, 170
pets, traveling with, 178–79,
    190
phones, 148–50, 155, 171–73,
    188, 198–99
pivot points, 77
places to stay, finding, 138–45.
    See also campgrounds
Pocketmail, 200
popup trailers, 30–33
power, conservation of, 146
power consumption of appli-
    ances, 116, 146
power-management system,
    115–16
power supply, 111–20
prescriptions, filling, 177
price incentives, 58
propane fuel
    generators and, 147
    heating and, 108–10
    refilling tanks, 109
    refrigerators, 104–6
    RV storage and, 159
    safety and, 153–55
    stoves and, 103–4
    tunnel restrictions, 140, 155

purchasing RVs. *See* buying RVs
PV (photo-voltaic). *See* solar power

rain, driving in, 73
raised roof, 15, 17–18
rallies, 220–21
refrigerators
    about, **42**–43
    caring for, 104–7
    levelers and, 78
    loading, 163–**64**
    propane tanks and, 109, 155
    RV storage and, 159
    size of, 17
registration, vehicle, 60–61, 221–23
regulators, 99, **100,** 101, 108
rentals RVs, 7–8
repair shops, 150
reservations, national campgrounds, 141–42
Resort Parks International (RPI), 138
resources, information, 226–30
retirement, 176, 223
reversed polarity, 113
Roadtrek (Class B), **16–17**
roofs, caring for, 122
RV Anywhere, 205
RV driving school, 66–68
RV organizations, 227–28
RVs. *See* motor homes
RV Safety Education Foundation, 132
RVs-R-Us, 56–57

Safari Trek (Class A), **26–27**
sales tax, 60–61
satellite finders, 196
satellite Internet access, 202–6
satellite phones, 149–50
satellite radio, 197–98
satellite TV system, 191, 194–97, 204
security, 151, 158
sensors, water-in-fuel, 127

side mirrors, **68,** 69–70, 75
sinks, 41
sleet, driving in, 73
slideouts, 17–18, **20–21,** 23, 28, **51**–52
smart chargers, 118
snowbirds, 10, 142, 183–84
snow, driving in, 73
solar power, 114, 119–20, 146
stabilizing hitch, 33
state income tax, 223
state parks, 140–41
steep hills, 73–74, 136
stopping/slowing RVs. *See* brakes
storage space
    in bathrooms, 43
    in bedrooms, 47
    decanting food items, 163
    features in RVs, 52
    leaving RVs in, 158–60
stoves (cooking), 40–41, 103–4, 153, 155
subscriber identity module (SIM), 150
sulfation, 118
surge protectors, 111, 115
suspension, 134

tax considerations, 60–61, 223
television, 193–97, 204
temperature conversion, 186
30-amp service, **48,** 49, 111, **112,** 114
Thousand Trails campgrounds, 142–43
tire protectors, **133**
tires, 60, 131–33, 159
toads, 84
toilets, 31, 43–44, 92–94
tools, emergency roadside repairs, 128–30
towables, 12, **30**–38, 50, 76
towing, 83–88, 150
tow packages, buying, 84–86
Trailer Life, 61, 99, 138, 213
trailers
    about, 30

backing, 76–77
generators and, 119
hitching, 90–91
levelers and, 78–80
propane tanks, 154
steep hills and, 74
wind and, 72–73
transmissions, 137
travel trailers, 33–**34**
trips, long, 182–84
truck campers, **13**–15
trucker campers, 12
truck stops, 132, 139
tune ups, 124–30
tunnel restrictions, propane tanks and, 140, 155
turning considerations, 67, 69–71
20-amp service, 112, 114

van conversions, 15–19, 81
vapor lock, 124
voltage, 113–14, 116, 119

wallets, stolen/lost, 146–47
Wal-Mart Locator, 139
warning lights, 130–31
washer/dryers, 44–**46,** 107–8
water considerations
    drainage, 95–99
    dry-camping and, 145–46
    Mexico and, 191
    supply of, 99–103
water-in-fuel sensor, 127
water-pressure regulators, **100,** 101
watts, 116, 119
weather conditions, driving and, 73
weighing stations, 132
wheelbase, 19
Wi-Fi (wireless fidelity), 200–202
wind, driving in, 72–73
Winnebago RVs, **24–25, 28–29**
Woodall's, 99, 138, 213